"We Ain't What We Was"

"We Ain't What We Was"

Civil Rights in the New South

Frederick M. Wirt

Duke University Press   *1997*

Durham and London

© 1997 Duke University Press

All rights reserved

Printed in the United States of America

on acid-free paper ∞

Typeset in Trump Mediaeval

by Tseng Information Systems, Inc.

Library of Congress Cataloging-in-Publication Data

appear on the last printed page of this book.

Dedicated to
David Cole
Robert Dunlap
Leonard Morris

With other Panolians,
they led the social change
that made the New South

Contents

List of Figures and Tables

Figures

Tables

Foreword

This book is a very important treatment of one of the greatest accomplishments of the American political and legal system—the elimination of the system of state-imposed apartheid in the South. The civil rights revolution in the South during the 1960s was one of the most remarkable social changes ever accomplished peacefully in a short period of time. It destroyed a comprehensive system of white control underwritten by all basic community institutions and enforced through monopoly control of government, law enforcement, and widespread toleration of racial terror. It was all the more striking because the period of intense federal pressure lasted only three years, from 1965 to 1968, before Richard Nixon became president and a very different political era began.

Because of intellectual myopia, ignorance of the nature of the pre-1965 Deep South, regional prejudices, and the concentration of intellectual resources in the urban North, there have been amazingly few serious efforts to study and describe the full range of the change in southern communities. We know more about individual neighborhoods in some of the cities where our great universities are located than about the civil rights revolution in entire states. This is particularly true of the rural South, where the old order was most rigid, the transformation most revolutionary, and the local research tradition the most feeble. In an important sense, when social conditions become sufficiently severe and widespread neither our political nor our educational system tends to provide much information about them. Since these were the very communities most intensively targeted by the civil rights movement and the officials enforcing the new civil rights laws of the 1960s, this means that we lack extremely important information about the possibility of social change through law.

Still another reason why little attention has been given to these issues is the fact that once the battle against apartheid succeeded it was almost immediately displaced by calls for much more far-reaching changes and by a division and radicalization of the civil rights movement. These changes directed attention away from the initial goals of the movement and toward battles that were often lost, leading to a serious underestimation of the change that actually occurred.

Professor Wirt had a rare opportunity among social scientists to intensively study social and political transformations in an area that was considered the most resistant in the country at the peak of the civil rights period and a unique opportunity to return to the same area a quarter century later. At a time when there is profound skepticism about the efficacy of government and almost no serious discussion of the transformation of southern racial attitudes and practices, this study is dealing with fundamental questions. Although social scientists always call for longitudinal research, few ever actually study controversial issues over a long time period. This book offers richly grounded observations by the same scholar of the same issues over a quarter century of profound and complex change and provides an important resource for historians and those trying to think about the capacity of law to resolve aspects of the American racial crisis.

It is a terrible American mistake to try to evaluate profound reforms within a year or two. A deep social change often appears as a disruption in the short run and requires years of transformation before a new equilibrium is firmly in place. Assessing the durability of a reform also requires analysis of what happens after the political coalition that pressed for its accomplishment no longer holds power. This book has a very long time horizon and follows the complex pathways by which a basic reform actually restructures a community and is built into the consciousness of succeeding generations.

Panola County, Mississippi, was part of the most rigidly traditional part of the South, the three hundred "black-belt" counties that were the center of white resistance. The book takes on the full range of issues from the civil rights agenda and measures change in unique and creative ways. It shows a deep familiarity with the county and the context of national policy changes.

Northerners typically looked down on the South as an area of backward social customs and inferior education and used these factors to explain its profound poverty. The civil rights revolution was imposed by the North on the South in a sense of righteousness, and it had the ironic impact of making the South a much stronger economic competitor. Economic development even in a poor section of the nation's poorest state, Wirt shows, has been related to responses to the civil rights revolution. In important ways, those imposed changes freed the South of some of the most severe limitations on its economic possibilities. As long as the region was determined to undereducate and underutilize a large segment of its people, it voluntarily condemned itself to many of the characteristics of an under-developed nation. As long as there were very severe unresolved social and legal battles, there were heightened risks to investment. As long as the political leaders were prepared to sacrifice economic progress to assure white domination, they could not be fully part of American capitalism. The civil rights revolution, where it was successful, greatly reduced those impediments. When these changes combined with the region's low costs and antiunion attitudes, the South became highly attractive to many firms. Wirt shows how social change increased these possibilities in a profoundly depressed and isolated area and led to new and more effective interracial coalitions for further economic development.

Readers should try to avoid our national tendency to take the civil rights revolution for granted and to underestimate its fundamental importance in bringing the South fully into the nation. Panola County's changed institutions today seem normal and typical, as if they have always been there. The fact that the revolution was one of law and peaceful protest and that any violence that occurred was perpetrated by the losers and is now widely recognized as illegitimate leads to radical underestimates of the change. Even students in Panola County have a very difficult time accepting the fact that their society was only recently one of rigid racial subordination, reflected in total white economic and political control and open degradation of blacks, and undergirded by racial violence.

If we deny where we have come from, we underestimate what we are capable of changing. As we think about the possibilities and the actual accomplishments of that remarkable, peaceful revolution and think about how much progress has occurred in this isolated part of rural Mississippi, we might well wonder whether there are lessons here about the possibility of change in what have proved to be the even more intractable problems of race in metropolitan America.

At a time when the country is inclined toward a profound pessimism, this book suggests that transformation is possible, even in the most rigidly resistant communities and that there are, as Gunnar Myrdahl suggested a half century ago, aspects of American values that can be built upon in achieving racial justice, even in the areas of the most deeply rooted racial subordination. The fact that many of these gains have been preserved and even extended under five conservative national administrations, which attacked the courts and civil rights laws, suggests something even more hopeful—that many Americans actually feel more comfortable operating in a society in which opportunity is less unequal and where coalitions and respect extend across the once absolute lines of caste. This analysis of rural Mississippi challenges us to think about the ways in which the seemingly intractable racial problems of contemporary American society might yield to law and leadership, as did some of Panola County's most intensely defended racial practices.

Gary Orfield
Kennedy School of Government
Harvard University
April 1996

Acknowledgments

Observing change in the American culture is rather like being the first worker at the onset of the Industrial Revolution. There is so much change you can't see all of it. The culture and changes we examine are southern traditionalism and the new and massive events that have occurred in that region in recent decades. My focus is on the consequences for that culture as a result of the implementation of federal civil rights laws after the mid-1960s. This analysis is made more significant by the comparison it makes over a quarter century within one southern locale—the Mississippi county of Panola—the subject of my first book, *The Politics of Southern Equality*.

In the late 1960s amid all the southern turbulence, often bloody, preparing for field trips to this county was rather like preparing for night scouting in combat. Those trips were protected indirectly, at a distance, by the Federal Bureau of Investigation, but the county sheriff extended a good word to others on my efforts. Moreover, I kept out of trouble by not traveling at night and by avoiding small service stations that were centers of Ku Klux Klan activity. It is important to recall, even though it sounds dramatic, that southern people were dying all around me. Three civil rights workers were killed in the deep Delta before I arrived in Panola County, other blacks died in surrounding counties, and a fiery cross was erected on the lawn of the county courthouse just before I arrived.

Most whites were either fearful, angry, or both at this second invasion of federal troops and their civilian followers. My dialogue with them and their leaders was remarkably frank and open, but shot through with racial hate. Offered frequent invitations to address clubs to report what I found, I deferred until the last day of my last field trip; then spoke to the chamber of commerce, took a fast car to the Memphis airport, and was home in Berkeley by dinner time. I thought I would never return, but I did—much to the relief of my family.

When I next ventured to this county in 1989, it was like visiting another world, where the powerful pull of traditionalism on all institutions was yielding to the new, surprising, often frightening forces of a modern trend. Many factors affected the basic economy after 1960, and both private and public sectors were intermeshed in the changes that followed; but parallel to them were new federal policies and the shaping role of law. I will argue that the force of this outside law over time altered individuals and institutions in their behavior and cognitions.

In 1989, a new generation of both races were in positions of influence. The county seat of Batesville was flowering in a new burst of business activity (complete with a McDonald's), its schools had been thoroughly desegregated, and in the county the historic dominance of cotton was fading. More important, though, the blatant racism of a quarter century before had vanished into a more complex set of feelings and behavior that this book analyzes. But some things continued: the deep and widespread poverty of the poor of both races, white dominance in all institutions, and the influence of the dead clutching from the past. The past still had effects in the present, such as restricting new industry in the northern section of the county and inhibiting whites from admitting blacks to any but the most formal relationship compelled by law.

The last point is important because the county evidenced two significant cultures among the whites, while blacks themselves had different attitudes about other blacks. It is these cultural divisions, especially among the whites, that serve as a conceptual lens to track the influence of civil rights law in politics, education, and job opportunities. There has been much writing about influences on the black community and their gains. But it is the impact on the whites—those recalcitrants who opposed the outside law—whom we will also review here, in their interactions with blacks. The implementation of law and its impact on individuals and institutions are the central theoretical focus of the work. This analysis seeks to clarify exactly how it is that with these whites, law changed their behavior, and, in time, their attitudes.

So many people have contributed to this work that listing them by name would not represent their individual contributions. Of prime importance has been the financial sponsorship of the Spencer Foundation for eight field trips, and of the University of Illinois's Research Board for four others and for computer analysis. For many weeks, the owners of the Oliver-Britt House in Oxford generously provided a Tara-like home for quiet and comfort.

Much evidence in this book came from long hours of interviews provided by almost one hundred persons among Panola's blacks and whites, sometimes on several occasions. Businessmen, bankers, educators, ministers, politicians, and ordinary citizens had special insights on recent events, and they opened up their experiences, reflections, and sometimes files. All spoke freely under conditions of confidentiality; of this hundred Panolians, only one ever refused an interview. Of special help were graduate students from Mississippi and Illinois, who performed content analyses on hundreds of weeklies from this county since 1960. The superintendents of three school systems were very helpful, giving me the use of their faculty and buildings in testing about 1,200 students. Two members of a jury panel expressed their views about the 1994 trial of the assassin of Medgar Evars.

There were some Panolians who reviewed certain chapters for factual errors on developments in politics, schools, and jobs. These include the three superintendents of the two public schools and one private school: David Cole, South Panola School, James Harris, North Panola School, and Henry Crain, North Delta School. Reviewers of economic development were Richard Darby, mayor of Sardis, and a Batesville businessman who desired anonymity. Reviews of local politics were provided by Leonard Morris, realtor and state legislator, and Hunt Howell, former editor of *The Panolian*. Any error in the book is attributable not to these people but to myself. They did everything in their power to explain what was happening and why.

Intellectual assistance came from different local sources. Local historical accounts were provided by Bobby Carlisle, school administrator and council member, in Batesville. Bibliographic and research assistance came from the University of Mississippi Library, demonstrating its cultural richness. I learned much from several sessions of lectures at the Center for the Study of Southern Culture and its director, William Ferris. The extremely rich *Encyclopedia of Southern Culture,* edited by Charles Wilson and William Ferris, is so detailed that almost every element described in the present book can be studied further in its pages. And the professional assistance provided by the copy editor converted a rough draft into a polished one. Eric Admiraal provided the index with great care.

Finally, but always foremost, appreciation is extended to my wife, who endured my weeks away from home — and my return with a curious, southern accent. As I wrote in my first book, she is a "woman of valor . . . whose price is far above rubies."

*In narrating history, you are speaking of what
was done by man; in discoursing laws, you are
seeking to show what course of action, and
what manner of dealing with one another, men
have adopted. You can neither tell the story nor
conceive the law till you know how the men
you speak of regarded themselves and one
another.*

*And I know of no way of learning this but
by reading the stories they have told themselves. . . . I must hear their sneers and gibes . . .
with what grace they obeyed their superiors in
station; how they conceived it politic to live,
and wise to die . . . when they were prone to
resist oppression and wherefore—I must see
these things with their eyes, before I can
comprehend their law books.*

—Woodrow Wilson, *Mere Literature*, 1896

*[Regarding his patient, Vergil, who had been
blind since birth, given vision for the first time,]
the rest of us, born sighted, can scarcely imagine
such confusion. . . . When we open our eyes each
morning, it is upon a world we have spent a
lifetime learning to see. We are not given the
world: we make our world through incessant
experience. But when Vergil opened his eyes,
after being blind for forty-five years . . . there
was no visual experience to support a perception; there was no world of experience and
meaning awaiting him. He saw, but what he
saw had no coherence. . . . [H]is brain could
make no sense of them.*

—Dr. Oliver Sacks, *An Anthropologist on
Mars*, 1995

Part I | The Context for Change

Individuals and the institutions in which we live and interact can be understood in two ways. One involves finding them in a single spot of time, when all is understood from a singular encounter. That kind of discovery is rare, often the domain of the poet who suddenly perceives that "two roads diverged in a wood" and attributes meaning to that fact. This way of arriving at meaning is attempted in this study in its use of accounts of local people that also indirectly illuminate the community.

Another way in which meaning arises comes not from snapshots but from the study of broad forces that over time alter people and institutions. Like a motion picture, the piecing together of events provides meaning by grasping a wide array of behavior that can be judged across time. Such meaning arises from a preliminary understanding that today's institutions—like the economy or education—are not what they were even a half century ago. Developments external to each institution have produced changes in their goals, personnel, and roles. Of course, the institution's basic functions—making a profit or teaching—persist because that is what institutions do. If some time machine were to bring former members of an institution to the present day, they would grasp its continuing functions; but the methods of carrying the functions out would differ from those they once knew.

Other individuals who have lived through the

years of institutional change would have altered not simply their behavior. Rather, any behavioral change would have been preceded by yet another change in their understanding of the reality around them. As external forces alter the reality that has been so familiar, individuals are caught between the old and the new realities, creating a tension that is uncomfortable—even painful. In this change, they must recast their roles in life and reshape their goals, but there must first be new perceptions and new cognitions about how to operate within the new reality. Older perceptions are often retained, reflected in "golden myths" about an earlier day. Thus a sense of place, even of the same place, for the adult is not what it was for the child. The "old neighborhood" or the "home town" exist only in mental images of a past that we use for contrast with the present. Often, we lament both the old and new realities.

Our focus is on the process by which individuals and institutions change as a result of these new influences outside the familiar reality. We focus on the role of a complex national law seeking to alter a traditionalist culture's racial reality, an effort that challenged the very heart of values and perceptions in that culture. We view its consequences for one collection of individuals—a county in Mississippi—constituting a community that had to respond to external change. We view that community over a quarter century of time, comparing early and recent generations of individuals and institutions. We seek for agreement in what happened and its consequences, obtaining internal validity through standard survey methods and other records of those individuals. As to how well this community also fits the larger community of others in this region, that is, to obtain external validity, we find it in relating the community to the whole through use of summary statistics about the region.

The epigraphs that precede this part of the book contain two observations that provide us with an understanding of how individuals respond. The first, by the political scientist Woodrow Wilson, explains that in "discoursing laws, you are seeking to show what course of action, and what manner of dealing with one another, men have adopted." That is best done "by reading the stories they have told themselves . . . before [one] can comprehend their law books." That is both my purpose and method here. But in observing individuals, I was struck by another observation, for it was clear that they saw a new reality that they found confusing. Like the poet, A. E. Housman, each could say, "[I was] alone and afraid in a world I never made." As with the once blind man who can now see, as the physician Oliver Sacks notes, "there was no visual experience to support a perception; there was no world of experience and meaning awaiting him. . . . He saw, but what he saw had no coherence." In this book, I attempt to provide that coherence.

To begin, we must view first what the experience and perceptions were that existed in the local community before the introduction of federal law, and then the changes that occurred within the larger community of the South. The local perception of the world—the local reality of place—that once was, and how that has altered, help us understand the changes that are reviewed in later chapters on the political, educational, and economic worlds as they are perceived in Panola County, Mississippi.

1 | Setting the Community Scene

In 1865 the officers of the federal army finally left Panola County, Mississippi. The agents of Washington, seeking control, would not again walk its hot town roads and country lanes until 1961, when officials of the Department of Justice set foot there. Both federal appearances brought enormous upheaval to lives here and elsewhere in the South. They brought excoriation from whites who saw the federal agents as invaders, but they also brought hopes in blacks as their secular saviors.[1] Both interventions changed cultural traditions so basically that in each century the "Old" South became a "New" South, with both black and white citizens having to adapt to new lives. But the first federal presence withdrew, leaving freed slaves on their own to find their mean fortunes. During the century that followed, the "dark journey" of Jim Crow brought blacks not slavery but feudalism.[2]

In the second federal appearance, however, its agencies purposefully remained on the scene. Staying the course has created a significant difference for both races, which this book explores, especially in the civil rights laws that shaped new experiences and behaviors. At the core of the matter in both eras is the issue of race. The writings and actions of the earlier period shout to us across time of the fear and hate of whites and of the fear and hope of blacks. In the last third of this century, the mass media have portrayed just how intense feelings remained—and just how violent some whites were about it.

The intensity of these events demonstrate something more basic that lies outside this region, namely, a conflict in basic values at the heart of American political ideology. The pursuit of freedom once meant, among other things, the freedom of whites to use slaves and later to exploit them in numerous and familiar ways. But against that value, the pursuit of equality energized black efforts to gain respect and resources for achieving a better life. This clash between freedom and equality was first noted in the earliest of writings on our Constitution in the *Federalist Papers*, sixty years later in Alexis de Tocqueville's *Democracy in America*, and a century later in Gunnar Myrdal's *The American Dilemma*. The power of this conflict of values can be understood as driving men to megadeath in the Civil War and to later labor-management conflicts. In effect, that conflict is like a running skirmish that persists across our history.

Amid all this, the law can be an instrument, now supporting one value, now another, as political leaders seek to lead or moderate the passions of values in conflict. To complicate matters, of course, Americans have always been ambivalent about the role of law. Witness the folk wisdom "There oughta be a law!" versus "Government off our backs!"

Thinking about Theory and Method

To demonstrate the role of law in shaping this conflict over basic political values, this book employs the lens of one southern county. The laws are the civil rights acts from 1957 to 1965 that were successively stronger efforts to implement the goal of racial equality. Their implementation tells us much about law's influence on social change and on behavior and attitudes. That relationship, we propose, involves a theory of law's influence that encompasses several stages working over time, each of which requires the modifier, "under some conditions."

Presume that *strong* implementation of any new law does the following:

1. It can produce changes in the reality that confronts ordinary citizens, no matter how distasteful they may find it.
2. Such changes create new social interactions in community life.
3. Citizens' perception of those interactions lead them in time to accept, albeit grudgingly, the new behaviors newly touched by the law.
4. Such acceptance can bring attitudinal changes not only about the reality but about the law's objective.
5. Finally, this process can accelerate in new generations, for whom old values and attitudes are not sufficient to meet present needs.

A fuller elaboration of these points appears in the last chapter, where I draw together the sets of experiences involving new rights that came to be in politics, education, and jobs in Panola County. But the theme is the same:

> *Law when enforced can change reality, which can change perceptions, which can alter behavior, which, in time, can alter attitudes.*

The book is an effort to specify the meaning of this theory.

To understand this theory of law and social change, we will explore major questions in evaluating civil rights law, although we will remain aware of other modernizing influences upon the traditional culture, noted later. Our particular questions remain: How did implementation affect the civil rights of blacks? What were these laws' impacts on all citizens' political, schooling, and economic behaviors? What were citizens' perceptions and judgments about the commands of new laws and about the resulting experiences? Answers to these questions are compared across time. Earlier and more recent events in this county are explained in the words of its people and in records of their deeds.[3] But this analysis is about more than just one county, and so I will regularly relate events in the county to others in the state and region. In short, the effect of law on social change can be understood broadly by this narrow focus on one locale, which will then illuminate in turn the larger context.

The choice of Panola County may be conservative, as it is one of the hundreds in the most racist section of the South and nation, namely, the "black belt" where for a long time the worst things have been done by whites to blacks. Here one would expect considerable resistance to any law changing that racial culture, here would be the greatest violence against federal implementation, here would be the least presence of local leaders to moderate resistance, and here would be the least modification of attitudes over time. Here would loom large the presence of white citizens we will later term the "recalcitrants." The choice of this county, then, provides a valuable test of the influence of law designed to change an older culture.

The approach of this study is primarily qualitative, with a heavy lashing of quantitative data and measures. This multiple approach seeks to avoid three errors that can occur in research: believing what is untrue, not believing what is true, and asking the wrong question. The study thus seeks theoretical validity through use of different methods of revealing experiences, even though any particular method may have a characteristic weakness. When such different measures attest to the presence of the same reality, there is greater validity than when only one method is used. This method for assuring validity arises from the limitation of the researcher, as one scholar has noted: "Typically the qualitative researcher arrives on the scene with considerable theoretical baggage but very little idea of what will happen next. Using theory, common sense, and any resources at hand, the researcher attempts first, to survive in the field situation, and second, to work [his or her] self into a position where both observation and interviewing of locals will be possible."[4]

Different sources of information serve different purposes. Sources for this book include over one hundred interviews on common racial topics, which are triangulated in order to obtain validity; content analysis of two newspapers in the county from 1960; digests of records on voting, schooling, and jobs; and a lengthy attitudinal survey of public and private school students. In this fashion I hope it could be said of this study that "various errors were [avoided] by multiple exposures of differing kinds to the problem area."[5]

If these are the theory and method requirements of this book, we need to explore what happened, which first requires understanding this county as a social reality—that is, as a community that existed before the outside force of modernization and law appeared.

Panola as a Social System

When the federal government entered Panola County for the second time in 1961, it found a closed society whose race relations and economy had not changed much since Reconstruction days.[6] In most respects this county was a microcosm of the South. Race dominated all its institutions in a set of complex taboos and behaviors that had generated separate ways of life for each race. Much of this pattern owed more to caste than to class, as scholars have long noted.[7] As the classic analyst of the Old South, V. O. Key, noted, keeping blacks in their place had become the central motif shaping the region's "peculiar institutions" after the Civil War.[8]

Geography and Demography

Panola's history shares many features with other parts of the South. There had been the removal of Native Americans in pioneer days, the rise of "King Cotton," the dreadful human losses in the Civil War, followed by decades of Reconstruction that locked in white supremacy and produced hard times for the poor, and, finally, the massive migrations of blacks after both world wars.

Like many other counties in the South, Panola had a rural and small population that was poor by any measure and clearly biracial.[9] Located between Memphis and Jackson, the county lies at the intersection of two lines running fifty miles south of Memphis and east of the Mississippi River. As Figure 1.1 shows, the county is almost square, and it is bisected diagonally by the Tallahatchie River, which once bore steamboats carrying away cotton bales. The flat and fertile Mississippi Delta carves out a bow-shaped notch on the county's western edge, which rises abruptly up the Chocktaw Ridge to reach gentle hills and fields that roll beyond. Running north and south, Interstate 55 now parallels the historic State Route 51, down which came Yankee cavalry over 130 years ago. These routes are today crossed by State Route 6 that reaches from Oxford in the east to Clarksdale and the Delta in the west.

Panola's demography is simple on the surface but complex underneath,

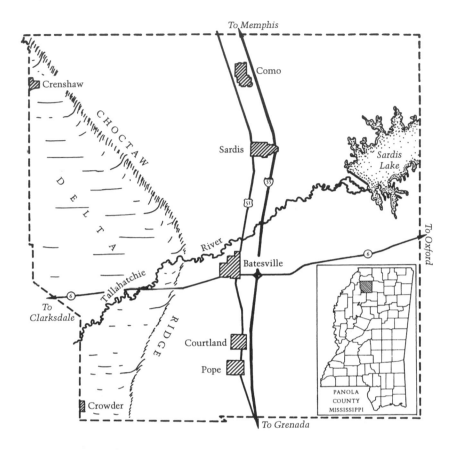

Figure 1.1. Panola County, Mississippi

like many small places in America. When federal civil rights officials first drove into Panola in 1961, its population was under 30,000, and its largest sites, Batesville and Sardis, had populations of about 3,300 and 2,100, respectively. But, while separated by only twelve miles, both were county seats that, because of historic hostilities, had produced two white cultures. This white cleavage is explored more fully in this book, because it affected how new laws were incorporated into their respective realities.

Racial demographics give a familiar account of the rural South, especially in the "black belt." Over half the county in 1960 was black (56.4%), a proportion larger than for the state. Black income—family and personal—was much lower than income among Panola's whites and three-quarters less than the average income of the state's blacks. A few blacks held some of the limited manufacturing jobs, but more worked in the cotton fields or in household service. These inadequate incomes and occupations for blacks were matched by their lesser education, housing, and health, mirroring the poorer conditions in the whole state. Thus:

— 8.4 percent of Mississippi's blacks had no schooling at all compared to 1.2 percent of whites;
— 45 percent of black housing was "dilapidated," compared with 28 percent for whites, and
— 62 percent of the blacks were on public assistance by 1964.

For many poor whites—those lacking land, occupation, or business—life was also a hard scrabble, though less hard than it was for blacks.

The hard times were causing changes for both races by 1960. Just over half the adults in this county had been farmers (54.7%), and another third were in rural nonfarm jobs (33.9%). But population was decreasing. In the 1950s, about one in six of both races was no longer living here, one in twelve households was gone, and one person in eleven had migrated. These raw figures of rural depopulation imply innumerable stories of frustration and deprivation that could be handled only by leaving home, with all the loss of community that such uprooting entails. That pattern, generated first by the introduction of the cotton-picking machine that overturned share-cropping, caused millions in the South to move north to the "Promised Land," with all its embittering qualities. Nor was the change purely local or even regional. As a close scholar of this transformation has noted, "Already several areas of the national life have changed completely because of the decoupling of race from cotton: popular culture, presidential politics, urban geography, education, justice, social welfare."[10]

The Economic Order

But to return to the origins of the traditional culture, much of it rested in the economy. In 1960, two economies had coexisted for over 125 years in this county on the Tallahatchie River. Above it, to the north, plantationism had dominated, while below it, small farming and industries were central. Plantationism had always thrived on cheap and hard labor that blacks had traditionally provided here and throughout the South. An extended analysis of Mississippi showed that the system produced a "great mass of black agricultural workers [who] remained a dependent, propertyless peasantry, nominally free, but ensnared by poverty, ignorance, and the new servitude of tenantry."[11] But the plantocrat of earlier times had to alter after World War II by using newer farming methods that relied heavily on machines and chemicals. Those changes stripped blacks from their meager jobs and incomes (and often living quarters), which in turn sent them north by Greyhound bus and Illinois Central's "City of New Orleans."

Farming changes also created other consequences. Agriculture had become very expensive, as equipment costs rose sharply, but cotton prices fell badly after World War II; cattle raising expanded as land was removed from crop production under federal control programs. But the commercial banks at the center of Panola's plantocracy—Sardis and Como—were still dominated by large landholders; they had been so strong that they had assisted Memphis banks in the Great Depression. Elsewhere in northern Panola, some small farms had remained, and blacks owned a few, although all were relatively small. Not surprisingly, then, the plantocrats dominated all the institutions of the rural society, not simply the economic, and their attitudes and behavior toward blacks was—at best—paternalistic.

Below the river, on the other hand, the economy rested on small farms and small industries, all focused on Batesville, which lay at the intersection of the county's major roads and the railroad. Economic development had been encouraged for decades under Mississippi's law to "Balance Agriculture with Industry." Local municipal bonds—tax free—had transformed farmland into industrial parks that in turn attracted firms whose rents paid off the bonds. While such small-scale industrialism had not been encouraged by the plantocrats of Sardis, it had thrived in Batesville, where the business community had pursued it energetically. By 1960, this town ranked first in industrialization in northern Mississippi after the larger towns of Tupelo and Corinth. By 1967, Batesville alone had eight small plants with the largest hiring over 400 persons. Not only had local businessmen liked this program, but voters also did; a bond issue to extend an existing industry was passed 623 to 3. Sardis pursued such development very slowly, and on a smaller scale.

Batesville, however, was in the throes of greater economic growth. Its merchants had half of all retail sales in the county. Besides industry, it had attracted electric services, federal grants for streets, new public buildings, a livestock show building, water improvements, a state highway office, a major sewer system extension, a new public library, and a gas distribution system—most of these before 1960. Also, the town's income had surpassed the income of the northern part of the county for the first time in history. Local merchant leadership in Batesville, especially the richest, had provided this stimulus. As a consequence, between 1960 and 1967 there emerged below the river more whites with higher incomes and fewer with the lowest incomes.

The Political Order

The essence of politics lies in the clash of private groups over access to public resources and symbols that can reinforce their special values and interests. The political system is the arena for this "authoritative allocation of values and resources."[12] It is the struggle over such allocations that creates the political order, and Panola County and the state share the pattern.

Cultural Divisions. The politics of Mississippi was exclusively Democratic, the deepest rock in the Solid South, until recent decades. The Republican party had left the state in 1875 and would win nothing until Barry Goldwater's presidential candidacy in 1964. This left control with a Democratic party that was rooted in the Delta elite of plantocrats, bankers, and railroad owners. At first they had recruited poor, white "hill" support by waving the flag of racism. Later, though, hard times for these small white farmers had mobilized them in a "revolt of the redneck." They expressed their frustrations through the demagoguery of leaders like, first, James Vardaman and, later, Theodore Bilbo, who controlled state politics for a half century after 1900.[13]

The political system was simple to describe before civil rights laws appeared in the state and this county. Blacks had no role in any of it, nor any benefit from it. White political rule involved low citizen activity by white voters and limited publicity by local leaders who distributed resources to favored groups—always white and always Democrats. However, there was a traditional tension among the whites between the poor and the merchant-planters, reflected in Panola County, that had generated two cultures, "the Delta" versus "the hill people." These contrasts were rooted in differences in the economic order and in lifestyles. In all this, Panola was a clear mirror of the South, as it had been in 1960—and in 1890. V. O. Key's reference to "states of mind formed long ago" fully applied to this county's attitudes of white supremacy and Delta–Hill tensions.[14]

Politics was about whites and their divisions, but those contestants fully agreed on white supremacy in matters of race. Delta people disapproved also of mass democracy, by which they meant those "rednecks" in the hills. The former pursued a code of honor that meant little to the latter, who sought an economic toehold for survival. Delta contempt is clearly captured on this characterization by planter, scholar, and poet William Percy: "They were the sort of people that lynch Negroes, that mistake hoodlumism for wit and cunning for intelligence, that attend revivals and fight and fornicate in the bushes afterwards. They were undiluted Anglo-Saxon. They were the sovereign voter. It was so horrible it seemed unreal."[15] This disgust was matched by that of poor whites from the hills and their leaders when they looked at the economic elite, and the animosities were pervasive and long-lasting in the state's political history.

But over this century the poor whites' leaders knew how to negotiate with Delta elites; of course, no negotiation over the conditions of blacks was ever considered. But deals could be cut to raise money for electing the champions of the poor whites. The appeal of this southern populism had diverse sources: hostility to industrialism, support of white supremacy, and taxing the big farmers for revenues to meet needs of small farmers, mostly white. Therefore, for decades before 1960, a running skirmish in politics had meant the dominance by Delta interests over those of small farmers, but within the Delta region itself there was great local power. "Rednecks" of the hills and "honorable gentlemen" of the Delta fought hard, often cruelly, in the field of politics, but they also united in keeping up a wall against the blacks standing outside and looking in.

Local Politics. Panola County over this period was more Delta than red-neck, as can be seen from its votes for two leading populists in the early and middle century. Vardaman won here only three of seven times and never in later years, and five of seven times this county's vote for him fell behind the state average. Later, Bilbo's record was quite similar. As guber-natorial candidate, he got no more than 50 percent in Panola County in his best year (always below his state average), but even as a U.S. senator he lost here in his first run (though he won in the next two elections).

But the white Panolians always united against the possibility of black voters. When the national civil rights movement began in the 1948 presi-dential campaign with the Dixiecrat candidate Strom Thurmond, Panola gave him 78 percent (among the ten highest counties in Mississippi, mostly clustering around Panola).[16] Black voting was a rarity across these years, as the state had the lowest registered percentage of blacks of the old Confederacy states. As elsewhere in Mississippi, blacks had registered during the Reconstruction era (over 1,600 in Panola), but their numbers shrank later with Jim Crow laws (only 114 in 1890). By 1960, however, only a single black was eligible—a minister who had registered in 1892.[17]

White party politics had taken somewhat different forms in counties in the Delta. Tunica County, to the west of Panola, had been run for some time by a millionaire planter and an elite faction, leaving the county the poorest in the state. In Panola, however, the Democratic party had served to bind the two white cultures to the north and south of the river. While the pendulum of voting strength had swung to the southern "hill" section by 1960, factions did not emerge within the party. There were no reports of any "boss" or "machine" for the county as a whole, although some per-sons did hold long elective careers. Locally, the mayor of Batesville after World War II, Daniel Ferguson, was quite powerful (as noted in chapter 7). He was loved by poor whites but ridiculed privately by merchants, yet still controlled political matters. There was also the county registrar, who flatly controlled black registration, as seen in chapter 4.

Local politics here, as elsewhere, was about the distribution of public services, even though there were few of them. This was a local politics of friends and neighbors and of face-to-face contact, a politics that was highly visible and vital for the quality of life in farm or town. These factors, not that of party, more likely shaped accountability and responsiveness than did elections. But as blacks lacked any influence in such matters, services for them were last to be noted and least to be provided.

Political power lay with county officers. The sheriff had been a powerful figure in Mississippi, and was often associated with graft from gamblers and bootleggers in a state that was dry until after 1970; gambling to raise state revenue was rejected as recently as 1991. However, it was the rural supervisors of the counties, in their respective "beats," or districts, who were of greatest importance. Their constituents in Panola County were surprisingly varied, being mostly rural but including some urban population in the small towns of Sardis and Batesville. Collectively, representatives of the beats formed the county's board of supervisors who handled more money than did any other public agency. Its spending for roads, bridges, hospitals, and public buildings meant vital services, jobs, and contracts for many white Panolians; blacks got whatever was left over, if anything. Competition for supervisor elections was fierce and often mean-spirited. Graft in distributing these services by supervisors was the norm in many beats in the state. In the 1980s, a state officer rose to the governorship by cleaning out much of this graft, and one or more supervisors in Panola were removed.

The Order of Community

On the farm and in the small towns, the people of Panola County had established two communities—black and white. Their intricacies, within and between them, have been well analyzed elsewhere,[18] but here our focus is on what "community" meant for these citizens. Part of it was the social reality—people's interactions in belief and action—that helped shape one's role in that community. The physical factor was yet another part of the community that shaped it—farm and town, school and church, or home. Much writing by those from smaller towns in the South evokes images of how the social and physical interwove in their early lives and created a sense of place that did not leave them years later. In Mississippi, the writings of Eudora Welty, William Faulkner, and Willie Morris are brilliant in their description and understanding of this sense of community. Later we will study the traumas of change that altered the social, economic, and political orders sketched above and that reshaped the meaning of community.

"Community" can mean either the "physical concentration" or the "social organization" of a group of people; the first is an empirical description and the second possesses a normative quality.[19] Community is no concrete entity; rather, it lies immanent in people's minds. It is a subjective concept that is "indivisible from human actions, purposes, and values. It expresses our vague yearnings for a commonality of desire, a communion with those around us, an extension of the bonds of kin and friend to all those who share a common fate with us."[20]

But community must also exist in a world of tensions that may threaten its once secure walls. Whether it is economic change, mass migration, war, nationalism, technological innovation, or other trauma imposed from the outside, the larger world threatens the community. The community thrives on isolation and intense interaction, but external forces break down isolation and interaction and distract both. Thus the internal stability of community always wavers, in tension with the instability of external changes. And the tension builds when external influences increase in number and in velocity; more things today seem happening much faster to upset the established order of community. Indeed, for some observers, Americans have lost any sense of community except maybe in the smallest places.

As a result, there comes a personal adaptation. Where once values were narrow—"parochialism" originally meant views within the church parish—now they are pushed toward universalism. The local community is forced to confront other values, brought in by these external forces, that may change traditional and stable perceptions. This is always an extremely painful process. "Broken habits are as painful and difficult as broken bones," as essayist Eric Hoffer once noted. That pain is aggravated by its speed. Change, and ever more change, not only challenge the comfortable and hence protective view of life that the community had built, but— worse—change threatens it.

This book is about the alteration of a community and its social reality, brought on by the external influence of law as one of a number of modernizing influences the South has known. We can capture that normative sense in what people say and do, and in the events that worked on these views. Earlier, there was a stable community, formed in farms and businesses that existed among both white and black races. Much of that stability is suggested in the following account of a Saturday afternoon in August of 1968, as observed by the author:

> The main square of Batesville . . . presents a scene which in many respects has remained unchanged for decades. The lung-draining heat hangs everywhere, a curtain through which everyone must struggle, hoping not to sweat—the heat is unbelievable. A westering sun floods the somewhat run-down town square, bordered by its tiny

shops and bisected neatly by the old Indian trail lines of the Illinois Central to which clings a small depot. A county courthouse, nearly as old as the town, with high corridors and rooms, broods over the scene on the north side. . . .

Both races parade back and forth on the west side, which is more of a shopping center, while around the square the cars slowly move. Clustered between this side and the old depot are parked cars filled with Negroes watching the passing parade. . . . On this busy western side, people march to see and to be seen, much as in any hamlet anywhere in America, or, for that matter, in an Italian village. Stores range in quality from dilapidated to the town's best. . . . Whites and blacks pass one another, but neatly separated clusters of the races gather along the street, sometimes in the way of cars whose drivers wait patiently for the pedestrians. No one is in a hurry, no one rushes, but everyone sees everyone else. The heat abides. . . .

The lines of people on the sidewalk counter march, a slow parade of autos counterpoints the marchers, and humans cluster around trucks and cars watch this village reel. Money is exchanged, acquaintances renewed, romance sensed and lust sparked, hostility begun and hate pumped—all on the streets of Batesville in the crushing heat of an August day.[21]

Beneath this calm lay a tangle of feelings, a structure of status and race, and a sense of an unchanging community that southern writers capture so well. White dominance was a central feature of this scene, rooted farther back in time than even the Civil War and implemented by daily contact. Nothing within the community could ever be perceived as changing very much. But outside forces were gathering. Arrowing through the county was a new superhighway, a symbol of the outside that had brought some economic changes by 1960. Down that road was to come the second federal encroachment on the community. As before in the Civil War, life would be changed.

2 | Regional Changes in the South, 1970–1990

What was to happen in Panola County was the end result of massive changes within the South in its economy, politics, schools, and—ultimately—culture. These modernizing influences challenged the traditional culture that the South had always known. This chapter summarizes those changes in the last three decades in the South so that we can understand their cognitive consequences in this county. The total change from these modernizing influences, not simply in civil rights, was so great that no other region has altered in such a short time. Shortly after the emergence of new federal laws in 1970, I wrote of a new black outlook emerging in this county from its own culture. The outlook was reflected in a saying among blacks, "We ain't what we should be, and we ain't what we can be, but by God, we ain't what we was!" In 1996, that hope became a greater reality.

A Traditional Society Undergoes Change

Southerners could see the change all about them in their new big cities and shrinking rural towns. Expanded state and federal services surrounded them, new industries provided more jobs than had agriculture, and farming people had moved to big cities. Everywhere newly empowered blacks were now in evidence in the new political system. Time after time, on the coast or inland, southerners of both races would look around them at these changes and exclaim, "I'd never thought I would live to see this!"

However, while the South became much like the rest of America, as some averred,[1] attitudes about race and politics at the century's end still resembled some older attitudes. Nonetheless, what had occurred here was a basic change in the regional culture, one that Daniel Elazar had termed "traditionalistic," that is, where control was focused within an agrarian order.[2] Led by an economic elite in the countryside or the county seats, the white leaders had believed that the world was ordered with power existing at the top and held by themselves—the plantation owners—who ran all the institutions. Participation in public decision making was limited to themselves, while the outside national economy was resisted for threatening elite control. Whites controlled the blacks, of course, but some whites controlled most whites. An old Louisiana family once put it bluntly: "We were secure. We were the old families. We had what we wanted. All we wanted was to keep it."[3]

This culture influenced public policy, which, with some state variations, embodied the following principles:

— Fight off industry and unionism, whose wages, low as they were, would compete with black rural income.
— Resist state welfare programs because the elite paid for these in the form of taxes but received no benefits.
— Keep educational costs low and avoid reforms because school professionals might introduce new ideas—and no help was needed for blacks.

As for any role by blacks, elites could both mobilize poor whites against them with calls of basic racism or advise white office holders against any change for blacks. Add to this set of policy stances a deep belief, shared by most whites, that blacks could not do anything as well as whites could. For many whites, it was hard to perceive a black as a "person." Despite the calls early in this century and, more recently, by southerners seeking economic reform, the traditional elites had resisted all change.

Against this centuries-old culture, traditionalism was suddenly—almost abruptly—forced to yield to a new culture, still emerging, but with a new black role. Here, economic development happened as a local response to a new culture, in which a market system was expanded to provide more jobs. A new morality in public life was forced on southerners by blacks voting and attending desegregated school. The disruption caused by changes is immense when an old culture is swayed by new forces.

In this disruption, induced by changes in law and economy, the old culture yielded to the New South. Let us begin the account of this alteration, not with civil rights, but with the southern economy early after World War II, when an agrarian society changed its mind about industry, tourism, and federal funds.

The Newest Economy

After World War II, national business had changed from its characteristic emphasis on heavy industry. The national economy had once required factories close to raw materials with transportation nearby for shipping finished goods by rail and water. But the new industry that emerged in the nation was not limited to railroads or waterways, because roads could carry products. That became evident after the mid-1950s, when the huge network of interstate roads began to be built under the National Defense Act. Using such roads, a business firm could build plants away from the central city—firms in the Northeast could move to areas of cheaper labor, cheaper land, limited state regulations, and fewer taxes. Clearly, the states of the Old Confederacy filled precisely these new requirements.[4]

When the civil rights movement began around 1960, the South was not at all a good investment in market terms. State services were inadequate, federal funds were limited mostly to defense, and there was little infrastructure on which business could build. There were also racial attitudes that did little to attract outside businessmen; the latter were concerned, not because they preferred tolerance but because of the uncertainty that racial tensions can create. However, in the coming years, especially after 1970, all these conditions changed dramatically. The new economy of the "Sunbelt States" emerged, one of the fastest growing in the world, and it was traceable to outside changes.

Causes of Southern Growth

Federal funds poured into the South, arguably at the expense of richer northern states. Earlier in the Great Depression, the golden flow was small, but after World War II it became a cascade. The cold war and the Vietnam War expanded military establishments. Long established in this region—due to political influence in Congress, better weather for more training, or cheaper costs—these military bases and camps meant that new wars poured billions of dollars into southern states. Moreover, after 1960 a new use for federal money appeared in the building of a new infrastructure.[5] Central were new transportation systems with airports and freeways. Between 1960 and 1970, the mileage of new southern freeways tripled, representing 44 percent of all new additions in the nation. Such developments made it easier for tourists to visit (a growing source of income), for businesses to relocate and transport goods, and for a huge growth of new housing to occur in big cities.

If the South's policies of low taxes, few services, and weak welfare might attract new business, why had they not done so decades before, when these conditions already existed? What had happened in the postwar period was that for the first time Washington had provided infrastructure funds. The beneficiaries were large farm businesses, defense building, extractive industries, new technology, realty interests, and tourism, while retired elders in their leisure filled its new pleasure domes. Southern political elites had mobilized in Washington to obtain this federal largesse by applying full pressure on all levels of government.[6] So the major economic interests in the South joined state and local power elites toward a larger idea of *economic development*. Much of this alteration was a different—not the traditional—approach to the political economy.

Further, new federal social policies had helped the South with its larger numbers of poor citizens. As federal welfare funds increased, especially after 1960, these poor were benefited by Washington even though their own state leaders had done little to assist them by using local resources. In this poorest of American regions, the states desperately needed such funds. Compare Mississippi with New York in 1981 in the federal money spent for just two programs: Aid to Families with Dependent Children (the largest welfare item) and Medicaid. Both are geared to each state's per capita income. Mississippi, with lower income, put up a smaller percentage of the costs and so had 78 percent of its costs covered by Washington. New York, on the other hand, with its higher income and larger percentage of costs, got only 50 percent of the costs from Washington. Yet New York's poor received over three times more per person in dollars, due to their state's higher contribution.[7]

Along the way, these economic changes led to new industry and commerce in the South, with the advent of small plants in small towns and larger ones in large cities, and with new *urban* southerners living in the newly big cities.[8] All these external forces had transformed the region's economy, as well as the new political system that would emerge here. Small-town industries of the past (e.g., textile mills) gave way to new, fast-growing enterprises where labor was cheap and plentiful, and the future was always open to growth under government support. That was the essence of a new culture that some southerners came to call "progressive."

Unequal Growth in Development

Much of the foregoing, however, is hardly true of the large population in the rural counties of the South. By the early 1980s, little development had occurred in the rural South, as reports of southern development agencies began to find.[9] Even the few rural plants that existed were closing down as industry turned more toward service activities. Rural population was shrinking, unemployment was higher, and rural governments could not provide conditions to attract new businesses. Traditional farm work was in sharp decline; it was especially weak among agricultural workers who supplemented their meager farm income with industrial jobs. Rural counties were also hurt by a workforce with poor incomes and lower levels of education, especially among blacks, and these rural places lacked a freeway to move finished goods. The better jobs were appearing in cities, and the bigger the city the better the wages and the less the housing segregation. We may see here an instance of an international phenomenon, using comparative data from abroad: "Everywhere in the world, industrialization has tended to break down barriers of nationality, class, and status in industrial democracies."[10]

Southern blacks, despite this growth in the southern economy, suffered more than whites, by any measure of their condition. Analysis of census reports finds these limitations:

— When farming changed after 1950, blacks adapted less because they had less education, which led to less efficient farms.[11]
— In the southern job market, better jobs went to white men, while minorities and women filled the lower occupational ranks.[12]
— In the rural South, black and white men had differences in wages that no explanation tested could account for except the practice of discrimination. Blacks ended up in jobs that were subject to low employment, low status, and low growth potential.[13]
— As over fifty years of analysis show, the linking of race and income in the economy give little optimism that new changes in the market will help the blacks and poor. Indeed, "Black labor market progress [will] no longer guarantee improvements in economic welfare, especially for the black underclass."[14]
— On sixteen measures of the quality of life that existed in 322 cities in the United States, southern location was less favorable for blacks because no single measure gave them a better result on economic development.[15]

These racial data show how both change and stability make the South a region where the economy cannot be described simply. It is not just simply that whites, both the wealthy and less wealthy ones, got more, and blacks got less. On the one hand, there was growing economic development, which raised the region's income, spread its economic diversity, and offered jobs for millions. On the other, the South's average was still below that of other regions across the board. There is great change in the big cities, while out on the farm economic life is still in decline. As these results show, whites have benefited more than blacks from this change. Using the measures of racial disparity that had existed before the civil rights era, we find today that the gap still remains; that is true, even though income and jobs have increased on an absolute scale for both races. For many blacks and poor, change has meant taking the "chicken bone train" for the North, or moving from rural to urban society within the South.

All this change has been accompanied by the emotional upheaval that comes from any change in the sense of community that shapes one's life.

This sense is both physical and psychological—we say, *my* county, *my* town, *my* neighborhood. Our sense of community also provides a judgment of self ("I'm from Tupelo"), a level of knowledge (such as the back streets or side roads), and a response to the threats of an external world ("You can't overcome me!"). On one side, it is comforting, so secure, to be rooted in one's place. On the other, it is also conformist, a freezing of lines of race and class that arise from even one's youngest years. Much of this is seen in Willie Morris's memoir *North to Freedom*, an evocation of how physical and psychological strands wove together the spells of childhood for a young Mississippi boy. But for many, to lose this sense of community would weaken a means for surviving in a world that was not always friendly. As one southern author wrote: "So what we are talking about, I think, when we talk about a sense of place [community] is how do we fit in? What we are talking about really is survival. . . . [W]e are not talking some romantic nonsense. We are talking something very realistic and very hard nosed. We are talking about survival in a technological and post-technological era."[16]

However, once having moved and adjusted to another place, usually a big city, one is left with the feeling expressed in the words of a black country singer, Charlie Pride (from near Panola County), considering "home town":

> It's nice to think about it,
> Maybe even visit,
> But I wonder
> Could I live there anymore?

A Racial Politics Emerges

Since 1970, the dynamism of change of this region's economy was paralleled in the political system. Economic development spreads when market conditions and government help it emerge, and it can be surprisingly prompt. But political change can be resisted for decades or even generations, and the traditional society of the South was much like that. However, federal laws, when enforced, did change some aspects of that older culture, especially by guaranteeing suffrage to the blacks. As a result, across the South a new political system emerged—much of it biracial—while the blacks' traditional fear for their lives for participating in politics has almost gone.

When V. O. Key's classic work on southern politics emerged in 1949, it found "no system or practice of political organization and leadership adequate to cope with its problems."[17] After all, that system was designed much more to cope with what it defined as the central problem—white control of blacks. The region was held tightly in all its social institutions by white elites; they controlled the political system by blocking blacks from all aspects of a democratic society: voting, nominations, elections, and public office. While white leadership failed to deal with the high-cost, high-tax needs of the poorest region in the nation, it nevertheless dominated any matters dealing with blacks. With this focus on race, by 1890 the political energies of the southern whites had created the largest regional power bloc in Washington. The traditional one-party system had enabled white officeholders to continue in power, which in turn bred seniority and hence power in the legislative committees of Congress. Until the 1930s and a rule change, presidential nominating conventions were dominated by a minority veto from the South that had checked candidates who were too liberal. All of this control turned away any national efforts to redistribute resources for the poor and blacks, or to provide votes for blacks, which whites always saw as the key to their own dominance. "States rights" was the battle cry, of course, except when national resources were needed to meet the economic interests of the state elites.

At the state level, southern governors were the weakest in the nation. In matters of race, they were usually and proudly demagogues, and their policy services were usually placating to some—but not all—white voters. Registration barriers against blacks also limited the turnout of poor whites. State legislatures represented only local elites, state and local judges supported segregation with no concern for the Constitution, and bureaucracies lacked any order, competence, or plan except to serve the powerful. All this was done without any recourse to the Republican party, to blacks, or to dominant national reform currents that had swept other regions after 1890.[18] All things considered, this societal arrangement was a modern version of medieval feudalism—one that national laws would change in a surprisingly brief period after 1965.

Voting and Partisanship

When that change came, there was a disorganized reshuffling all around the Old Confederacy. The debate continues whether racial attitude changed southern party identification, or whether other issues generated the change.[19] Nevertheless, more black registrants were followed by more white registrants, new groups moved down from the North to enjoy the economic development or to retire, and new activities spread to both political parties. Republican membership grew because some voters were converted, some were a new generation, and some represented new economic development.[20] As President Lyndon Johnson said in signing the Voting Rights Act of 1965, the law would turn the South over to the Grand Old Party; it did just that within thirty years. In the end, the Republican party became revitalized through votes for the presidency and in the Congress; by 1995, half the South's House seats were Republican. Governors were elected, but the GOP held little power at the state legislative or local levels. The Democratic party retained state and local office, and, depending upon black strength, a new form of biracialism emerged in state legislatures.

After 1965, the surge of black registration peaked and then fell slightly, with a small boost for the presidential candidacy of Jesse Jackson in 1984 and 1988. Almost 36 percent of black voters were registered in 1965; the number rose to 52 percent in 1967 and 64 percent in 1972, but dropped to the mid-50s percentage level until Jackson's primary campaigns. While his effort stimulated new black registration, little of it carried over to the general election.

Rather, the consequences continued to affect newly politicized blacks who saw a chance to gain more office.[21] The number of blacks in office increased enormously, but the rate of increase dropped steadily after the early 1970s. Two-thirds of these black office holders were in the South, especially in local administrations, yet blacks still held offices proportionately fewer than whites.[22] Winning for blacks in any locality had developed a new pattern. A large black majority was needed because blacks' lower voter turnout reduced their power to elect, and the estimate was that 60 percent registration was a minimum for a black victory. Even so, there still appeared more blacks holding public authority. By 1993 in Mississippi there were 751 blacks in these positions (or 15.2% of all offices). One was a congressman, 9 percent were in the state senate, over one-quarter were in the state house, and one was on the state supreme court. Locally, under one half of the elected officials were mayors or city aldermen, and 17 percent sat on school boards.[23]

In the 1980s, blacks were heavily Democratic (about 80%), whites were still Democratic, although their numbers were declining (about 75%). However, by the mid-1990s in presidential elections the two parties had polarized racially; the Democratic voters were heavily black and the GOP just as white. Voters not born in the South were far less Democratic (only about 30% voted Democrat); they had earlier rebuilt a once-moribund Republican party (along with the help of Democratic defectors). As the GOP grew in strength, the southern states went Republican: after the 1996 election, Republicans held 13 of 21 seats in the U.S. Senate and 60 of 128 seats in the House of Representatives. Republican state governors controlled 30 of 50 states across the nation. Variation in Republican strength was also considerable, from little in Arkansas to a lot in Florida.[24]

For Republican presidential candidates the impact was massive. Recall that in 1940 the Democratic presidential candidate in the South got 80 percent of the two-party vote, but in 1980, only 45 percent; in 1972, the Democratic candidate received only 29 percent. That recent shift in voting patterns has brought a Republican to the White House in every election but two—Jimmy Carter and Bill Clinton—and both were governors from the South. In 1988, all the southern states gave at least 54 percent of their vote to George Bush, with most states five percentage points higher; most of the voters were white.[25]

The linkage between this partisan change and support of civil rights for blacks became quite clear. In the Bush and Reagan administrations, federal pressure to protect voting rights was eased. Administrators in the Justice Department offices slackened in their enforcement of existing rights and the solicitor-general weakened his support of civil rights before the Supreme Court—all signs of a different emphasis. Affirmative action enforcement eased even more, as public opinion came to identify this policy with "quotas," a view strongly encouraged by Republican leaders, including presidents. Support for desegregation in these presidencies disappeared in court actions. As one scholar notes, presidents like George Bush created "a kinder, gentler racism."[26] By 1995, Supreme Court members appointed by Republican presidents were overturning school desegregation plans, affirmative action programs, and heavily black congressional districts. The Republican majorities elected to both houses in 1994 sought to eliminate affirmative action entirely, leaving a Democratic president to suggest that only small changes were needed in the law.

Congressional Changes

On this and other matters discussed below, *southern* opinion on public issues came closer to the *national* viewpoint. In short, what had been a distinctive regional viewpoint had faded into the national cultural outlook.

The new black voters had helped the survival of the Democratic party, but white reaction against the party had also stimulated the Republicans in this region. By 1970, with the Voting Rights Act then only five years old, an observer found a reversal in Congress of the deep resistance to civil rights that southerners once had. Enfranchising blacks locally had caused basic changes in congressional actions:

— Southern Democrats were losing power in Congress.
— More of the Democrats remaining now supported that party's national views on civil rights.
— The newer southern Republican members were supporting the national party more than regional interests.

All these forces worked to change the traditional southern view on civil rights.[27]

Further, when the Voting Rights Act came up for a seven-year extension in 1975, the two parties in the South split in a pattern counter to its past. In the House's large vote supporting that extension, southern Democrats supported it two to one, but southern Republicans opposed it seventeen to ten. The newest southern Democrats were even stronger in support; for example, the 1972 class had voted ten to two and the 1974 class twelve to one in support. In the Senate the same voting proportions prevailed when southern Democrats supported the extension nine to six; those elected before 1966 opposed it five to one, but the post-1966 group supported it eight to one. Republican senators tried to limit the bill, but finally supported it by a large majority.[28] Seven years later in 1981 in again extending the same act, the trend continued. Southern House members supported it by 91 percent compared to 73 percent in 1975; Republicans supported it also, but by 64 percent.[29]

The point was clear.[30] The restrictive laws that had once kept blacks from registering and voting were now opposed by the new southern representatives. There is good political sense in this new attitude. Once blacks did get more votes under federal law, to oppose black interests would have escalated the political costs for representatives. Consequently, full support of black civil rights on votes was established, despite opposition by Presidents Reagan and Bush. But there were trade-offs. The cost for the Democratic party was that many whites moved to the Republican party in national elections. That loss gave blacks a larger role within the Democratic party, which helped them win even more local offices, although still fewer than their proportion in the population. However, the end result was a weaker position for the South in national politics, and a stronger Republican representation in federal voting due to new arrivals and transformed Democrats. In sum, national legislators' positions have been reoriented by the new black voting power, even though that power is not a majority in any southern state.

On this, as on other policy matters, the South is moving toward the national viewpoint on ideology. Behind such change has been an ideological realignment in southern voting and representation. For example, from 1973 to 1986, overrepresentation of the South in Congress had been corrected so that southern senators now served on major committees only in proportion to the size of their region (except for military, farming, and labor and welfare issues).[31] Or witness the change in ideologues within each party. Between 1972 and 1984 conservatives moved from the Democratic party to the party that better fit their interests. Southern liberals and moderates remain within the Democratic party, but it hardly forms a working majority in any federal election.[32]

Changes at the State Level

Below the national level, other political changes in the South have recast its political system in equally dramatic ways. A review of these changes shows that they were not always linked simply to growth in civil rights but to other social changes as well.[33] It is clear that old notions of southern governing have been replaced with new structures and personnel. Modernization forces have begun to move the South away from its old culture.

Governors

State executives were once widely known as weak offices, essentially dupes for elites and "good-time Charlies." Changes in governors over three decades, however, have developed "a new breed of more professional and energetic state chief executives in that time."[34] These New South governors had a recurring theme in their reformation of the encrusted policies and practices that had been left by the culture of traditionalism. The leadership change meant that the governors needed to work with new black voters or officials in order to create new jobs and raise tax revenue; but they also had to remain fiscally conservative, to protect the environment, and to promote better education. These governors were younger and were always men; electing a woman was still too much for this culture—until the 1990 election of Democrat Ann Richards in Texas. This group was educated, often outside the South, and expressed a mission to create in their states a management-oriented form of "good government."

Governors produced changes that in turn helped produce in part the New South. Everywhere they accepted a new vision of race in the modern South, maybe their most important contribution to reducing group conflict. They also gave leadership to the powerful legislatures in order to generate new public service programs, sometimes with new taxes—but not too much. They turned southern schools away from excessive local control—with its emphasis on low costs and hence low results—into state mandates reinforcing better quality. They developed a fuller relationship with Washington agencies, as the "states rights" emphasis faded due to a pressing need to seek federal help for growing state problems. Many of these gubernatorial reforms were in management, using new ideas that were traceable to the Progressive movement of the early 1900s. Thus they sought efficiency, honesty, executive control, and equity in administration. And as their influence grew, they also sought national influence. An earlier New South governor—Georgia's Jimmy Carter—became president after 1976, and a later one—Arkansas's Bill Clinton—did the same in 1992. "Good-time Charlies" had become as time-bound as the "Solid South."

Legislatures

Change has also emerged among southern legislatures, which became less Democratic and less homogenous than before. Traditional elite influences slowly waned as more women and blacks appeared in these offices. Consequently, newer issues appeared on legislative agendas, and governors mobilized to collaborate in supporting them. What is most striking is the new composition of the legislatures and the new issues.[35]

Partisanship had changed these bodies across the South. In 1953 the Democrats held 93 and 96 percent respectively of the seats in the upper and lower houses. Thirty years later they still dominated, but they had 10 percent fewer seats in each house. The range of partisan control among the southern states today is surprising. There is still 90 percent or more Democratic control in the legislatures of the deep South—Alabama, Arkansas, Louisiana, and Mississippi—but in Virginia and Florida an evenly balanced situation is approaching.

Yet other changes appeared in legislative capacity. Twenty years ago, southern legislatures were ranked the worst in the nation—they were part-time, unstaffed, and poorly paid. Much has now changed, as legislative reform was part of the New South's political system. Legislatures now meet annually, and fewer committees operate, have less turnover, are better paid, hire adequate staff and facilities (including computers), use more office space and research agencies, and expend more money. These are signs of a new institutionalization of rational principles in which concepts of order, planning, and knowledge are slowly brought to bear on new agendas. However, issue politics in these new bodies are just as bitter—only not linked to an overt racism.

More issues arise in response to these changes. There are the new representatives in the legislatures, such as women, blacks, environmentalists, and one-issue advocates. As a result of response to change, more bills are now enacted than in other regions, and a new interest in legislative oversight of agencies has emerged. That is particularly seen in the interest shown by some states in "sunset" laws, which are those requiring state agencies authorization to be reviewed periodically by state legislatures. Southern states were the first to adopt this control over bureaucracy by making agencies justify their continued existence. The old suspicion of bureaucracy in traditionalism still carries over in the new agenda.

While these legislative changes are less dramatic than the new governors, who are more highly visible, the legislatures have improved more in two decades than they did in their prior existence. Legislators appear willing to start dealing, as other regions have already done, with both new issues and old ones that they had ignored in the past. New events, such as environmentalism, would acquire a greater salience in the 1980s, as did efforts to deal with a major recession in the 1990s. Yet a new-style legislature does give members better training and greater competence in facing a new agenda, whatever their policy differences.

Bureaucracy

Given these changes, state administration had to be reshaped from the traditional past in which citizens had viewed it with great distrust. Change has indeed been great, but one review finds that this movement has altered from focusing on one set of problems to yet another, that is, "from traditional fragmentation to administrative incoherence."[36] In the past, bureaucracy had existed with many, plural-headed agencies, with government services fragmented, and an executive with no control over their activities. Between World Wars I and II, southern reform of bureaucracy had begun—but only modestly. A second reform movement after 1960 had begun to deal with new problems arising from new urban problems, black politics, and reapportionment.

Part of this change was the stimulus of Washington in the Great Society programs and later in the General Revenue Sharing Act. These programs sought and obtained upgraded standards of public services, such as requiring civil service and equal opportunity policies. Central to this national stimulus was a call for state planning in the spending of federal money; state agencies and governors were to plan more in dealing effectively with social problems. In the decades that followed, most states strengthened their developmental and redistributive programs by developing a close intergovernmental bureaucracy.[37] To accomplish these tasks, southern states by the early 1980s had hired more employees, well above national averages, and had expanded programs in planning, education, and welfare. In addition, civil service reforms matched those in other states, providing higher pay and benefits and more training than in the past.

But such reform is still not fully in hand, for southern bureaucracy has not become a focused instrument of government for executive and legislative leadership. After all, few states undertook a new overhaul; indeed, South Carolina and Texas resisted such local reform in the two reform waves already noted. Curiously, the strengthening bureaucracy had weakened governors who were operating amid a maze of new agencies; they must now fight agencies strengthened by reorganization and civil service. Crisis management is the best that many governors can do with a fragmented system. That result may be why so many have done rather well in reforming the weak condition of public education. However, bureaucrats are now providing better services of other kinds than ever before through more planning, resources, and equity. Of course, the levels provided are still low compared to other regions, but nevertheless, there are indeed more services.

Judiciary

State courts also reveal changes, but much less than other branches of government. The courts are still dominated at all levels by whites, Democrats, Protestants, and males who are locally educated. Little research on such courts exists below the level of the state supreme court, but the system, as one scholar noted, still remains one of "robed elites."[38] Selection to the courts by elections goes back a long way, starting with Mississippi from before the Civil War. In the current era, blacks or women enter office only by gubernatorial appointment, as did the first black supreme court justice in Mississippi appointed in the 1980s. There are more blacks on the state benches today in the South, but their proportion is shrinking now; it is still lower than their proportion in the population though far higher than a quarter century ago.[39] Far more black lawyers (whose number doubled in Mississippi from 1970 to 1983), and more cases involving black lawyers, now appear in state courts.

But the professional nature of the judiciary remains much the same in the South as before, despite its efficiency reforms and more litigation on the dockets. The fact is that partisanship and control by state and local leaders still dominate a judiciary that changes much less than do other branches. Despite widespread elections, accountability for decisions still seems unclear. Judicial elections get little public attention, and so the voting turnouts are low. However, court resistance to changes in civil rights is not evident today; indeed, efforts by whites to use state law to "dilute" votes for blacks have been checked by these courts.[40] There are reports of more openness to public needs in Mississippi courts, as elsewhere in the South today.

Political Changes and a New South

The combination of new economic development, new civil rights laws that opened voting to blacks, new movement of population, and new ideas about an improved political system—all combined to create a New South that observers agree is unprecedented. No one thinks that this change is complete, for blacks complain about needs that are still unmet. But it is equally clear that an understanding of the region's politics must go beyond what V. O. Key once knew and what national opinion once held. There is now a new political system with changes still under way.

Racial Adjustment in the Schools

While litigation and legislation moved the South to change its political system, in matters of schooling there was change but a different pattern of response. Clearly, there was a very dramatic change in what had once been the most deeply segregated educational system in the nation.

Litigation and Change

Rooted in an acceptance by state and federal courts, black schooling was always separate but never equal, as scores of studies and court cases have pointed out. For example, money for white education exceeded that for blacks many times over; in Mississippi in the 1940s, white students got seven dollars spent on schooling versus one dollar for blacks. Indeed, blacks paid more than their share of public school costs, as they also paid part of white costs; that is, taxes from blacks were used to finance the better white schools. Underlying the white practice was a fear that more black education would have destructive consequences. Schooling could lead to challenges against existing racial restrictions, could reduce the supply of black farm workers, and could subvert an ancient traditionalism about working relationships. Separate but equal education was just a legal façade for whites; indeed, as Neil McMillen noted, it was just a "mere faint gesture" before the Supreme Court decisions of the mid-1950s.[41]

The thunderous explosion from the South in response to the *Brown v. Topeka Board of Education* decision of 1954 overturning segregation also precipitated the closest to anarchy that region has experienced since the firing on Fort Sumter.[42] The "massive resistance" following this decision had generated scores of state responses in the first decade: a freedom-of-choice policy, closing schools, selling of school property, giving of public money to private schools. Opponents even used the hoary "interposition" argument that was thought dead after Appomattox; that is, states could interpose between Washington and citizens to protect them.[43] That resistance ended with a set of definitive Supreme Court decisions from 1968 to 1971. These decisions sought to abolish any racially identified systems, to drop slower corrective approaches for more immediate corrections, and to use busing to overcome segregation.[44]

The result of this litigation—backed by supportive federal law in the shape of the Elementary and Secondary Education Act of 1964—stimulated a historically high proportion of desegregation. Ten years after action began and twenty years after the *Brown* decision, federal reports found that the South—compared to other regions—had done the most.[45] Desegregation in the metropolitan areas had created most public attention, but in the small towns across the South the U.S. Office of Civil Rights had pursued change quietly and doggedly. There were years of resistance, but slowly the old system responded to a new form of schooling. Then in the 1970s, the challenge moved outside the South to the big cities in the Supreme Court's efforts to overturn urban segregation. But in the 1990s, a new Court, convinced by demographic changes and a new conservative philosophy, began dismantling older desegregation orders; their grounds were that the task had now been done, and no action was justified unless there was an official intent to segregate. These reversals involved cities that had started desegregation following the *Brown* case forty years earlier, including Topeka. By 1992, the Court gave district court judges guidelines to drop orders where demography, not political decisions, had prevented any more desegregation. Within three years a number of long-standing desegregation orders on big cities were disbanded by district court action.[46]

Changes from Desegregation

At the heart of this debate, especially in the South, were two challenges: Did the South actually desegregate? If so, did it cause southern white reactions that actually blocked educational change? Popular and scholarly confusion reigns here, but a brief review of recent research will cover these questions.

Desegregation and Stasis. The fact was that there was indeed much desegregation under the new law, but much more did not occur—and it often decreased—after the mid-1970s. Gary Orfield, a close scholar of desegregation, finds that between 1968 and 1980, segregation had declined nationally, especially in the most segregated schools. This was still an enormous change, given the deep passions that whites had exhibited when the issue first arose. By then, one-third of all blacks attended all-minority schools (i.e., a very high reduction in segregation), and over 60 percent were in schools with over half minority students (again, a very high increase). But the rate of decrease in segregation was slowing down by 1980, and by 1987 these percentages remained the same.[47]

Nevertheless, the largest increase in desegregation came in the South. Between 1968 and 1980,

— the black percentage in mostly minority schools dropped from 81 to 57 percent;
— blacks in 90–100 percent minority schools dropped from 78 to 23 percent; and
— predominantly white schools dropped to 43 percent of all schools.

However, there was still much variation within this region. By 1980, the figures for blacks in predominantly white schools were 91 percent in Kentucky and 60 percent in Florida; but in Mississippi only 24 percent, the lowest ratio in the nation.

Despite this great change, desegregation froze and little change has occurred since the earliest 1970s. In confirming this standstill, Orfield and his colleagues point to the failure of any national leadership to do much more:

> Three of the four Administrations since 1968 were openly hostile to urban desegregation orders and the Carter Administration took few initiatives in the field. There have been no important policy initiatives supporting desegregation from any branch of government since 1971. Advocates of racial change have found themselves reduced to defensive positions devoting most of their energy to prevent a rollback of what has already been achieved. . . . When all the positive and negative forces are added together the aggregate statistics make it appear that nothing has happened.[48]

Clearly a slowdown, if not backsliding, did occur in the South. Most of these states between 1980 and 1984 actually saw desegregation *drop* a few percentage points. However, Mississippi did improve its proportion of blacks in mostly white schools, bringing the number to 27 percent (still the lowest in the region).

At the level of metropolitan school districts, even more variety had existed by 1987. If asked what proportion of whites attended schools with black students, the answer was 61 to 66 percent or more in places like Tampa–St. Petersburg, Louisville, and Greenville. In Greensboro and Orlando, blacks attended schools with 50 percent or more white students. At the low end, though, as few as 16 to 19 percent of whites attended school with blacks in Miami, Atlanta, New Orleans, Memphis, and Houston. The most successful effort had involved using a broad plan, incorporating city and suburbs for some period of time. Note that these most segregated districts had never employed any plan to change (except Memphis).

But as the 1980s ended, the effort was weakening. Atlanta's plan had been rejected by the Supreme Court, and Houston's was dropped by courts without much desegregation having taken place. Memphis used only voluntary methods, New Orleans had no plan, and Miami had made few efforts that did little, even though faced with overwhelming numbers of minorities. Elsewhere, big southern cities were declining in desegregation; Augusta, Little Rock, Tampa–St. Petersburg, San Antonio, and Atlanta fell by 5 to 11 percentage points in desegregation rates from 1980 to 1984.[49] And the Supreme Court in the 1990s began allowing districts to drop desegregation plans where every effort had been made but no more change was possible due to demography.

These desegregation results flow from changes in political will and in demography. After 1980, presidents of both parties, a majority of Congress, and a new Supreme Court majority agreed not to do more with this effort in the South, just as northern white citizens also resisted. The federal agencies of government provided limited, if any, funds for making desegregation plans, there was no national leadership to encourage change, and little record keeping was available to deal with changes. The evidence is clear that all these negative signs represented a lack of political will by leaders and citizens alike. Moreover, on the demographic side, population movements had brought huge numbers of blacks and Hispanics from rural to metropolitan areas. If an urban school system's population reached a majority made up of minorities, it was hard to produce much more desegregation when there was an ever decreasing proportion of whites. The movement of human beings had blocked any more change. Even with careful plans in some cities, and with officials working hard, the desegregation figures changed little—and even declined—after the first decade of change. Both political will and demography blocked further change.

Challenges to Desegregation. Challengers have raised serious questions about desegregation where it did occur. These critics claim that whites flee schools, that "resegregation" arises within remaining schools, and that white voters reject new school levies that could make desegregation work.[50] Understanding the truth of these claims is made difficult, however, because research on these challenges often uses diverse methods (e.g., measures of school or periods of time), and measures of change are often quite different. Also, not much is published on such challenges in the South, as the North gets the attention. The necessary study would have to focus on the same schools over the same time period, asking whether there was evidence of desegregation costs, like white flight, resegregation, and financial losses. Such a research design actually did inform an analysis of 345 school districts in Alabama, Georgia, Mississippi, North Carolina, and South Carolina—truly the heart of Dixie.[51] Three findings in this study question all these challenges about desegregation costs.

First, white flight to private academies, often for religious reasons, did indeed occur everywhere, especially in school districts where black enrollment was high. However, a full review found that as little as 8 percent of public school enrollment—usually the affluent—had actually moved to private schools. Despite all the publicity, this change was not a large wave of whites abandoning public schools. Second, in the resegregation of blacks (i.e., segregated treatment within schools with white students), it was shown that the usual measures downgraded many blacks. They classified many blacks as "educable mentally retarded" (which meant moving them to special classes), or as having behavior problems (i.e., dismissing or expelling them in large numbers). However, when these measures were used to analyze southern states, research found that very little of this downgrading actually occurred there, and what did, took place in affluent white schools. In racially mixed schools, proportionately fewer blacks were assigned to special classes, or dismissed, or expelled. Finally, the loss of fiscal support that is often alleged (i.e., whites not voting for tax referenda that support desegregated schools) was also found not to exist. Very little fall-off in financial support actually occurred, and few if any theories could explain why such a drop might occur, except for the practice of discrimination itself. After all, whites in most southern schools needed these tax levies to support funding their own children. The point made by this review, then, is that the consequences of desegregation are little substantiated in the South although northern, big-city districts may differ.[52]

Other broader challenges, often popular, claim that under desegregation white students lose in achievement and school systems fall apart under the pressure over this issue. But a large body of research does not support this judgment. Indeed, an extensive overview of this evidence appeared in a brief filed before the Supreme Court in mid-1991.[53] Here, fifty-eight scholars of this field signed a petition showing that widespread research had found desegregation was not the failure that its critics had alleged. Indeed, they found that desegregation

 — is made more effective when authorities use major plans to cover all grades from the youngest and to cover large geographical areas, and persevere in the implementation;
 — provides minor academic gains to blacks but no loss to whites, while offering both races a clear sense of their involvement with each other;
 — produces improved instructional effort by the staff within the existing school resources with a resulting greater influence on their students.

The complications of what happens with desegregation are extensive, but much of the research summarized here runs quite counter to views of the public and politicians about what happened in the South. There is considerable difference about this program's effect—some states and districts do less well at desegregating—and it is clear that the South also reflected these differences. Two conflicting views of reality in desegregation exist, that of many white (in all regions) versus that of empirical scholars. But what is interesting is that, over time, this region had adjusted to an educational change, any small part of which was dangerous to discuss—much less to start—barely a quarter century ago. Few people disagree that only a national court could have started a national policy change for the region.

Social Changes and Personal Changes

We know much about the regional change hitting the South's economy, politics, and education from the analysis of government documents, voting records, and survey polls. These reports tell us that in less than three decades the South altered its many systems to form the New South.

Indeed, that change seems to have moved many southerners to accept viewpoints that come close to those of the nation as a whole. For example, on many opinion surveys southerners' views are no more or less conservative than others on policy issues concerning governmental job guarantees, health care, and aid to education. But in the South some older traditional views still linger; their views differ from the rest of the nation's on crime control, use of force to control urban unrest, women's rights, and affirmative action. The growth of conservatism across the rest of the nation in recent years has clearly reduced this gap between the South and other regions.[54] The clearest survey evidence exists on southern attitudes toward the blacks and on segregation attitudes over a few decades. In 1964 and 1976, 90 percent of southern whites felt threatened by the civil rights movement, but a dozen years later in 1976 the fear fell to 44 percent; the 50 percent who earlier had wanted a segregated society now fell to 20 percent. As one analyst noted, "In this regard federal policy in the South has been a dramatic success. . . . *As political and legal structures have been changed over time, attitudes have changed to accord with these new realities*"[55] (emphasis added).

That last sentence will undergird the section that follows, which investigates such changes in a typical county, one that lies on the flat Delta and rolling hills of Mississippi. How did behavior change, what were the consequences for institutions, and how were individual attitudes affected? That is, as external law worked its way down into the lives of people, when the traditional culture of whites was sharply challenged by such law, the accounts of both races can help illuminate a larger proposition. How does law change a reality that changes people's perceptions and cognitions? When that occurs, how do institutions change and individuals come to see another world?

3 | Panola's Pre-1970 Response to Civil Rights

This tight little island in Panola County, like so many in the South, would be stormed by the civil rights acts from 1957 to 1965 that were designed to check and dilute, but never conquer, white supremacy. By 1970, though, a new biracial society was just emerging. The first task is to review the immediate events after these laws, when the traditional culture experienced root shock, and the possibility of a new reality first arose.

Expansion of Black Voting

After the mid-1950s in the South, ever-tougher civil rights acts slowly expanded black suffrage through litigation, until the 1965 Voting Rights Act appeared to do the job effectively. The weak acts of 1957 and 1960 required litigation in every county or state to demonstrate the existence of a "pattern and practice" of denying blacks the vote. However, obtaining such evidence was laborious, drawn out, and eventually ineffective. But in the face of southern power in Congress, little better was feasible.

Litigation in Panola County

Panola County was the first in Mississippi in providing black suffrage, but it took a long struggle. Agents of the U.S. Justice Department's Civil Rights Division (CRD) began fieldwork there in April 1961. The CRD had guessed that counties with more than one half the population black, but with few or no registered voters, were likely sources of discrimination, and Panola County matched the criteria. The CRD and FBI secured information from voting records and interviews, their agents moving on obscure, dusty roads over Delta and hills to interview blacks who had been refused registration. In October 1961, then, these data formed the basis of a federal complaint against the county (plus six other counties) that was tried before a federal district judge, but cross-filings took another eighteen months. Then in mid-1963, the judge rejected the CRD claim against

Panola. But on appeal a year later, the Fifth Circuit Court in New Orleans overturned that decision.[1] A week later the district judge issued an injunction against the county registrar with specific corrections that had been suggested by the CRD almost three years earlier.

Clearly, earlier litigation supporting a "pattern and practice" of discrimination took much time and expended great resources for even this small change in voting. In the Panola case, from spring 1961 to mid-1964 the trial data required 110 pages of tables, copies of registration books since 1932, primary election poll books, microfilm reels of these records, interviews with several hundred persons, and scores of subpoenaed witnesses. The charge of discrimination rested on the white registrar's discretion in judging how applicants had answered certain questions that he selected. Record analysis was necessary to show that whites had received easy questions while blacks did not. From these tests, the registrar had wide discretion in judging the applicant's writing, which favored whites exclusively.

The primary remedy sought by the CRD in the Panola case was to "freeze" the old standards used for white applicants and apply those to black applicants. While subsequent enforcement by Panola's registrar did not go smoothly, the CRD did not seek a contempt order against him because blacks were indeed registering. Thus, even before the appellate decision, 40 blacks had been registered and 59 rejected; but in the two months after that decision, the figures were 340 and 59 respectively (the figures for whites were 118 and 1). Another reason for leaving Panola alone was the strain on CRD resources. This was the "long, hot summer" of 1964 of heated, often violent confrontation, especially in Mississippi, between supporters of the traditional culture of the South and challenges by northern whites and southern blacks.[2]

The Politics of Implementation

This first stage is notable for the use of litigation, with all its delays, but it was the only strategy available to implement national law. While litigation often delays resolving massive social and political problems, it was all that was feasible until public opinion changed. The desirable is often not possible until new conditions change perceptions of what is feasible. Indeed, it took one president's assassination, another's energetic pursuit of new laws, and the publicized violence of some southern whites—officials and citizens alike—in order to generate a supportive public opinion in the nation. Those conditions built a national legislative coalition that finally made the desirable into the feasible in the Voting Rights Act of 1965.

However, litigation had three uses in supporting voting rights. First, it provided a forum for whites who were slowly adjusting to an emerging political order. For example, as black registrants increased in Batesville, white candidates dropped the language of racial demagoguery and provided paved roads and streetlights in the black section. This response was also widespread in local areas across the South, as we will note in later chapters. A second use of litigation was that it ensured that its first results were legitimated. Both sides understood that accepted constitutional procedures in litigation had been followed in bringing on the change, even though it was detested by whites. That legitimation had helped ease the pain that whites felt for their threatened culture; litigation did not change whites, but it mollified them.

Finally, litigation expanded awareness outside this county and the South of just what was happening in this region, creating a national recognition of what it meant to be black and to live in the South. Other factors contributed to this new awareness, especially coverage by the media, whose fascination with things going wrong in society made them find southern events very attractive. It was this understanding by a general public outside the South that generated pressure to change conditions by the use of new laws. These events fit a characteristic pattern in the innovation of public policy. That is, merging political streams of ideas and interests allow representatives to seize "windows of opportunity" for policy change that has been created by recent events in order to realize their goals through that new policy.[3] In the case of civil rights, there emerged other instruments of implementation to bring about change:

- a constitutional amendment (the 24th), which outlawed poll taxes in 1965;
- federal statutes, such as those banning literacy tests or the 1965 Voting Rights Act; and
- administrative oversight under the Voting Rights Act of 1965, so that counties with less than 50 percent of nonwhite adults unregistered would attract federal registers to do the job.

With all this national swirl, what was the scene in Panola County in the 1960s as these laws changed?

Black Political Power Arises

The first opportunity provided by law to increase registration and voting was promptly taken up by Panola's blacks and by outside volunteers who appeared on the scene to challenge white supremacy. There was much activity and great fear among both races, yet after a few years, a newly politicized black community developed whose power was still uncertain by 1970. Amid all this drama and pain, Panola's whites were slowly accommodating to the court injunction on registration. The CRD's move to

extend the injunction another year actually found the local attorneys sug-
gesting an informal agreement to that effect. This was first occasion in
CRD agents' memory of such cooperation, but Panola was also the first
county to get this far in implementing the earlier 1957 law.

First Changes in Panola's Voting

Mobilizing black voting in Panola began with an outside biracial group
who saw themselves as "agents of change."[4] The Council of Federated
Organizations (COFO) was one part of the national civil rights coalition that
appeared throughout the South in the turbulent summer of 1964. About
forty COFO volunteers came to Panola from across the nation in order to
register blacks. Using churches as organizational centers, faced with hostile whites, harassed by local officials (including the voting registrar), certain that the federal government was indifferent to their efforts—these
young whites and blacks believed that the leverage point in racial change
was the ballot. Consequently, their efforts focused mainly on encouraging local blacks to register and then to vote. But COFO workers agreed that
their efforts were less important than what the local black leaders did
within their community.

Among these, a farmer, Robert Miles, and a minister, Ray Middleton,
became key mobilizers, despite living with considerable danger. "Danger" was no exaggeration, as some Panola whites responded with hostility
in actions and words. The action included vandalism of black churches,
threatening drive-by of cars, constant verbal threats of violence, a cross
burning, objects thrown into black homes, bodily assaults, and the use of
firearms (Miles's home was shotgunned from a passing car). There were
also economic reprisals against black registrants on some plantations, who
were fired when notices appeared in the local paper with their names.
Local officials used police and court officials to arrest and sentence the
white volunteers and local blacks on various charges, most of which were
overturned on appeal. One of the first signs of changed attitudes in Mississippi appeared later, when the district attorney active in this effort, Clifford Finch, was years later elected governor of Mississippi on a platform
of being "for all the people." He was among the first Mississippi governors
to call for racial peace and to appoint blacks to public office—changes that
did not sit well with whites back in Batesville.

There was also much white verbal hostility by recalcitrants against the
volunteers. Locals saw all of this as an "invasion" by "outside agitators"
who did not "understand the South"; they were probably "Communists"
who were driven by sexual desires. Local whites who thought they were
personally close to blacks (usually their domestic help or field hands) were
astounded when blacks registered despite white denunciations of out-

siders. More violent reaction by whites existed outside the county, such as the murder of three civil rights workers in Philadelphia, south of Panola County, but locally there developed an awareness of new restraints upon recalcitrant whites. These constraints were seen in the presence of federal agents of the FBI and CRD, the swarm of national media looking for violence, and the reluctance of many whites to be this violent, no matter their deep disgust at changes. The last group was quietly mobilized by business leaders in the White Citizens' Council. These local formations could air fears, spread caution against violence in "their" county, and deputize a "citizens' militia" to back the police to resist demonstrations. The last came to nothing, although it tells much about how strongly whites felt about this storm of change.

Registration and Electoral Results before 1970

What were the results of this black mobilization across the dusty hamlets and merchant towns of Panola County? The record demonstrates a presence of new groups, tactics, and bloc voting. In this summer of 1964, the Freedom Democratic Party of Mississippi (FDP) organized across the state to send its own delegates to the Democratic national nominating convention and to hold a mock presidential election. Robert Miles and two other Panola leaders were FDP convention delegates, and Miles sat on the FDP state committee. A program of "Freedom Registration" registered 80,000 blacks in the state (4,000 in Panola), foreshadowing what later civil rights acts would accomplish. There was a black slate to a local federal farm organization, which, even though it was defeated, was the first local biracial contest; it was also a foreshadowing of future elections. But it was a gain in that it marked increasing political sophistication for a group new to being full citizens.

When the 1965 Voting Rights Act appeared, however, blacks quickly registered in large numbers under the stimulus of COFO and, in Panola, a Voting Rights League. By August 1965, blacks had enough votes to contest a state legislative election, although their candidate—a white—lost. In early 1966, the first black candidate for any local office ran, but also lost, the contest for the South Panola school board; there was only one "incident" at a polling place. The 1966 shooting of James Meredith, a national civil rights figure, just north of Panola stimulated greater black registration locally. By the spring of 1966, over 2,000 blacks were registered, as were over 6,400 whites. However, in the 1966 U.S. Senate election, the powerful incumbent, James Eastland, was returned in a statewide vote. A black candidate, Clifton Whitley, pulled a very cohesive bloc of votes in Panola's black sections—almost two-thirds in Batesville's west side. But these votes were few; only about 500 black votes were cast in the election, compared to the white votes of about 3,500. This election was the first sign of black apathy that would continue to hinder black political effectiveness in decades ahead.

In the primary and general elections of 1967, Panola's blacks mobilized their first large-scale effort since Reconstruction days. The Voting League explained to newly registered blacks the mechanics of the polling booth, provided guards at polling places, and endorsed white candidates. This last was done quietly so as not to antagonize white voters—the "kiss of death" problem, as blacks termed it. Candidates were endorsed due to their earlier record of treating blacks fairly. They actually appeared before black caucuses to explain how they would be "fair to everybody" and "give justice." Even District Attorney Finch repeatedly called on Robert Miles to secure his support.

How effective was the effort in this 1967 election? In the first primary, thirteen of fifteen candidates endorsed by black groups won a majority or had the highest plurality; but their gubernatorial candidate lost statewide. In the second primary two weeks later, four of six endorsees won; the eight heavily black precincts gave them a larger majority than they received county-wide. But racial interests were parallel in some races; the Voters League and Rotary Club (as a local paper noted) agreed on nominees in five contests in this second primary. Yet cohesive bloc voting by blacks was clearly emerging in the vote for white candidates.

But would the bloc vote be enough if black candidates ran for local office? The county's board of supervisor elections provided the first test in early 1968 when Robert Miles ran for a seat. He was first in a special election but with only a plurality (25%), and then lost heavily in the run-off against a well-known white. The winner focused only on getting out the vote in an election where whites outnumbered black registrants. In some black precincts, Miles did not get even a majority, and he clearly attracted only few white votes. That last outcome would be repeated throughout the South in years to come.

So in these early elections after suffrage, the blacks' problems were clear. Their lower registration rates and reduced electoral turnouts sharply cut their ability to elect black candidates. But the successful alternative was to support white candidates who were more supportive of black concerns.

Summary

In the mid-1960s, then, unusual forces had impinged upon Panola and other southern counties that would alter their political system dramatically. The federal enforcement of more effective methods of implementation, the mobilization of registrants by courageous local blacks and white outsiders, the constant media attention to white violence—all combined to bring many blacks to Panola's courthouse to register. However, black voters in the early days showed electorally that the black candidates could not win, while backing supportive white candidates worked much better. Nevertheless, in the minds of both races the law had brought on three clearly recognized changes. Law had first eliminated violence from elections, then had produced white candidates more willing to recognize black needs and to forgo racial demagoguery, and, finally, had oriented local agencies to meeting some black service needs.

Over the next two decades, as noted in the previous chapter, these first consequences of the new laws would expand into something even more significant for the politics of Panola and the South. The acquisition of black suffrage would affect the political cognition and behavior of both races in a fashion that, in turn, altered their political system so that it slowly adjusted to these new influences. Further, the local context, including its leadership, would differentiate this external influence of law.

Federal School Desegregation

If schooling brings people to a better life in America, the two systems in the South—black and white—failed because of weak standards. Characteristically, Panola's schools prior to 1965 had ranked very low on almost any scale—funding, staff training, instructional services, and student achievement.[5] Even more noticeable, they were rigidly segregated in the pattern of the traditional culture. To challenge this deep-rooted condition, other federal agents were to appear, again using litigation.

Pre-1965 Schooling

Two school districts, north and south, centered on Batesville and Sardis respectively with the Tallahatchie River serving as a border. On most measures, these schools were ranked as middling or lower among districts in Mississippi (e.g., achievement, attendance, instructional costs); they ranked even lower on supplies and libraries. On such scales, black schools always ranked much lower than whites. Typically, only Batesville had a four-year high school for blacks, and there was none in Sardis. The state reported in 1955 that white students had more faculty, more school buses, more foreign language training, and higher per pupil expenditures. Black schools in the county lacked equipment, their curriculum was limited, and their teachers were less trained and taught more than one grade.

The total result was mediocre student achievement for whites, with blacks achievement even lower. Thus, by 1960 almost 63 percent of the blacks had finished school at grade six (39% by fourth grade), compared to only 15 percent of the whites. The proportion of blacks to whites having no education at all was enormous, 4.5 times greater than whites; the ratio for graduation from college was even worse; and twelve times as many whites as blacks finished high school. Had census data been broken down for the two districts, the black conditions above the Tallahatchie would have been even worse; there, as local observers noted, plantocrats saw teachers as no more than baby-sitters. However, before the firestorm of the 1960s, whites in north Panola had begun to rebuild black schools, not to achieve parity with whites but to fend off court challenges. This, then, was segregated education in an average county in a poor state and region, where the will and the resources to improve education for either race had always been limited.

The Initiation of Desegregation

As interviews and administrative records demonstrated, the two school districts would react in different styles in the first stage, but both also fought off federal guidelines. Two federal laws were involved, the Civil Rights Act of 1964 and the Elementary and Secondary Act of 1965, and both interacted.[6] The 1965 ESEA forbade the use of federally funded programs in segregated schools, while the 1964 CRA banned discrimination based on race, among other criteria. While southern districts might ignore the latter, they could not ignore the federal grants that Washington could provide or withhold.

Consequently, these two Panola districts, like hundreds throughout the South, submitted their desegregation plans to meet federal guidelines to the Office of Civil Rights (OCR) of the U.S. Department Health, Education, and Welfare (HEW).[7] The two districts agreed they would desegregate two grades a year for six years, which was the state's suggested strategy. Within months, however, the OCR rejected them and required prompt revision. A north Panola representative then agreed with OCR to desegregate four grades a year; but the south Panola school board wrangled over such a plan for several months. Both federal and local officials held meetings to acquaint some whites with what lay ahead, but there was no outreach to the blacks.

The first strategy of southern desegregation under the OCR stimulus involved white school boards adopting "freedom of choice" schemes by which either race could go to any school, even one dominated by the other race. But it was clear in the first few years that not much changed. Thus, desegregation in Panola's 1965–1966 year generated little publicity, few blacks applied to white elementary schools (seventeen students in north Panola and thirty-four in south Panola), and no whites entered black schools. Nevertheless, in that spring of 1966 both districts' officials filed assurances of compliance with the OCR, using documents heavy in data and plans. Panolians now knew what was transpiring because local newspapers published these results. In the next two school years the same pattern and result occurred in the middle and high schools; that is, there was little movement by blacks and none by whites.

As early as autumn of 1966, the OCR signaled its disappointment with these results. Their officials at first reported satisfaction with the sincerity of effort in north Panola but not in south Panola, where they recommended improvement. But these OCR efforts were delayed in the latter by the white superintendent and board, and so in winter 1968 the OCR charged them with seventy-one complaints of discrimination contrary to existing law. All pending grants for federal funds would be deferred, and other federal, and even state, agencies would be notified.

A hearing on the complaints six months later produced substantial OCR data that four of seven schools in south Panola were still segregated, that all faculties and bus transportation were segregated, that facilities for white students were superior, and so on. The district's defense was that for many reasons it could not comply, and so segregation should continue. Not surprisingly, a federal hearing examiner in spring of 1968 supported the OCR, finding that only 2 percent of the black students had enrolled in the white high school. Accordingly, the examiner judged that freedom of choice had failed to desegregate, and so this district was not entitled to federal funds until the situation was corrected. While the board's attorney raised a few minor objections, in autumn of 1968 this decision was approved by HEW; Congress was then notified, although it could not overturn the judgment.

Meanwhile, recognition grew among south Panola whites that this federal judgment meant that their favorite reaction to desegregation, freedom of choice, had failed. Its newspaper, *The Panolian*, which was to play an important role for the community in fully reporting these unfolding events, had laid out the OCR complaints, the federal funds that were to be lost (half a million dollars a year), and the hardships likely to result. Also, the superintendent reported to business groups on those results. But as the 1968–1969 school year opened, there was still no local planning for further desegregation. But elsewhere, federal courts were invalidating the scheme used in south Panola. The U.S. Supreme Court earlier that spring had clearly overturned such plans; the purpose of desegregation, the Court declared, was not "a 'white' school and a 'Negro' school, but just schools."[8] Clearly, this was not the case in south Panola.

As for the district north of the Tallahatchie River, the same pattern was repeated but lagged for about a year. Freedom of choice there had attracted only a few more black students to white schools (4%), which was not even the proportion (10%) that local officials judged (wrongly) as being what the

OCR had in mind. After observing little change, the OCR filed complaints in autumn of 1968 with evidence much like that found below the river.

In American federalism, a policy battle lost at one level can be pursued at a higher level for yet another skirmish. Southern whites did this in autumn of 1968 by seeking a new national law to overturn desegregation, an attack led by Panola's own congressman, Jamie Whitten, a powerful figure until the early 1990s. His repeal would forbid any fund cutoffs for "forced busing" or any other scheme that compelled students to attend schools not chosen by their parents; but his effort failed in Congress. In the 1968 presidential election, southern whites supported Republican Richard Nixon, expecting him to ease up on OCR's early constraints. But shortly after being sworn in, Nixon did not do so. Rather, he upheld the fund cutoffs of five southern districts, including south Panola; but he did provide a two-month extension to settle the current disputes.

Despite Whitten's indignant response, Panola school officials feared much less the loss of federal money (most went to blacks anyhow, they claimed) than the Department of Justice seeking a court action to desegregate. Within a week after Nixon's action and mindful of this fear, south Panola officials began a series of meetings that lasted two months to discuss a new plan. Wrote *The Panolian*, "School Board Needs Divine Guidance. . . . We have no advice, no solutions." Out of these negotiations did emerge a plan that HEW accepted in March 1969 containing three parts:

— There would be only one high school in south Panola, serving *both* races, but enrollment in middle and elementary schools would reflect racially their neighborhoods.
— All faculty would be desegregated, but none would be dismissed if schools were closed or encountered lower enrollment.
— The plan would commence in 1970–1971, but a year before that 20 percent of the blacks would go to white schools and the faculty would start desegregating.

Reactions were decidedly mixed. OCR Director Leon Panetta (later congressman and President Clinton's chief of staff) found that south Panola was the only one of the six districts with threatened fund cutoffs that had arrived at an acceptable plan. Newspapers and group discussion locally provided a clear signal to both races from authoritative local sources that desegregation would commence and not be delayed. About seventy white families then withdrew their children from south Panola schools to form a private school. These modern recalcitrants had realized the failure of their strategy of resistance to desegregation in freedom-of-choice plans. So instead of fighting to adjust, they fled to their new private schools.

However, that strategy had already caused two problems for black parents. Those whose children attended white schools were shocked and frustrated by their poor records in the new site. Inadequate schooling in the inferior black schools had not prepared many black parents for enforcing good study habits or for those white teachers who were contemptuous of their children. It was a crushing realization for blacks to find that their children's tickets for a better life through education went nowhere. A second problem for black parents was the fear—and sometimes reality—of white owners on plantations who might (and in some cases did) fire them if their children went to white schools. "Freedom of choice" meant little when there was also the freedom to fire those who exercised it.

As for those whites who could not abandon public schools, freedom of choice had meant that their worst fears of desegregation were *not* realized. They had feared desegregation even more than voter registration because racial contact in the schools would be daily, continuous, and detested. Their opposition to any further desegregation was rooted in fears of violence and in a certainty of the reduced quality of schooling for their own children. Yet surprisingly, few white families in south Panola withdrew from even this limited racial contact that the first plan created. As noted in chapter 2, few whites withdrew from public schools in the South.

However, neither race knew what to expect of the next stage of desegregation, when many students would interact in both districts after 1970. As shown in chapter 6, in north Panola the plantation whites fully abandoned public schools for a small private school, leaving behind an almost-black public system under ineffective leadership. But in south Panola, both races desegregated the public system under effective biracial leadership. Thus an understanding of the implementation of law was affected by differences in leadership, even in a seemingly similar local context.

Economic Rights: Subsidy and Regulation

Opportunities for the good life in society are always maldistributed, so that a dynamic element of societal life is the struggle of some to secure more opportunities. The old "redneck" saying "Them as has, gits" recognizes that maldistribution. Many of these opportunities arise from the interactions of a market economy. The public sector can promote or defend those opportunities through use of two major legal instruments—subsidy and regulation. That is, law may result in the transfer of public funds to individuals in order to expand their opportunities for a better life (i.e., subsidy). Or, law may restrain certain economic behaviors that restrict those opportunities (i.e., regulation). Not surprisingly, then, in Panola County and the South in 1960 most of those economic opportunities were concentrated in the hands of white plantocrats, merchants, and businessmen. The mass of both blacks and whites, on the other hand, had economic opportunities so limited as not to exist. However, as the civil rights era opened, that maldistribution was to be mitigated by federal laws using both subsidy and regulation. A review of that earlier period now will set the scene for an analysis of the expansion of Panola economic opportunities for both races over the next quarter century.

Federal Subsidy of Economic Rights

While the South rejected any federal regulation in civil rights, it accepted federal subsidies, mostly for whites.[9] Mississippi had received so much federal money by the mid-1960s that it constituted 25–30 percent of its total receipts. No wonder, then, that state governors and private businessmen struggled for a larger federal share of subsidies. Such income was one of the few ways to close the gap between the economies of Mississippi and the nation. A clear sign of this need occurred in the late 1960s when a private corporation of fifty highly influential white and black business and professional men (the Mississippi Economic Council) was organized to increase the flow of federal funds to the state.

What happened with this national largesse when it flowed into Mississippi is typified in Panola County, where federal subsidies expanded economic opportunities. During the full flush of Great Society spending (1966–1968), in this county alone there were twenty-two *new* federal programs announced, as well as even more money for continuing programs in schools and agriculture. It was a golden cascade—military contracts, job and farm worker training, poverty studies, Medicare assistance, industrial park development, city planning, promotion of economic growth, more recreation facilities, and the building of a new library, bridge, hospital, and five water systems. Into the underdeveloped economy of Panola County these programs spilled down from thirteen federal agencies to produce $8 million (over half from military contracts). Whether it was money shared with other counties in loans and contracts, these direct grants required some limited matching funds from county or state. But at the personal level, the federal largesse meant $245 for each individual or $1,000 a family; its multiplier effects on the local economy were incalculable.

In the politics of American federal policy making, subsidies can promote economic opportunities at both ends of the income scale. Thus in Panola, some thirty federal farm programs (totaling $6.9 million in 1969 alone) assisted a local agriculture that was dominated by a few plantocrats. At the other end, the poor obtained help in school milk and luncheon subsidies for children and food stamps for adults from just one federal department—Agriculture. But there was a maldistribution along this income scale, because these farm funds meant that a few plantocrats got the most and the many poor got the least. However, many plantocrats and local business-men here and elsewhere had a different perception; they thought that the distribution was loaded more heavily toward the poor. Maybe that perception arose from finding the poor, especially blacks, obtaining increased economic opportunities in other federal programs such as farm co-ops, water and sewer services, hospital facilities, job retraining, and infrastructure services. Yet few blacks at that time believed that they had got much help from these subsidies, especially the equal job economic opportunities provided by the Civil Rights Act of 1964. Certainly, such effort could touch only a few when a very large pool of unemployed blacks continued to exist. The same was true for poor whites.

To deal with this pool there were federal subsidy programs, often termed "public welfare." Where few in Panola County received even a middling income from private sector jobs, blacks and whites had an income maintained primarily by public assistance. The total subsidy for Panola was over $500,000 in 1964–1965. These funds went to the aged (the largest beneficiaries), dependent children, and the blind or disabled; two-thirds or more of such federal funds went to blacks. Food stamps appeared in the county in 1967, and 85 percent of the $855,000 went to blacks that year. Even then, malnutrition appeared, arising as much from an inadequate understanding of nutrition as from lack of money. Health care in hospitals was even less certain, as blacks' ability to get treatment was restricted by segregation. However, Sardis had voted overwhelmingly by referendum to provide a desegregated hospital. That happened due to a federal prerequisite to obtaining funds for health care; local officials referred to this as "strings." Nevertheless, even with subsidized funds, both races still lacked adequate medical care, however one measured it.

It was clear at the beginning of civil rights laws in the mid-1960s that federal subsidies had benefited many economic groups and both races, despite their maldistribution. Economic opportunities had been improved, even if marginally. Washington had already become a major factor in allocating these economic opportunities from which both the rich and the poor benefited. While southern whites would look upon federal regulation as an assault on their culture, federal subsidy, on the other hand, was a case of mutual seduction.

Subsidies can also work to broaden economic opportunities through development programs that attract or maintain local businesses which, in turn, subsidize jobs and generate local revenue. As noted, Batesville had made some strides in this regard. Yet employment was still limited for both races, and more so for blacks. It was as if two races lived together geographically but existed in different stages of economic development, that is, a third-world nation surrounding an advanced nation. Despite its volume, federal subsidies touched only lightly on black poverty while slightly increasing black economic opportunities. Yet it was not the only path to redistributing those economic opportunities, because improved economic development could produce more jobs with greater income.

There was a potential conflict between such development and white supremacy. Civil rights controversy and federal involvement would threaten development if white supremacy prevailed. As always, business was nervous about investing capital in an uncertain social order. However, to choose development under federal guidelines would mean weakening the traditional discrimination that, in turn, would arouse white opinion. In the event, when new plant construction in this state dropped 25 percent during the civil rights turmoil of 1964, the white Mississippi Economic Council promptly issued a clear stand: *The national law must be obeyed or else the state economy would decline.* In the decades ahead as we will see, both private development and federal subsidies improved economic opportunities when they were pursued energetically, although differences in local cultures would alter the results.

Federal Regulation of Economic Rights

While subsidy is an instrument to improve economic opportunities,[10] regulation affects behavior by proscribing traditional market practices that had blocked development. Preventing economic discrimination in use of public facilities was the most publicized feature of the 1964 Civil Rights Act, even though it would occasion few compliance problems in Panola County and the South. The law's ban on using federal money in programs that discriminated was significant in providing at least a few more economic opportunities for blacks in this region. A ban on job discrimination and a presidential executive order promoting equal opportunity among employers with federal contracts would become the two major forms of regulation.

However, by 1970 the promise of such federal action had been little realized. The federal Equal Employment Opportunity Commission (EEOC) that was designed to administer the regulation was weak. It would use only the compliance method of conciliation with employers, and it would select as targets only individual, rather than group, discrimination. Few gains for blacks were reported. As for the executive order against job discrimination by private contractors, its administration was fragmented among many agencies so that its implementation was buried under these other agendas.

Panola County perfectly reflected this early implementation stage when there was only limited regulation. Enforcement of Title VII of the 1964

Civil Rights Act was started in early 1965 with an organized effort to integrate a Batesville cafe by young blacks "sitting in" to request service. What happened thereafter fits a pattern noted elsewhere.

At first, the white owner refused service, then the blacks were ejected by whites, and the police arrested a black leader. This incident precipitated a drama familiar for that time. Black picketers assembled around the county courthouse, some were jailed, a larger demonstration involved crowds of both races, a resulting free-for-all broke out, and the blacks got sentences that were later overturned on appeal. All in all, this was pretty normal for the period, when blacks first flexed their group muscle to challenge the old order of white supremacy.

In the next few years, however, black complaints from this county to the CRD for six cases of refusal of service were negotiated with the white owners who, when urged to comply, did so without court action. They complied relatively promptly because other businesses were doing so and because not many blacks were using these facilities anyhow. Those whites, while complying, could condemn "the feds" but still remain in business and fit the traditional culture. Consequently, this part of the law did little to expand economic opportunities for blacks here or elsewhere in the South.

By 1970, even less had been done to enlarge job opportunities for blacks using the 1964 Civil Rights Act. Economic changes were squeezing labor off the farm at a rate too fast to be accommodated by the available non-farm jobs in Panola County, even though the latter were increasing. Even job opportunities in local branches of federal agencies found few blacks in these positions. Industrial jobs might have offered more job opportunities, but their supply was limited; there were about 50 percent more of both races seeking work than there were jobs.

However, racial discrimination was also at work. Few of those hired in local industries were black, and other blacks had to commute to work in Memphis forty miles away. Some firms—including the largest—would not provide the author with figures on black hiring; the four that did had hired one to three blacks. The limited schooling of blacks also worked against them, providing a justification for employers to hire whites. While figures before and after passage of the 1964 act do show some improvement in hiring blacks in some firms, the estimated percentages were still small. However, two plants did report that 50 percent of their job-holders were black—all in entry-level positions. But even had these hirings been doubled or more, black unemployment would still have been large because of the excess labor supply, their lack of training, and white discrimination.

Blacks themselves tried to use the law. After 1964 they reported to the EEOC instances of alleged discrimination in hiring. Indeed, one woman took two Panola plants to court after the EEOC had found evidence to agree with her complaints. While the EEOC might help, its efforts were limited and involved no harsh penalties for the recalcitrants. Other federal agencies were just as slack in enforcing the regulation of economic opportunities. The Defense Department gave little effective oversight to the 1964 Equal Employment Opportunity Act's requirements about nondiscrimination in military contracts. A $4.6 million contract with one Panola industry provided no evidence of DOD compliance with the president's executive order; reports throughout the South were quite similar. Those results are suggestive of the power of national and regional forces over in southerners' business interests, legislators' influence in Washington, and the large military presence in the region. There was an implicit *quid pro quo* working here over federal funds and nondiscrimination requirements. That is, keep the money, but do little about discrimination, which would, after all, interfere with the traditional culture.

In retrospect, by 1970 federal subsidy programs had accomplished more than regulation in increasing black economic opportunities, but neither had done all that much. At least, subsidy did provide a flimsy floor for providing income, food, housing, and health. But measured against resources available to local whites, to the South, and to the nation as a whole, the gap in economic opportunities for Panola's blacks was staggering. Regulation had appeared, but it involved only a weak law and an even weaker national implementation. Enforcement was further diffused by the political and economic power of white southerners resisting changes in old patterns of segregation. But the most critical problem for the poor—black and white—was the absence of nonfarm jobs for those driven off the land by other federal laws (e.g., the minimum wage law) and by the increasing mechanization of agriculture.

Federalizing Conditions in Panola: A Summary

The application of federal civil rights law for blacks in this county and elsewhere had varying results, running from the wide reaching and totally unsuspected to the minimal. Voting laws had registered and mobilized a majority of eligible blacks. But none had been elected to any public office, even though here was a potential for using the vote to obtain further resources from white office holders. As for schooling, this county and the South took different paths to desegregation. However, all schools were still poor by any measure of regional and national standards. In the economic order, federal subsidies had done much more than regulation to expand black economic opportunities, but these improvements were far from impressive.

These changes for Panola's blacks can be characterized fairly as only minimal, either in scope or consequence. Yet both races felt overwhelmed by another sense of a dramatic change within a short time. All attributed this to the emergence of federal law in the county's social order. In each institution blacks could point to how far they needed to go, and some whites still feared they would do it. But suffrage had not elected blacks to office.

New perceptions of a new social reality were emerging, although it was quite a confused one. While the old order of the traditional culture had been challenged by new law, both races had overestimated how much real change had taken place; the change involved was not as big as either opponents or supporters thought. As with any person who is struck, the familiar reality was jarred into a scramble of perceptions, and people had a poor grasp of what had happened. The new social reality and new perceptions based on it were not yet evident. But clearly there was a sense that something basic had changed in the social order.

In the old days of King Cotton, the monotony of plantation life was broken only by the steamboat's whistle around the bend, which created anticipation that something important was to happen. Over a century later, most Panola blacks who looked around also believed that something important was coming around the bend. This book now turns to explain what came later, and how it altered behavior, perceptions, and resources in this county and the South. We will find this account of social change to rest in hard data as well as in the stories that locals tell, who, like those once blind, began to see a new culture.

Part II | Institutional and Individual Changes in Panola

The changes that were to occur over the next quarter-century in this county and the region focus primarily on social reactions to the intervention of law. However, other forces of change were also at work. The economic order also altered, due to external forces, so that income from agriculture dropped well below that from industry, tourism, and intergovernmental funds. New industries emerged to provide the largest source of jobs. Also, state government became energized, sometimes with federal stimulus, to expand and control local services in their quality, equity, and efficiency. Indeed, from one perspective, "outsider" influence stemmed much more from the state capitol than from Washington. Further, the norms of urban professionals, rooted in universalistic concepts and covering most of the nation, became guidelines that helped shape "local control."

It is the changes brought on by federal—and increasingly state—law that is our focus here. The purpose is not to prove that law caused all the changes noted in this section of the book. Rather, it is to focus on how law changed the traditional reality and, in so doing, changed whites' racial perceptions and, ultimately, their cognitions. However, there were also nonlegal influences to note in this analysis.

The changes that took place locally rose from two sources: the institution and the individual. Institutions—regular ways of thinking and acting about important matters in life—focus and embody individual energies and goals. The interaction of individuals and institutions requires studying, so we may learn how new institutions are formed that go on to dominate the social reality, and how individuals provide these new institutions with energy and goals.

We will focus on three aspects of social reality in this county, although they are linked to the larger culture of the state and region. The aspects are, first, government and politics; next, schooling the young; and, last, expanding economic opportunities. In each area, we explore how individuals responded to ongoing changes in what had once been familiar. Whether using personal accounts or analytical statistics, we can construct the influence of a new culture that arose from the old. In judging the "reality" of social change, we need multiple sources of information on those experiencing this change.[1] Multiple sources permit us to find agreement on who did what to whom with what results. Moreover, a span of time is needed to study the changes. Time is a curious taskmaster. Too narrow a time span means that the overall meaning may be lost, but too broad a span means that one may lose the details. The time span used for this book is the quarter century after the passage of the Voting Rights Act of 1965, which allows us to observe two generations of Americans, both public officials and ordinary citizens, through changes in politics, schools, and jobs.

The public record is one source of knowledge about Panola County. It includes voter registration rolls, voting results, school programs and student achievement, local economic indicators, and development activities. These records document the quantitative changes, but tell little about its subjective context. For that dimension, another source was used—interviews with local people.[2] Because it relies on impressions of past and present, this source is more subject to bias, although the triangulation of many views helps confirm what happened. But this source is also more complex, more useful, and more informative on the subjective reaction to change. A third source of knowledge is what local newspapers report—or ignore—about local events, which can reflect change when viewed over time. While newspapers serve to mirror some aspects of society, all scholars who use them know they also mirror certain biases of local culture, including those of the newspaper owners. But in a study focusing on cultures, this source can be quite useful.

Using these sources of assessing reality, which are different but related, we will explore in this section the reach of federal law over time into the traditional culture of the South, as reflected in this rural community. Once the significant details have been established, we can turn, in the last section, to their consequences for the new world of perception and cognition that now exists in Panola County.

4 | Local Politics and Black Empowerment

From the perspective of Panolians and southerners since 1960, the nature of the political system, born and bred in traditionalism, has drastically altered, including the new role of blacks in the system. These changes struck both races quickly after passage of the Voting Rights Act of 1965 because blacks soon registered in sizable numbers. In the decades that followed, black empowerment altered not only the party system. It also led to basic changes for blacks, by enabling their entry into officialdom, by granting them more public services, and by earning them more political respect among some whites. The tone of politics had shifted from violent to collaborative racism by both groups on some issues of mutual benefit. In the process and over time, new white leaders arose who accepted this empowerment and worked with it. They did so, however, without much loss of power, so in this aspect the old style of politics had not changed. But to understand the change that occurred, we must understand the past.

Politics in the Old South Style

Parties had long been a major instrument of white control, not only over blacks but over poor whites as well.[1] White power had excluded blacks from voting and improving public services. Earlier accounts have detailed that traditional process in Panola County in the 1960s,[2] but an illustration will help show how a culture of personalized power once created local fiefdoms over blacks and poor whites.

When southern blacks actually attempted to enter politics in the 1960s, they found other and informal controls on their lives that were rooted in violence—cautions, threats, intimidation, beatings, and even death. Not all whites had used these methods, but all levels contributed. Poor whites would use violence, the middle class would politely caution their black cooks or farm hands against any effort at voter registration, and the affluent would block federal actions seeking to implement change.[3]

Many white Panolians of today are shocked to hear about the violent events that occurred over voting registration in their county a quarter century ago. If they are dissembling, they are exhibiting a characteristic feature of the Old South attitudes, namely, control the blacks but be discreet about it to outsiders. But if they are honestly shocked, it shows how the older traditional influence still suppresses their understanding of just how raw the threat of violence was in sustaining white dominance.

Old Politics in the Ferguson Machine

When the civil rights movement hit the South, the traditional system reacted in a uniform pattern:[4] town ordinances were drawn up against protests, individuals and officials resisted voter registration, local judges condemned offenders, police and sheriffs used intimidation or actual violence, state and federal elected officials fulminated, and people covertly threatened beating and death—and in some cases *did* beat and kill blacks.

Many of these reactions were seen in Panola County in that period, although violence was much more restrained here. Local residents reported on these activities in interviews in the 1960s.[5] Southern politics was typified in Batesville's mayor, Daniel Ferguson, who had held office for years before 1973. In resisting the new federal civil rights laws, he acted out the classic model of the Old South white politician controlling a one-party system. That system had always rested on a "friends and neighbors" approach with white voters. It was a closed system of acquaintances in which a few friends were encouraged to vote and be rewarded, while their enemies were not.[6]

Ferguson's power in Batesville, built over the years, was linked to other structures of power at county, state, and congressional levels. But at all these levels, decision making was closed, not just to blacks, but to most whites. Ferguson's tight control was to be checked, however, first by federal law and court, and then by new, young white merchants seeking economic development. The latter's values were less in support of black rights to vote—although they also did that—than they were in favor of economic development.

Ferguson's aims were to limit black empowerment and to oppose new industry. He had used county supervisors to restrain growth by not altering ordinances that could have attracted new business. His efforts paralleled those of the largest property owners around Batesville and the big planters who feared wage competition for their black field hands from new industry.[7]

But there was also an aura of corruption about him, never charged and never proven. Those who knew him tell today of "back room deals," "money under the table," "satisfying his own little group of old men," and so on. "For years," said a longtime observer, "much of city business was carried in Mayor Ferguson's coat pocket," sometimes without recourse to the city council. No problem with that, however, as the council members were his cronies. As a local judge, he held irregular sessions and kept few records.[8] This corruption touched also the county's board of supervisors, where Mayor Ferguson had some close supporters. Statewide graft in these offices was widely publicized in the 1980s following enforcement of the law by the state comptroller, Richard Mabus, who later became governor. His investigations found that the state was filled with local fiefdoms, fragmented and often corrupt, including Panola. For friends, supervisors built culverts, provided fuel, dumped and spread gravel on home driveways, and built county buildings on their properties.[9] In the wave of investigation and fraud cases,[10] some Panolians went to jail.

Reaction to these scandals later led most counties (including Panola) to adopt a structural reform to introduce some elements of honesty and efficiency. As part of the great change in local government after 1980, the post-Mabus reform for counties included the "unit system," in which county services were placed in the hands of a county-wide administrator.[11] After five years of trying it out, Panolians voted in 1992 to retain it, although by a slim margin.

Earlier though, this mind-set of Mayor Ferguson and the Delta leaders, of keeping the existing economic order and running a game of favors, had been opposed by the slow emergence of a new group of Panolians with a different agenda. The larger Batesville merchants and those new to the area, often younger businessmen, and a local editor wanted to open the town to economic development to create a sound local economy and to overcome poverty. By backing a young probusiness mayor—Bobby Baker— these new men, working with black and white leaders, ended Ferguson's tenure in 1973. Thereafter, they supported candidates who were open to economic development and were in turn supported by voters of both races. It is important to note that this new development orientation was first heard about in local politics from a black civil rights leader in 1968. In an election that year, the first black candidate in over a century running for the board of supervisors, Robert Miles, Sr., announced that he sought "the economic development of Beat 5 [his district] and Panola County, which will include more jobs for the unemployed, better schools and welfare programs for the poor. I feel that these are our greatest needs at this time."[12]

This overturn of traditional power illustrates one pattern that emerged in the South when federal laws supported blacks voting. The entrenched local whites were challenged by other merchants who favored the boosterism of economic development. But blacks also joined in, for they were interested in jobs that paid more than farmhand wages. The major factors that started this transition were a new white attitude about growth, a new black vote, and, behind it, federal law opening up new possibilities of a different reality.

As the voting law worked down into the context of local life, one source of that influence is found in how newspapers reported events over time, and a second in the views of participants. We will use this perspective next, and follow it with a case study of broader changes.

Newspapers' Mirror of Change in Politics

One window on the community is opened by local newspapers. It is not a perfect view, though, but over time newspapers reflect a rough image of events affecting both the plain and the powerful.[13] Newspapers indicate the overt public agenda, that is, those issues thrust on the community for decision making. Of equal interest is what public issues are *not* featured, that constitute a hidden agenda and a hidden face of local power. These combine to obscure latent public problems.[14] Also important is the fact that in selecting certain local events over others, newspaper editors in small towns reflect locally dominant values; if they did not, they lost subscribers. Consequently, newspapers provide one—but not the only— sense of the law's effects and, by inference, their meaning for the community. One judgment is clear from this review of local newspapers. Over the quarter century of Panola's history in which blacks voted, white reactions have changed from bitter recalcitrance to a subdued pragmatic acceptance of great social change.

Two weekly newspapers serve this county, in north Panola the *Southern Reporter* and in south Panola *The Panolian*. The circulation of *The Panolian* is larger, and its success has won it awards as the state's best weekly in the nineties. The *Southern Reporter*, however, is much older and serves the values of the Delta culture, as we will see. In both papers there is woven the regular rituals of citizens' lives—a bulletin board of weddings, births, and deaths, of church, school, and commerce, and of local sports. No issue of either paper ignores these indicators of personal and community life. Interspersed among these human-interest items there is also local "news," that is, local and outside events of politics, schools, economic affairs, and government activity that the editors believe important for community life.

In earlier times, however, the newspapers failed to discuss any of the ordinary rituals in the black community; that omission indicates which race was involved in defining "the news." Later, when external events began to empower blacks, the papers once again reflected the values of the whites by resisting change. But there were some differences between the

Table 4.1   Summary of Editorial Stances of Two Panola Newspapers, 1960

Stance	The Panolian	Southern Reporter
Opposed to civil rights protests	7	9
Opposed to Communism at home or abroad	2	7
Supported "unpledged" democratic slate for presidency in state	4	0
Supported white control in Africa	0	2
Total	13	18

two papers, which reflect the underlying differences between the Delta and Hill cultures, mentioned in chapter 2. We can open these windows on the two communities by summarizing the news coverage in the two papers (table 4.1), focusing on each decade and starting with 1960, before Panolians felt any outside influence.

The 1960 Community

Prior to 1960, there were few references to blacks in any part of the local life except in an occasional echo of the outside world, such as the "Dixie-crat" revolt in 1948. But in 1960 the papers still had no reference to blacks in local politics, or much of anything else about this group. Yet the outside world was getting closer now, as seen in resentful editorial comments on national racial "threats."

Those views were expressed directly through news stories, while editorials and outside columnists were even stronger. All reflected fear and indignation at racial change. These themes included

— fear of black "agitation" over civil rights (demonstrations had just begun);
— support of laws to avoid voting for the Democratic presidential candidate, John Kennedy, and endorsement of his Republican opponent, Richard Nixon;
— fear of the Communists at home and abroad; and
— the Old South's distrust of Washington and politicians on other issues.

The sharper edge of these views was expressed in the *Southern Reporter*, the Delta newspaper, although it was still close to the Hill-based paper. The *Southern Reporter*'s coverage differed little from *The Panolian*'s on anti–civil rights editorials, but it argued that more white threats were coming from Communists or from black awareness rising in South Africa. Both papers supported unpledged presidential electors, so that former

Democrats in Mississippi could vote in a bloc, but the *Southern Reporter* used stronger words and ran more stories. However, on other policy issues, the two had different agendas but still with a southern outlook. Both supported an antiunion "right to work" referendum for the state constitution (the county later supported it overwhelmingly). Both papers also

— opposed larger federal budgets and labor "featherbedding" (the *Reporter* had twice as many stories);
— condemned violations of the state alcohol prohibition and supported local option to permit alcohol (*The Panolian* had twice as many);
— lamented funding welfare costs for those not deserving it (*The Panolian*); and
— saw federal aid to cities and education as an unwelcome growth of federal power (*Reporter*).

In short, this was the world of the traditional political culture, unaware of the black community and unconcerned about racial inequalities in votes, schools, and jobs. Our world is safe, was the dominant view, but those outsiders were becoming a threat.

The 1970 Community

A decade later, though, the threats had become realities. In 1960 there had been only a single black registered to vote, and by 1964 there were still only a few hundred. But under the Voting Rights Act of 1965, two years later, the total of black voters registered in the county was 2,060 and in the third year 3,500.[15] Moreover, by 1970, school desegregation was fully under way in south Panola, while whites were fleeing north Panola schools.

By 1970, the two white cultures of the county were clearly evident in their newspapers, as the two had sharply differed in their coverage of racial issues. Of the 28 racial stories and editorials in both papers that year, one-half focused on a single subject—criticism of school desegregation in Panola and the South. But *all* of these stories were found in one paper—the *Southern Reporter*. The Delta culture underlying that paper was clearly reflected in the widespread embitterment of the plantocracy. It had stories supporting tax credits for private schools, twice as often as *The Panolian* (Delta whites were creating such a school); fearing that whites would lose control in South Africa; and condemning the U.S. Senate's rejection of a southern conservative for the Supreme Court.

The flavor of the *Reporter* was seen in a single mid-January 1970 issue, which ran the following three stories:

— Senator Stennis's criticism of the unfair treatment of schools in the north and south United States, which he hoped would soon cease under a Nixon administration;

— a national editorialist applauding the Nixon administration's even-handed and conservative approach on these matters; and

— a local editorial condemning the federal courts for abandoning "freedom of choice" in the desegregation of schools, and fearing that tax exemptions for private schools would be denied.

Anyone reading the paper that day would be reinforced in the average white belief that enormous changes were attacking ancient traditions. These changes were clearly objects of fear for the whites and of hope for the blacks.

But note what was missing in these 1970 files. The voting rights struggle of the 1960s had now simply disappeared, barely five years after the 1965 act. There were no stories on who could register or vote. Indeed, stories were now appearing of blacks running for offices in major contests, such as U.S. Senate, House, and the local judicial circuit (all the black candidates lost, of course). The first of these appeared in the *Reporter* early that year but then faded, while *The Panolian* picked them up; the latter had probably the first story of black candidates appearing at a black political rally (October 29, 1970).

There were other signs of change in 1970. There was probably the first guest editorial by a white who *supported* biracialism, condemned segregation, and urged biracial cooperation for state problems (*The Panolian*, June 25). Those stories emerged in the Hill culture's *Panolian*, but not across the Tallahatchie River. The white Panola of 1970, then, had grudgingly swallowed one basic change in its political culture—black enfranchisement—but in its northern section was still resisting desegregation.

The 1980 Community

By 1980, another dramatic change was evident. Schooling conflict had now disappeared because desegregation was established in the public schools, while affluent whites had fled to private academies. Moreover, there were more signs of a two-party system emerging and of black candidates in local political contests. Stories, with accompanying photographs, dealt with blacks in municipal and school board elections, the caucuses of both parties at local and state levels, and state and national candidates who were appearing locally. The Republicans held their first state presidential preference primary in June 1980, and later a state Democratic caucus supported Jimmy Carter. That autumn in Panola County the Democrats won in both congressional and presidential contests. These events were covered by both newspapers and showed an emerging party activity that would set the pattern for future election years.

But in 1980, there were yet other signs of political change. Governor

William Winters had pledged at his inauguration that there would be no racial prejudice in his administration, a promise later confirmed, for he achieved a biracial record beyond that of any previous governor. This story was reported in the Hill's *The Panolian* (January 24) but not in the Delta paper. The Republicans had become an all-white party, while the Democrats had become biracial in federal elections. Democrats were also biracial at local and state levels, a sharing of leadership that was initiated in 1976 by the black leader Aaron Henry and the white governor Clifford Finch (himself a Panolian).[16]

Also, some blacks were winning seats in local office. In the March 1980 races for local school boards, a black won in north Panola although another lost in south Panola. Major problems in these schools were little noted in the county's newspapers, but black students in north Panola had engaged in a boycott over white school leadership that was mentioned only once in the *Southern Reporter*. Its editorial claimed neutrality but also feared that the boycott would cost state funds and was "dangerous by creating community antagonism to defeat the necessary bond issue" for a new school (October 23).

As a result, this world of 1980 saw more changes in the preceding decade than in any other period. There was now a new party that was biracial, the Democratic party, while the Republicans appeared as all white. A few blacks were elected to office but always from a heavily black district. And new state leadership had marked the first changes from the older culture of Mississippi politics. Behind it all lay a new federal law guaranteeing black enfranchisement.

The Post-1980 Community and the Federal Presence

The federal presence was still in Panola county a decade later. Table 4.2 summarizes local stories of federal influence in the dozen years after 1980. It shows that there were more black efforts to use the law to affect local elections by improving their representation and preventing "vote dilution." The federal influence had touched even the smallest hamlet—Crenshaw—as well as agencies of city, county, and state. Legislative seats were mostly involved in this change, but even elections for offices seemingly remote from the political scene, such as for circuit judges, were altered to make black votes effective.

Local power systems reacted to this influence not with the recalcitrance of outright rejection, characteristic of the 1960s, but by pragmatically using consultants and federal offices to adapt to the new political system. It is clear that blacks now had additional resources to challenge white control, even to the point of using a federal law to control a close election that blacks had first thought lost. The results show that by the late 1980s

Table 4.2   Federal Involvement in Voting Cases in Panola County from 1980

AUG. 1980	Batesville aldermen remove at-large representation to city council to avoid U.S. Department of Justice (USDJ) disapproval.
OCT. 1980	USDJ overturns Batesville's redistricting, so that a black ward could, by assigning whites to another ward, give blacks larger representation.
MARCH 1985	Federal court decree against county board of supervisors from black plaintiffs that left two of five districts majority black.
JUNE 1987	Federal court requires special election in hamlet of Crenshaw, abolishing at-large election.
MARCH 1989	Federal court issues statewide elections for primary and general elections for the circuit and chancery judges (including Panola) to be held in April and June; court criticizes the diluted black votes.
MARCH 1989	Legal challenge by civil rights attorney against Como and other communities for their at-large systems, which dilute black voting. Como's subsequent election showed a strong two-party system for first time.
FEB. 1991	County board of supervisors, through attorney's statement, seeks a consultant for input on ordering redistricting with dispatch; in the past, its reputation had been to delay change.
JULY 1991	USJD approved county's redistricting plan, leaving a filing deadline of only one week. But the USJD rejected the state's legislative redistricting (opposed by 20 black and 38 white legislators) because more minority districts were not provided. The north Panola school board asked the USJD for new ward lines (later approved), and the southern school board was also required to do so. If special elections were called in north Panola using paper ballots, they must be cleared by USDJ.
DEC. 1991	A failed school board bond issue in north Panola raises possibility of a suit over miscounting voting totals, with a threat to use the Voting Rights Act of 1965 to prosecute.
MARCH 1992	After numerous plans were attempted and rejected, the state of Mississippi obtained USDJ permission for its congressional district lines. In Panola County, this will affect blacks in western Batesville.
MAY 1992	Batesville was still discussing with USDJ new redistricting lines. By putting blacks in one district (77%), the population size would differ from others that are larger. Later, precinct lines approved by both sides for the May 1993 city elections, lines that *The Panolian* set out in two-page spread.

Table 4.2 *Continued*

AUG. 1992	Batesville black Leonard Morris won Democratic primary over a white in court-ordered state legislative election. Later endorsed by county and state teachers associations (October 7), and then elected in general election with 62.4 percent of votes. Fifty-six percent of voting age population turned out in county compared with 53 percent in state.
OCT. 1992	U.S. League of Women Voters commended Mississippi for making it easier to register to vote due to expanded hours and mail in provisions; the states adjoining were on the "worst list." In the May 1993 elections, registration hours at city hall were open eleven hours weekdays and a half day Saturday.

county blacks were winning a few seats on the county board and town councils. By 1992, a black Democrat from Batesville had won a state legislative seat, joining a score of other blacks in Jackson.

In 1990, then, when black office holders throughout the South had increased (although the rate of increase fell sharply), there were also more blacks in office in Mississippi (669 positions of which 136 were women); 44 percent held positions on municipal councils. With more representation, blacks now used the law to attack continuing discrimination. Thus they learned to identify the problem, to provide evidence of discrimination, and to convince federal courts and officials of the need to make changes. Their strategy followed closely the attacks pioneered thirty years earlier by the U.S. Justice Department when its chief agent, John Doar, had first walked the dusty back roads of the South.[17]

The events set out in table 4.2 suggest yet other changes in white strategies to control black votes. Earlier in the 1960s, one generation of whites had sought physically—by threat or violence—to block registration or voting by blacks. The strategy of the next generation was to alter voting jurisdictions in order to dilute black votes. In Frank Parker's legal analysis this was done by "creating at-large and multi-member districts, redrawing district boundaries, and even changing some offices from elective to appointive."[18] All were eventually defeated in this state and throughout the South.

Two of these forms of resistance also appeared in Panola County (see table 4.2). However, some white Panolians were more aware of the need to facilitate changes in order to meet federal requirements. For example, in early 1991 the attorney of the county board of supervisors, after citing the past delays in meeting challenges to representation, declared it was necessary to move immediately to meet new claims. Two decades earlier, that viewpoint would never have been contemplated or expressed.

Another form of resistance was also defeated in Panola County. White resistance in the South defended at-large elections (where candidates run across a whole district), which had historically always been status-based; white, male, middle-class voters won those races, which had policy implications for the community agenda.[19] But in the South this form of resistance, like all others, had become racial. Black struggles to replace at-large seats with ward systems had occurred throughout the nation by the end of the 1980s and were successful in Panola County. But, with a ward system (in which candidates run from one section), a proportion of blacks could win one or more seats in black areas. Accordingly, that shift occurred in the 1980s in the county's local councils and school boards after blacks attacked redistricting and at-large practices. The Supreme Court upheld this change; in one case (*Allen v. State Board of Elections*, 1969), many Mississippian counties were successfully challenged. But Panola County was omitted from the challenge due to its earlier reform, which reflected its new cultural awareness of the black role.

The Newspapers' Mirror of Change

Over time then, the newspapers mirrored Panola's two white cultures by responding differently to these major changes. Since 1960, their local reports on the political system had traced the emergence of the New South. This change involved not simply new actors like blacks, but a new agenda of priorities about race and politics. Over time, these papers had less to say about the agenda of the Old South on race and power. The old recalcitrance once lodged in the culture's foundation has given way to a more pragmatic working with the black community.

One sign of this shift in agendas over time is seen in tables 4.1 and 4.2. In 1960, complaints about black protests were the largest category of stories (forty-six), but this particular total had dropped to twenty-eight and twenty-six in 1970 and 1980; by the last date, voting changes had already begun altering politics. Later, in 1989–1992, when attention was focused on new black candidates and on changes in representation, there were only about fifteen stories each year on race and politics. This decrease leads to an important conclusion about the vote for blacks as guaranteed by federal law. The papers had few stories on this matter because the reality of the change had become more accepted—even though grudgingly—in the white community. In the pages of these newspapers, as well as in the attitudes of white interviewees, recalcitrance gave way to pragmatism. After all, "news" means reporting what is exceptional, but over time the fact of black voting was not that at all. A quarter century after the Voting Rights Act of 1965, black registration and voting were normal and expected in the New South.

Returning to our original analysis of law's effects, we see here that federal voting law had sought to change the reality that newspapers and interviews reported among whites. Some southerners tried escape through a white Republican party or in private schools. Others altered their attitudes to form a biracial party of Democrats and to form a large minority of white voters to elect (as noted later) a "qualified" black to office. This last event tells much about these changes in reality and perception. Over time, then, law certainly has changed some perceptions of reality on the part of a new generation of whites who were not fully entrenched in the Old South.

Community Leaders' Reactions to Political Changes

The evidence of paper records—documents, newspapers, government actions—is not the only indicator of this basic racial change. There was a subjective context to these events for both races that needs understanding. For that, we turn to observations of community leaders on political developments over the last quarter century. While both races spoke often out of some bias, it is their biracial agreement that is of interest here. Their reports are quite clear on one matter: a great deal had changed in racial relations in politics, schools, and jobs. We turn first to the empowerment of blacks, the political process, and public services.

Perceptions of Political Change

Among white leaders of Panola County there was generally a sense that the voting changes had benefited not merely blacks, but whites as well; only among the Delta leaders, especially the older ones, was there still recalcitrance. As one Batesville official noted, this change was not a "win-lose" situation because both races achieved benefits from the change. These benefits came when whites began working closely with newly elected blacks, which gave rise to greater white respect. The older racial image broke in the face of this change, behind which lay new laws. Also, whites reported that black empowerment had helped them overturn the old power holders and the planters who had blocked racial and economic change. New white leaders were able to emerge to expand business and assist in removing the traditional mistreatment of blacks.

Some whites spoke as if they had helped found a new society. Said one Batesville official:

> Everything is changed, and all of us have more, despite the area's poverty. We changed from an agricultural economy as much farm labor is now gone. Used to be, public decisions were closed, but now we have blacks voting, open meetings, more public awareness and

involvement. Now, blacks vote more, and they now get more city services and more quickly than they would have had. And I see the city board acting as equitably as possible; I hear little from blacks today about needing more services. Also, there are more blacks in city and factory jobs, even though before there was indeed discrimination going on. To do all this, there was some give and take to make it work.

One white male found the results a "mixed bag," but still recalled how he had seen traditional racism.

> Whites today remember how those things were [in the Old South], but the 1960s crystallized something to the surface. We could not have things continue that way. At James Meredith's march through the county in 1966, I saw an instance of deep feeling by whites. A row of cars had caused a breakdown caused by a car driven by old blacks, causing a traffic jam. Some whites came up and tongue-lashed them; the whites got all worked up and used this couple to object against changes. The bottom line of racism is when you vent your feelings on everyone because of skin color. I saw whites using race as a scapegoat—so immature—even though human. It was behavior at the lowest level—macho, compensatory, strong on running down others. I could get mad at outside agitators, but when you saw those local white reactions, you knew it had to be changed. I see a much more genteel atmosphere now.

But some whites are still resentful of the change, mostly in north Panola. Not pragmatic but still recalcitrant, a town councilor from there thought that today, "black candidates are not qualified; I think the black voters prefer their candidates to be unqualified to run. Look at the board of supervisors with a million-dollar budget, with two blacks on it! In Mississippi, I have heard of candidates for judge who can't even read or write. But today, supervisors get $24,000 a year, but pay little attention to board business and are not progressive."

But among black leaders, there is no doubt that blacks have been improved by the ballot. Without exception, they commented that enfranchisement meant they could run for and win public office, could represent both races' interests, and could achieve a sense of accomplishment from these actions. These attitudes had never before been known in the county's history except in the brief Reconstruction era. The experience of blacks around them underlay their attitudes about change. Blacks in Panola County had been running for local office since the late 1960s, some were on the board of supervisors, others on the town councils and school boards of Sardis and Batesville, and yet others were a majority on hamlet councils amid large black constituencies. Their circle of black friends reached to other counties where they heard of similar results.

Many black voters had first wanted their local representatives to be symbolic, that is, to be black like themselves. In time though, they wanted representatives to provide individual or group services and to secure the public policies that would provide sufficient resources.[20] Typically, a black representative in towns and the county dealt with a battery of black interests much like those from white wards. He also supported white business interests in promoting economic development, as noted later. Often, white interviewees reported blacks as also representing them.

These black officials are keenly aware of the difference that comes from having the ballot. One north Panola black remembers that registering to vote once meant that "you stood in city halls for two days to take the test, but never got the chance to vote. Registering meant having your name in the paper for two weeks [thereby opening one to white threats] and paying a two-dollar poll tax. Back in the early days, there was fear, but not now." Typically, this black's later career involved running for office in the black community with standard techniques of home canvasing and distributing name cards. Today though, as a local representative of his town, he notes, "More whites want to talk to him about business and its problems, because they need my vote on something. More whites seem to be for you and want you to be good." But black needs must also be met. A black woman official in a hamlet noted that "blacks feel that they can now come to me and get answers to problems; they have a connection with the system. Ten years ago, a black woman complaining of a city bill would not have gone to any white councilor but just paid it. Now, she is aware of options."

Consequently, from all this awareness of changes in political reality there developed a clear sense that blacks had gained more respect from whites—often begrudging—than their ancestors had ever known. Of course, it was not all perfect; being realists, they knew there were whites with covert racist attitudes, nor was their economic situation very strong. But on the political side, they reported that times had changed—and mostly for the good.

Not all in the black community enjoy the benefits of the New South, however. As a Batesville black leader observed in 1990: "The winners were the small numbers who took advantage of it, namely, the middle class. As for getting city services, they do if living in or close to white communities, just like whites. I live in an area that got annexed and now we have all the services except sewage. Now, there are more public jobs in Batesville in different offices. However, black contractors don't get many bids because they can't handle the costs due to a lack of capital."

These estimates of racial advantage are primarily impressions of how voting affected local life. It is time now to turn to an analysis of some data on the consequences of black empowerment as blacks sought public roles as elected and appointed officials. As we will see, communities with ward systems or with large black registrations could get blacks elected; and one case where a black professional candidate for state office attracted biracial support suggests another possibility for future political developments.

Political Alterations in the Racial Climate

In Batesville, both race's leaders confirm the appearance after 1970 of whites who spoke for the interests of both races, but particularly for white merchants and officials. Campaign slogans earlier had featured the phrase, "I will serve the interests of everyone in the community." This was the code of a change in representation understood by both races, and one that white merchants came to insist on. As one black leader noted, in the 1970s, these merchants "said in public that the voting right changes had to be accepted and carried out. They were the same whites who later pushed for more industries and who encouraged school desegregation. They said they wanted to change things."[21] That change also came, though later, in north Panola, as blacks emerged on the city councils of Sardis, Como, and Crenshaw. By 1990, a white mayor, Richard Darby, and others in Sardis had formed a biracial citizen committee to review a local problem, and officials of both races were eagerly seeking out new industries.

The once quiet support of blacks by whites at earlier times could now become overt. A black Batesvillian remembered how, in the civil rights conflict in the late 1960s, "a white farmer had stood up to protect them because it was right what blacks wanted." Some whites, who had been disturbed by how blacks were treated under the traditionalist culture, would nevertheless have remained quiet. But the presence of the external force of law emboldened many of these to accept without violence a massive change in racial relations.

Yet all are aware that race still shapes voting in any biracial contest. Thus, all elected officials interviewed knew the racial percentages in their own wards or beats, and had a rough sense of what proportion of votes they had received from each race in the last election. That such bloc voting can be used to form a new kind of political party is clear in the emergence of a strong and white Republican party in this state and region. The Democratic party emerged in Mississippi with a biracial leadership at state and local levels. In Panola County, both races led a Democratic party that, while it had the supporters, lacked campaign money to mobilize many of them.

Signs of political change were also evident in the emergence in Panola of black professionals, who usually are linked to political parties. As one veteran Batesville professional noted of this group, "They are now putting their fingers on the community, working through the back door." One black attorney had practiced here and when he left he was replaced by another in 1992. A listing shows several black professionals, including a doctor (who later left town but was replaced in the mid-1990s), an accountant, a dentist, state or federal bureaucrats in local offices, and as always the ministers, morticians, and teachers. But no blacks have wealth like that found in the merchant and farmer groups. Clear to all white leaders in Batesville, however, was the significant presence of one black professional: former city planner and board of education member, Leonard Morris, whose high standing will be discussed later.

In the Delta culture, despite some visible black leaders in politics (two on the board of supervisors, and others in town offices in the mid-1990s), there was no professional influence except among the teachers and administrators of north Panola's schools. James Harris finally succeeded to the position of superintendent; which he kept from the late 1980s to 1995, after the previous white leaders had failed to cope with a system in deep trouble, as noted in chapter 6. When he left, the schools were in fact in worse financial condition, which led to a state law to bail out schools in deficit. But there were few professionals in this section, which was still steeped in the Delta culture.

Even here, though, there are signs of attitudinal change among the races. As a black observer noted:

> The Delta culture was different on progress because those whites feared an impact on black wages. They had a different impression of blacks because they saw them only as field hands. But the younger Delta blacks and whites accept one another better than the older ones. *Attitudes were changing by [the two groups] doing the same things, even unknowingly.* Whites learned that not all blacks were ignorant in schools. Why, one of my family members even had an advanced college degree. (Emphasis added.)

Or a white professional in one of the "old families" of the Delta saying, "The old saying is that you can't legislate morality, and it is true except for civil rights in Panola County. *Without these laws, change would have come very slowly* as the county was conservative, willing to achieve change but slowly" (emphasis added).

Public Services Enfranchisement

A group getting political power always seeks to secure more public resources, including public jobs. The allocation of city jobs has been a continuing struggle, because minorities newly arriving in power (like the Irish 150 years ago or blacks now) see this work as an improvement, but immigrants from an earlier era already held them.[22] Did this pattern operate in Panola County?

In the 1960s, blacks had few public jobs of any importance; they were mostly laborers, tarring roads or digging ditches. For example, among police jobs in Batesville and the county, only one black was hired in the late 1960s, and only to patrol the black areas. All other jobs of any kind were held by whites as a matter of custom.

As law expanded the numbers of blacks voting during the next two decades, more jobs for blacks appeared, although primarily in small industries. White perceptions were changing slowly from the total recalcitrance of the traditional culture, and acquiring city jobs for blacks was still difficult. Traditionally, small town jobs have been nested in local subcultures, sometimes passing among family or friends; this selection process clearly improves new applicants' eligibility. Not surprisingly, then, by 1989 in Panola there were only a few more blacks in city jobs. Blacks may see this as the glass half empty, or whites as one half full; but it is clear that these few numbers were nowhere near the black proportion in the resident or voting populations. As table 4.3 indicates, by 1989 only one black appeared in the top positions of Batesville (Willie King, councillor), though another was significant in acquiring local grants (see below). While the city jobs were few in number, many blacks saw them symbolically as a sign of new respect for people in their community.

Most of these (appointive) jobs were entry-level, however, involving laborers, clerks, or police. But in 1994, a black was appointed police lieutenant in Batesville. There were also a few black assistants to county supervisors, namely, in the streets, water and sewer, and parks departments. As one elder black observer noted, blacks still balked at this problem of "oneness" in city jobs, that is, tokenism. Tokenism may be seen either as a continuing racism or as the lack of qualified black applicants who needed to be trained to do other work than just being field hands. Nevertheless, it is a general belief of whites that much more is being done for blacks by providing them with city jobs and services. Black leaders are less sure of that, however, as table 4.3 confirms.

As for city services, the change was greater. As a result of black empowerment, there emerged a needs-based model for distributing city ser-

Table 4.3   Number of Batesville City Jobs, by Race, 1969 and 1989

Job	1969	1989
City board	All white	4,1
Mayor	All white	All white
City clerk	1,1	8,2
Police:		
Chief	All white	All white
Patrol	All white	11,2
Dispatch	*	3,1
Fire	All white	18,2
Roads	1,4	2,1
Laborers	*	1,3 **
Gas	1,1	*
Water	2,4	2,1
Sanitation	1,3	*
Utilities	*	2,1
Public works	*	All white
Parks	*	2,4

* = Service is absent or has been altered in name.
** = Numbers conjectured.

Source: Interviews with Batesville city clerk, Betty Broome, and city alderman Willie King.

First number refers to whites, and second to blacks.

vices to both races. A veteran black office holder notes that in earlier times the all-white Sardis section got the better services; they even received the mail early in the morning. Now, not only is that distribution move even, but more qualified black job applicants are appearing, because black officials are acquainting their community with public job openings. The police in both Sardis (three blacks, four whites in 1990) and Batesville (see table 4.3) have been arresting members of both races for some years now, although one Sardis leader thinks blacks are arrested more for drinking and speeding.

Batesville councillors of both races agree that they review job applications provided by administrative heads. These jobs, advertised locally, were another departure from earlier hiring practices. Further, critical reports by the black community of one white applicant's past discrimination did prevent the hiring of that person. But the general impression is clear, as one black observer noted:

City services are definitely better. As late as 1980, cops used firearms in my community, but now we are not afraid, and we get better
services. I work to be sure that blacks get better roads and lighting. I
stimulated three housing renewals in my area. In the private sector,
blacks are beginning to appear in the front office of businesses, but
that is still a problem. It's only token appointments in the private
sector—a loan supervisor in a bank, an assistant manager in a local
plant, and an assistant supervisor in Piggly Wiggly [supermarket].

These observations attest to a constant theme in the democratic proposition: when citizens become mobilized, officials pay more attention. The
proposition fits V. O. Key's classic definition of public opinion as "that
opinion to which politicians find it prudent to pay attention." The change
is clearly seen in table 4.3 in Batesville, even though it was only minor.
Elsewhere, in north Panola's heavily black Como (70.5%), there were four
of five council seats held by blacks by 1990. Jobs were well distributed by
race; three of five police officers, the city clerk, two garbage men, and a
maintenance man were black, although a white police applicant was also
appointed.

Below the Tallahatchie River, blacks in west Batesville who had earlier
lived outside the town and were served by the county board of supervisors
found their power had been dispersed among many whites. But when their
community was annexed to Batesville and became a separate ward with
a council representative, they received much better services. Streets were
improved, and most houses had access to sewage and drinking water. As
one black educator wryly noted, "Voting numbers seemed to make the difference." However, there is a belief in the black community that favoritism
is still shown toward the affluent whites when they have service problems
or seek government contracts. This judgment is "street wisdom," reflecting class and race distinctions, for which little evidence exists aside from
occasional anecdotes. The blacks' problem is that with town administrators shifting to a needs-based criterion to provide services, there are still
not enough public resources to meet the needs of everyone, black or white.

Blacks have always been especially sensitive to the actions of the police.
In recent years, a black policeman arrested the son of a prominent white
Batesvillian for speeding. The son objected to being arrested by a black,
but his father was quiet on the matter even when his son went to jail before being released by bail and later fined. The mayor and city council
had backed the black policeman because their attitude had been stated
clearly and earlier about blacks arresting whites: "Arrest any lawbreaker."
Another recent incident involved the videotaping of a police action. A
shooting of a black man in the early 1990s found the department sensi-

tive to concerns in that community. It defended the action by displaying videotape recordings of the event and by holding community meetings to show that both black and white policemen had been endangered before the shooting. The community concerns then faded. In the traditional culture, there would not have been a black policeman, much less one arresting any whites. Police shooting of blacks was not then a major event, a fact that is symbolic of the little attention given to the black community's concerns.

White attitudes in both the city councils of Batesville and Sardis were that city services improved increasingly after black enfranchisement, a change due to the emergent influence of service professionals. Their influence was another of the external forces that was working upon the county, state, and region in the last quarter century. As elsewhere, professionals came to influence, but not determine, service distribution to meet community needs. By definition, professionals value quality, equity, and efficiency, which are engrained in their training and education. This modernization of city services has replaced Old South–style decisions that were based on party power or local influence.[23] A white Batesville city councilor noted that "the professional influence is now greater, using these criteria [of needs]. Thus a public works director came in the last decade. Hiring chief administrators now requires first certification by the state. That involves short-course programs in water or gas or environmental policies, with a training based on federal standards."

Other signs of the professional needs-based model have appeared throughout the county in recent years. As noted, state law helped break up the traditional, patronage-laden county board of supervisors by requiring new standards of service based on need. Even in the Delta culture of Sardis, the new white mayor has the reputation among knowledgeable blacks of trying to distribute services on an equal basis of priorities. When old houses in one black neighborhood became the lodgings of drug gangs, Mayor Darby used the power of condemning homes to remove them—to the delight of the black leaders.

Everywhere there are indicators of more professionalism in public service. As will be noted in later chapters, schools in both districts are run according to state and local professional standards. They are overseen by biracial boards concerned with improving educational quality by imposing school service standards based on professional training and on a modern curriculum responsive to state requirements. In local city jobs, Batesville employees seeking promotions must attend special professional courses. When a new police chief was sought in the late 1980s by Batesville, their choice had extensive professional training, was from outside the county, and promptly required new standards of performance in his personnel. We see here the new influence of professionals in providing urban services who in turn influence, if not constrain, local control in American communities.[24] When free to work, these professionals undergird the drive of blacks to secure better public services.

Law and Life Changes

Evidence obtained by different methods shows that Panolian leaders agree, without exception, about what happened when blacks became enfranchised. The vote had changed basically the nature of politics, enhanced somewhat the lives of blacks in their community, and altered considerably racial perceptions. A pivotal white figure in Batesville affairs put it with characteristic bluntness, "There would be nowhere the change we now have." There were some white reservations; a few thought that blacks were getting too much or that the quality of black leadership was doubtful. But the deepest white fear was of black majorities on locally elected boards. The successful changes in Batesville, for example, are thought by some in both races to stem from a "favorable" black-white ratio in that place (51 percent white in 1990). As one wealthy white noted:

> Whites would like to help, but there would be fear if blacks got the numbers to have control. Blacks would be very radical to us, unless they get educated to our system of the economy. There would be their need to learn to be fair to us when they got power. In towns I know across the country, there are the same fears we have. The people I deal with don't want to deal with them, and their children have no contact with ours. But, you know, blacks want what whites do, namely, a good place to live, work, and raise their kids. In the future we will improve even more, because here we have more sincerity about race and life.

Yet whites also saw changes in themselves as they had to deal in a new reality about racial matters. Note the following brief quotations of whites from across the county, on these changes:

— White perceptions are changing because more blacks are now better educated.
— To our friendliness, they are friendly, more on an equal level. No more the "Yassuh, Yassuh!" by blacks.
— There is a new perception of black leaders, namely, that they will try to do a good job.
— I once thought blacks to be lesser persons, but now, after observing locals [Willie King, Leonard Morris], I found something new about them.

A larger view of these reported changes comes from a white assistant to former governor Mabus of Mississippi.

> What you hear of the elites of Batesville reporting change is a pride that they have from adapting to change. Blacks getting the vote was the key to change. In the old days there was need for change. But people knew only what they were told locally, as there was no alternative source of information. So change was a long time coming, and much time was lost. Those federal laws and court orders ran up against a very personal relationship that Mississippians have as a caring people. But once they were forced to begin examining what they were losing, a change would have occurred.

Panola's blacks saw the law as the only means for achieving this change in behavior and attitudes, and for whites accepting them as citizens. Most white Americans think of themselves as citizens without giving any thought as to the meaning of that status. But for blacks, their history had regularly denied them citizenship status, even as fighting soldiers in all the wars since the Civil War. Their greater success in the Hill culture of Batesville has been noted, but even in the heart of the Delta culture in Sardis, an experienced black official comments on the changes:

> In Sardis, I'd hate to think of the condition we would be in without the law; we'd be forced to do different things. Laws can't change hearts, but it can change behavior. Without the law, Sardis would now be a junction, not a town. As a boy, I remember men burning a cross on the home of Mr. Edmonds [black farmer], but it's been a long time since there has been violence. I see in Mayor Darby [a white] a symbol of working [to improve] a deteriorating town, and both races see this.

Or another black politician from Sardis: "Without the law, blacks would have just waited. Even before the federal law, there were a few blacks here who worked at it. Now, though, the perception of blacks is that my vote does count and that most blacks do care. Now I [have to be] concerned about both sides of town and what happens."

A black educator saw that "the federal law backed the whites up against the wall to make a change, and the whites knew it. Some whites today still see us a little bit differently than before, because more of them come into contact with us and find what blacks can do." Or in Como, the home of wealthy Delta planters, a black city alderman finds now that both races support him. He found little evidence of voting along racial lines; looking at recent electoral contests, he notes that both races "seem to vote on whether you've got any common sense. Really, I can't see any issue that divides blacks and whites."

Could that racial blindness work among whites for a black candidate?

Leonard Morris, Black Political Leader

New black leadership appeared after the 1965 Voting Rights Act, when white recalcitrance retreated over the next quarter century into a pragmatic acceptance of black empowerment. By the 1990s, blacks could get elected to county and town offices, *as long as their constituencies had large proportions of black voters*—that is, about 60 percent or more. Bloc racial voting was thus the norm in Panola, as elsewhere in the South.

Leadership is hard to define, but we recognize it by observing those who respond to it. Some lead by managing an organization based on accepted values; others lead by changing others to accept their new values.[25] Leadership changes with differing situations, as the leadership skills needed, for example, in academia are quite unlike those needed in the military. In the turbulent 1960s, black leadership had required an ability to confront white dominance with courage and perseverance. Thus Robert Miles was an early effective leader, helping realize the basic black agenda, even though many blacks were fearful of the changes he advocated—register blacks, focus their strength on candidates, and mobilize their votes.[26] He endured great white hostility, even violence, for his home was once shot-gunned. However, he also stimulated blacks to find courage to meet the new agenda. (Still active in 1992, he again sought election to the county board of supervisor but this time lost. He died in 1996, amid great newspaper coverage.)

Another type of black leader can emerge with support from both races if the federal law alters white perceptions about some blacks. That was unlikely where voting districts were dominated by blacks, for example, in towns like Como or in the black wards of Batesville and Sardis. It was also unlikely where districts had just a few blacks, like the wealthy or middle-class wards of these two county towns, given the traditional white views. But Panola County, with a 51 percent white population, might test the thesis. Could a law change white reality so that new perceptions might support a black in an election? It stands to reason that such a black would have to have unusual qualities.

A test of this thesis arose with Leonard Morris of Batesville, whose record of leadership for both races is strongly affirmed through interviews of white and black leaders. Morris was a teenager during the civil rights struggle. His family had befriended the civil rights workers from outside during the 1960s. In 1971, Morris graduated from the University of Mississippi, one of the earliest black recipients of a degree. Subsequently, he created a Batesville business in realty and brokerage services and became a partner with white "progressives" in Batesville's economic development reviewed in a later chapter.

He worked first as a consultant on urban planning for Batesville and other communities where he employed ideas from courses at Ole Miss (the University of Mississippi). Morris was then appointed to direct the North Delta Planning and Development District, once the domain of former white mayor Ferguson. Covering ten planning and development districts within seven counties, this agency obtained grants at county, state, and federal levels. Working with others over a dozen years, Morris had helped others to attract small industries to the area and expanded new public services. These efforts stimulated Batesville's economic life and raised similar hopes even in Sardis.

In addition, Morris was elected to the south Panola school board in 1975, losing his first campaign but winning the second with 60 percent of the vote and support from black ministers, white board members, and other leaders.[27] His first efforts at policy making had died because there was no research to support them. One white member noted that when white members came early before a meeting it was to discuss policy; so he also came early and stayed afterward for the discussion.

Slowly, Morris began creating white support by voting to support white policy needs. In time, he was the one black who was involved in preliminary discussions on new policies that affected blacks and schools. Rarely treated as a black spokesman—a role that he rejected—he urged educational policy that both races needed as it was the best for all students; the board also agreed with that stance (a subsequent chapter reviews these decisions). Morris developed this essentially political ability to work with others to reach an agreed goal on the regional planning board. All white leaders interviewed regularly commented that he understood what service needs were without having recourse to race, that his experience was relevant, and that his judgments on decision were first rate. In time, his reputation spread beyond Batesville.[28] Morris next sought election to the state legislature in 1992, where he won both the Democratic primary and the general election. In those campaigns, he strongly emphasized the great need for community development in order to provide more jobs, and the willingness to speak for all groups in the society (echoes of Robert Miles twenty-five years earlier).

The results of the voting were striking. Morris won by 57 percent in a district that included two precincts in a nearby county (which were white and Republican); in Panola alone, he won by over 62 percent.[29] Since he competed during the presidential race of 1992, his election was not em-

Table 4.4   Democratic Vote, 1992 General Election, in Panola County's Black and White Precincts

| | PERCENTAGE VOTING FOR CANDIDATES | | | NUMBER OF VOTES | | |
Precinct	Leonard Morris	Bill Clinton	Michael Espy	State Legislature	President	Congress
Black precincts						
West Como	87.5	86.9	87.5	519	869	678
West Sardis	—	78.1	83.6	300	270	292
Crenshaw	—	66.2	84.9	—	420	449
Pleasant Grove	55.9	58.4	73.5	273	257	268
South Sardis	63.0	66.5	74.2	781	692	740
Curtis	73.0	72.1	87.9	397	359	141
Belmont-Hebron	72.9	76.0	83.2	332	300	310
Cortland	74.2	61.8	—	392	600	—
East Crowder	59.8	67.7	84.1	251	226	239
West Batesville B	80.5	76.5	82.9	809	705	725
Pleasant Mount	58.9	63.7	70.3	316	270	317
Median %	72.9	72.1	83.2			
% range	55.9–87.5	58.4–86.9	70.3–87.9			
White precincts						
East Como	35.9	37.9	58.5	365	351	342
East Sardis	—	34.6	—	—	436	—
Tocowa	43.3	33.4	—	420	362	—
North Asa	40.8	39.1	—	125	115	—
Batesville 3	35.8	25.9	—	159	320	—
West Batesville IV	42.6	39.0	—	242	228	—
Median %	40.8	53.8	—			
% range	35.8–43.0	25.9–39.1				
Total county vote	62.1	53.8	79.4	7,089	11,399	4,731

Note: Some voting tallies are not included due to jurisdictional lines; they are indicated by a dash. Candidates were not on the ballot in those jurisdictions.

Source: Mid-November 1992 issues of *The Panolian* for overlapping jurisdictions, confirmed by registrar records.

phasized in the local papers; but the voting record is dramatic, as seen in table 4.4. The precincts voting for president, congressman, and state legislator differ in their totals across the county because of new redistricting lines (observed and approved by Washington).

In the whole county, Morris got huge votes from black precincts but also a surprising plurality from white ones. His 62.4 percent was well above Clinton's 53.2 percent, but below that of the leading black politician, Congressman Michael Espy's 79.4 percent. Among the black precincts in Panola,[30] Morris topped Clinton in 8 of 15 precincts, but he never got more votes than Espy.[31]

Turning to the white precincts, the size of Morris's plurality is extraordinary. Of course, Morris lost them all (like Clinton), but he received *40.8 percent of the white vote*, a bit more than Clinton. In four of five white precincts, Morris had more votes than Clinton. While Morris's victory was soundly based on the black vote, he also received a surprising plurality of whites even when George Bush and Ross Perot carried those precincts by as much as 75 percent of white voters (e.g., note Batesville's wealthy district IV). Morris, however, is not an isolated black phenomenon, as shown by Espy's win in one of the white precincts in East Como.

Something else odd appeared in this vote, which may represent the intense interest in Morris's bid for office. By precinct, the largest number of votes was cast in his particular contest; usually one could expect the highest tally to occur in federal, not state, races. But in eleven of sixteen precincts in table 4.2, his state candidacy attracted the most voters (while one other person was nearly equal). More strikingly, this proportion appeared even in four of the five white precincts. A clear implication is that the presence of Leonard Morris had generated more voter interest than even the highly visible presidential race, and did so even in white precincts. The white precinct plurality was of a size that no black had won before, providing yet another indicator that some racial attitudes—for at least some whites—were undergoing adjustment as a long-run consequence of federal laws.

The Realization of Black Empowerment

The record of this county, illustrative of other New South areas, demonstrates that even amid the Delta's great recalcitrance, the goals of the 1965 Voting Rights Act had become realized. Legislation, court orders, and bureaucratic regulations had expanded the enfranchisement of blacks for those who wished to use it. This act was one of many in that curious period of national social reform that actually did work. It would be hard to discuss the years of effort, the will, and the frustration to achieve these results by black leaders. It also occurred amid criticism of them from both races and by their puzzled introduction to a new world of policy making. Their effort required a series of leadership tasks in the black community.

The first task was that of registering blacks, a goal nearing completion as early as 1970. The second task was to elect first those *whites* who would understand some of the black needs in community life. That occurred first in Batesville in the 1970s with the replacement of white elites in the city council, a new group who saw racial peace and economic development as the key agenda for the future. Sardis and other north Panola towns followed much later. The third task was to get *blacks* elected to public office, and that took place two decades after the 1965 act. Accomplishing these tasks resulted in the election of the following blacks: a majority of city councillors in Como; two city councillors in Sardis; two members of the county board of supervisors; an alderman in Batesville plus an influential black advisor; and (as noted later) members of local and county school boards. The climax for this era was the 1992 election of Leonard Morris to the state legislature, with a huge majority of blacks and over 40 percent white support.

However, assistance in completing these tasks rested with others outside the black community. White Batesville businessmen helped move the issue along by denying, first privately and then publicly, that the racism of the Old South would continue. (Another kind of racism would remain, though, as noted in the concluding chapters of this book.) One result of easing attitudes was the opening of black employment in the new small plants. Moreover, white leaders informally endorsed some blacks for public office who could fit their dual agenda of racial and economic change, defined as "progressivism."

Another outside agency, that of federal agencies, was a key partner in black empowerment. Litigation started the removal of white obstruction from black voting and representation, and in Mississippi it was the "necessary precondition to black political success."[32] Litigation weakened the effort to dilute the black vote by recalcitrant whites still thinking in the Old South mode. The U.S. Supreme Court removed at-large elections from local and state seats, thereby opening black seats in the state and Panola County. The Office of Civil Rights of the Department of Justice oversaw local implementation, but its records on Panola are skimpy over recent decades because the county was clearly adapting, however slowly, to the purposes of the national law. Still, the OCR in 1984 had required Batesville to redraw its districts, thereby increasing black voting power.[33] A later redistricting that annexed blacks in the West Batesville ward also required a similar redrawing under OCR oversight.

There was some criticism that these results had distorted the original act—a judgment thoroughly countered by others with more experience.[34] Nevertheless, the results were that more blacks appeared in elected office. These came mostly from redrawn majority black constituencies, termed "majority minority districts" in the 1990s. An increasingly conservative Supreme Court has, however, overturned these districts, and in 1996 they were deemed no longer constitutional. But as the Morris case in Panola demonstrates, some black candidates could garner surprising proportions of white votes when they shared a common agenda about economic improvement, could demonstrate basically middle-class qualities of ability, and had left the old racism in the past. Curiously, these criteria also applied to white candidates in the county and elsewhere.

The linkages between granting the franchise and achieving meaningful results for blacks are long and complex, as this chapter attests. What is central to this process is the agreement by a new generation of whites and a new cadre of black leaders to avoid the violent racism of the Old South in order to offer an agenda for the New South. Of course, problems remain. Black turnout is still low, whites and blacks still use race to vote in biracial contests, and new issues arise that voting itself is not sufficient to solve.

Nevertheless, the changes noted here, drawn from interviews, newspapers, and voting records, point to a new perception about living biracially, not in segregation but in community, that was quite unknown before federal laws. In the process, white voters support a black candidate, and leaders of both races learn the need to cooperate to deal with problems common to both. In the case of voting, then, law changed one reality of the traditionalist outline and gave rise to new perceptions and new cognitions among both races.

5 | South Panola and Desegregation

The clash between local cultures and outside law arose early in redefining the educational resources of both races. But the Delta and Hill cultures chose different routes, leading to three separate school systems: one all-white private system, and two desegregated systems, one all-black and the other racially mixed. The interaction of law with these cultural responses had consequences in how students, teachers, and school officials provide education today for both races. In this chapter we start with the desegregated response of the south Panola school system, for it alone achieved the parity of resources that court and Congress had sought.

Community, Sense of Place, and Schools

Americans as people and as communities are enormously diverse. Even before the American Revolution and despite the common heritage of descent from "Albion's seed," that is, from England, our regions were remarkably different then and remain so today.[1] The communities we founded generated for their citizens a sense of place that was cultural, that is, a form of reality known and experienced by all members. Even in big cities, people's lives are shaped by living in neighborhoods that are influenced by ethnic identity, status, or religious cultures; a similar—and often singular—influence is common in small towns. In the South there was an emotional attachment among both races to a rural ideal, as well as a contempt of an urban North, which was resistant to change until the period that we are reviewing. Many southerners write movingly about growing up in such places,[2] and historians justify the values of this outlook and the dangers that it faces in modern times.[3]

A powerful mechanism for transmitting this sense of place is the community's school. Locally based and financed—like few other public school systems in the world—schools involve more citizens than all other democratic local institutions (14,000 in the United States in the 1990s). For the young, schools provide a sense of place about their neighborhood or small town and later a sense of the nation and the world. In communities or neighborhoods, we go through all the stages of growing up from childhood to late adolescence in school. Of all urban services, most people in the community know most about some school functions; often, school football and basketball games help define for young and adults this sense of place.[4]

While American schools respond to the diversity of local cultures, however the curriculum and instruction offered in them are standardized through national professionalism and state law.[5] Local cultures often challenge these norms, but teachers and administrators learn to live within that cultural zone while still providing higher standards of knowledge. In small towns or religious schools, officials seek a "fit" between their local norms and public authority.[6] They seek a curriculum that does not challenge the existing sense of the community, religious or secular. Indeed, most teachers and administrators are reared and trained near their districts, and so they often share and hence reinforce these local values. But outside influences, such as new laws or national trends, can fall upon the community with an influence that transcends the local sense of what the school means. For example, school desegregation became one transcendental force with a subsequent influence upon the local culture and sense of place.

An Overview of Desegregation Responses

Mississippi's effort at black education prior to the 1960s, as Neil McMillen notes, was a "mere faint gesture."[7] Even before 1900, a tragic racial imbalance in finances had existed with the result that "no state spent less on black education." Indeed, black taxes were actually diverted to white schools. W. E. B. DuBois had found in 1901 that black schools had not cost white taxpayers anything because black taxes paid for them. As always, this policy reflected an underlying value, the dominant white view that blacks were not fit for "book learning." Accordingly, whites provided less schooling for black students, less preparation for black teachers, and lower qualifications needed for entry to low-standard black colleges. Such lower standards rested on a weakened school financial structure, always controlled by whites, that had pervasive effects upon black education.

The Federal Intervention for Desegregation

Against that background, then, later federal studies, court orders, and administrative actions easily found evidence of discrimination.[8] The subsequent history of responses by southerners shows significant changes over time.[9] By the fortieth anniversary of the Supreme Court's *Brown v. Topeka Board of Education* in 1994, there had clearly been some changes of importance for blacks, but serious problems still remained. In the early years of desegregation, there were large gains in black students moving into majority-white schools; there had been almost no movement in 1954 (0.001%), compared to 43.5 percent in 1988. But that number had fallen off to 39.2 percent in 1991. Elsewhere, however, in many large cities, such desegregation has never even been realized because white flight and resegregation have occurred. Today, by one of the curious ironies of American history, the South is the most desegregated region; only 27 percent of blacks were still in segregated schools in the South, compared to 50 percent in the Northeast. Some southern districts were highly integrated, though, while others had all-white private and all-black public schools. For example, in North Carolina, the Charlotte-Mecklenberg schools were highly desegregated, but one hundred miles away in Summerton, the schools were 98 percent black.[10]

Panolian Responses: Fight, Flight, Apathy

These patterns of resistance and accommodation also took place within Panola County. When Washington descended on the county in the 1960s, the white communities of both Delta and Hill cultures were outraged, in large part because their traditional sense of place was sharply altered. Amid curses and condemnation, white rhetoric correctly foresaw the undermining of that culture. Nevertheless, the two public school systems in this county—one above and the other below the Tallahatchie River— took different paths in adjusting to reality, a pattern that is found elsewhere in the South.

These different responses reflected the classic strategies in any confrontation, namely, fight, flee, or be apathetic.[11] The richer whites of north Panola, fleeing the public schools they had always dominated, created several private academies (later combined into one, called simply North Delta). However, the farmer and merchant whites of south Panola, under strong leadership, slowly fought out a desegregation plan to meet federal requirements and created an integrated school district. The poorer whites and blacks, lacking funds for any choice, could only go apathetically to whatever public school was available. Meantime, the school leaders in all cases were trying hard to fight to provide education under hard circumstances.

These three responses echo what was found elsewhere in the South. The "flight" strategy of the wealthy whites has received much attention in the press, but relatively few southern white students ever ended up there, only about 8 percent of them, depending upon the state. In the larger southern cities, whites could flee the central city for the suburbs, creating there mostly all-white public or private schools. But that was not the case outside the few metropolitan areas. In many places, much as in Panola County, white parents stayed, and either paid the high cost of a private school in the area or sent their children to desegregated public schools.

Where the ratio of blacks to whites was relatively high, as in north Panola—Como was 70 percent black in 1990—wealthy whites turned to private academies. However, even there they faced problems of finances and staff that finally gave way to a consolidated private school system in the 1980s. On the other hand, in areas where the racial balance was fairly even, like south Panola—Batesville was about 62 percent white in 1990 and the schools almost evenly balanced—desegregation could be fought with surprisingly little fight or flight by local whites. In this case, for community leaders the problem of mediating racial conflict would be the first concern and improving schools the second. Both problems were much more serious in north Panola. White voters defeated any tax referendum proposed to improve schools, and well-qualified teachers moved over to the academies. North Panola's problems arose not only from poor financing and a diluted staff, but from weak parental support by blacks. Simply catching up after over a century of educational deficiencies in black schooling would be a long-run matter.

To understand the human problems of this social change, we begin with the south Panola school system, the only desegregated institution in the county. As with the other school systems, veteran members of the board of trustees (or school board), administrators, and teachers were interviewed to piece together the history of this struggle. This period covers the earliest days of community conflict, the programs of school officials to desegregate, the reactions of teachers, and (in the next chapter) the attitudes of Panola's students. This range of information is important because, despite the attitudes of recalcitrant whites, the community was nevertheless led by whites to deal with a new reality for schooling children.

The Early Years of Desegregation

When the South Panola Board of Trustees, or school board, faced desegregation in the late 1960s,[12] they found two streams of opposition in the community. They had no support either from the whites who feared for their children, or from black educators, who feared losing their jobs. The board's first reaction was to adopt a policy then used throughout the South, namely, "freedom of choice." That is, open any school within a district for students of any race to enroll on their own. This policy was not a sudden commitment to equality. White leaders expected that blacks would not enroll in white schools and knew that their own children would not move to black schools. Their expectations were fully realized in practice.

District and Federal Interaction

The freedom-of-choice policy was challenged by the U.S. Office of Civil Rights throughout the South. In the late 1960s, Panola County faced the challenge when an OCR lawyer told the north Panola school board face to face that freedom of choice was not an option because, as one official recalls his statement, "We are not interested in education but in integration." Consulting with the OCR,[13] the board's attorney, William Corr, finally told the board that changes would have to be made. This was probably the first signal by an insider that resistance had failed. The board finally approved a new plan to distribute children of both races among the schools.

Facing this legal threat, and after much consultation with black leaders, the south Panola district adopted a novel plan. They closed the black high school in order to build a new but desegregated high school, and in the meantime used trailers for classrooms in the black neighborhoods. The blacks protested against losing their schools—but not the whites against a new high school—which caused some difficulty. Eighteen black parents signed a petition to sue the board on this ground among others, but in a few weeks the signers withdrew and instead sued the local attorney who had advised this course.[14] White residents were clear that their own race simply would not move into a black neighborhood. The only plan that could gain white support for desegregation was the one suggested here. Among many signs of the plan's success in the community was that in years to come south Panola regularly supported tax referenda for expanding desegregated schools.

So in the school year 1970–1971, total desegregation in south Panola began, with children on the move via buses and with faculty slowly integrating; the central administration remained white. However, in this first year about 1,000 students skipped school opening in this system, of whom 150 to 200 whites went to private schools. The rest were blacks whose parents feared what might happen; fear was widespread in both communities at this time. Slowly, most of these students returned in the next years, as the district fumbled with problems of busing and integrating faculty, but the community remained disturbed. Teachers and principals of both races remember today that they were constantly stamping out racial flare-ups among students (discussed later), while the board and central administration recall group protests over the change.

Key Changes in School Leadership

The South Panola Board of Trustees made a personnel move in 1974 that looked odd at the time but which became a key to the future. Composed of local men, born and bred in this traditional culture, the board appointed a new superintendent—David Cole—from the nearby hamlet of Pope.[15] The youngest superintendent in the state at the time, an Ole Miss graduate, and with only two years experience in teaching, he had earlier been selected by the incumbent superintendent to learn about administration. At age twenty-seven, nine years out of high school, and "green as a gourd," Cole felt he "was young enough to relate to the new problem and old enough to stand up for something when desegregation came."

Superintendent Cole and the board faced what today seems only limited opposition, but it certainly was not perceived as such at the time. There were a few major incidents that the community talked about; but, as one veteran trustee noted, "Little things were made big, but they didn't last long, though." The contentious matter of busing both races was gradually handled; for example, bus drivers were trained to deal with the expected racial turbulence of bus rides. It helped that many whites drove their own children to schools for some time as they feared violence. School officials learned to anticipate many problems by creating a new criterion of administration, unknown in the South, namely, *judging how the other race might respond to a proposed change.* To do that, leaders started keeping close contact with black, as well as white, parents. But, as one trustee recalled of the board's purpose at that time, "People had to learn how to do what the law required." When a familiar social reality is altering, and one must learn to accommodate to a new life, leadership is a central key.

One early problem arose in integrating the faculty. School officials looked for two qualities in their appointments, professional qualifications or experience, and a sense of self-control in working with students and parents. What that quality meant was calm and reason when dealing with the school turbulence when many in both races were very disturbed. On the first criterion, of professional qualifications, many black teachers and administrators would have lost out, and many did just that in Batesville and throughout the South. Older blacks in the town recalled how they had been hurt by the loss of a black principal from a formerly segregated school. But board veterans also recalled that they were faced with black principals and teachers who were often, in one board member's words, "loose disciplinarians." Discipline was crucial at a time of social change when control over the students was vital. This emphasis on student control reflected the familiar traditional culture of southern schools. But not all black faculty were dismissed. A longtime trustee recalled, "We once had black teachers who were not really qualified, but we kept them and tried hard to improve them. We got real flack on it [from whites]. Most of those teachers are now retiring, and so we are recruiting new black teachers, but that is hard to do."

In 1975 the black community produced a representative on the south Panola board in businessman Leonard Morris. Looking back on his role, all the trustees saw Morris, as one noted, "as the best thing that could have happened to secure support from the black community" on the need to adapt to the new reality. His obvious qualifications—local origins in the Hill culture, Ole Miss training, and the calm ability to use both—developed in Morris a maturity in meeting desegregation problems that whites noted and applauded.

Morris worked closely with local officials who had come to accept his judgment and perceptions of reactions in the black community. But he was also independent enough to oppose local black opinion, for example, in appointing the first black principal from *outside* the county.[16] Earlier, he had learned to accept the trustees' wish that all decisions should be unanimous when made public, despite disagreements in private. One trustee remembers that Morris told a newer white member, who disliked this principle, that "whatever he might say on a matter, when he left a meeting it is *we* who did it, not you or me." This principle of collective responsibility sought to avoid split decisions that would stimulate local groups who were always opposing something they did.

Group Responses to Early Desegregation

Amid this change in policy and personnel, community reactions in south Panola were surprisingly modest, given the deep emotions that their rhetoric demonstrated. Some whites whose children stayed in the public schools still grumbled, but they were not organized. They came to learn early that a complaint about a person's race in a conflict that involved a student would go nowhere, although these complaints were reviewed closely by Cole and his staff. Observers agree that students of both races seemed less concerned about desegregation than their parents; athletes were regularly seen as leaders among the students in adjusting to this social change.

Some blacks were reluctant about portions of the early plans, especially over losing "their" high school, a reality for generations. But these black attitudes faded when new schools and resources became available for both races. Many black parents faced a school staff that increasingly sought their support to facilitate their children's schooling. Many parents of either race, then and now, did little in response. But the small black

middle class (e.g., small landowners, professionals, ministers) was supportive of these efforts. As for black teachers and principals, they had problems
adjusting at first, not simply in facing white students, but in the increasing professionalism of the new schooling approach. However, the black
educators, despite worrying over changes, helped focus the black community to confront this major change in their reality.

Facing this change, Batesville merchants stayed aloof for about a year,
trying to see where desegregation would go. Later, the school trustees reported that the merchants came to express satisfaction with the efforts,
who then made their support public. Shortly thereafter, the business community in its efforts to attract new industry recruited Superintendent Cole
as part of the reception committee when plant agents visited Batesville. As
for the farming community, some large planters resorted to a new private
school. One trustee sent his own children there, but he never again ran
for reelection to the school board. Other farmers met privately to express
verbal resistance and threats, but nothing happened because many stayed
with public schools. Further south in the county, near Courtland and Pope,
a closely knit community of small white farmers were overtly racist and
often Ku Klux Klan members. Nevertheless, like the big farmers, their resistance avoided direct and violent action. A veteran board trustee recalls
once that at a rural gas station the attendant had muttered loud enough
for him to hear, "I ain't going to send my kids with those niggers." But in
time they did send them, because they could not afford private schools.

However, other institutions of the area were not heard from publicly.
Political parties did not deal with the issue; on this as on many other matters in one-party systems in America, parties avoid controversial issues.
Another institution, the white churches, made few if any public statements through their ministers. But as a devout trustee noted, many white
ministers calmed parishioners who were upset by desegregation, counsel-
ing moderation and restraint in the emergent reality. Regardless of race,
some neighborhood churches were used as meeting places to discuss desegregation. But the curious public silence of white church leaders amid
the community clamor raises questions about the limits of law when the
Constitution protects them. The white churches are dealt with in this
book's concluding chapter.

Another local institution, the local newspaper, always has to be careful
in taking sides. But a review of Batesville's *Panolian* finds that it supported
obeying the law and condemned violence over desegregation or other civil
rights laws; but it also carried news about private schools. For example, in
1970 its editor covered both the emerging desegregation controversy and
the founding of private schools. That year it also:

— expressed disappointment at a local black suit against desegregation plans (which was later dismissed);

— condemned bombing threats against churches and local schools (including one rural church burning);

— urged support of the school trustees' policies;

— carried a photograph of that year's senior graduates, including blacks; and

— expressed concern that school quality would decline.

For comparison, the number of school stories covered was at least twice that found in the northern county's newspaper, the *Southern Reporter*, covering desegregation in the Delta.[17] By preserving a calm face amid all the tumult, *The Panolian* not only presented the news professionally, but both its views on obeying the law and its support of private school were responsive to the racial contrasts in the community.

Reflecting on these early events, one school trustee notes that surprisingly few whites had directly or violently opposed these changes. There were *ad hoc* groups, sometimes loud, but as an observer noted about any such issue: "They fade and then another arises. Same people are in these groups, but not always negative—sometimes positive ['like the teachers,' noted the trustee's wife]. The opponents were often the affluent, those who think everything should be done exactly their way—no sense of compromise." Even today, there is still no group opposition, just the occasional parent complaint about the race of a teacher or principal; but the board, after reviewing the case, usually backs the professionals.

Curricular and Instructional Changes

Desegregating a school means more than just busing children to buildings. The policy is defined in terms of what happens in that building, that is, how students learn, and how teachers adjust to a new constituency. This adjustment requires hard work by everyone after the buses started to roll. A review of these events in south Panola reveals their leaders' interest in making an educational change to adapt to a legal change that had been designed to shape a new reality.

New State Mandates on Ethnicity

The local control of education in the last quarter century has been transformed as state governments have become a close partner.[18] Today's legislature provides far more funds and more mandates to carry out local schooling than ever before. A mid-1980s surge of state-centralized reform designed to enhance quality appeared in every state, including Mississippi. The result was an elaborate array of curriculum components for each grade, with subjects and "core skills" leading to more state testing of student achievement. Reforms in teacher training and student assessment also accompanied these curriculum additions. The subsequent results were an enriched, but often disgruntled teacher body, which had to change its lifelong orientation to courses and instruction.

Even earlier, though, southern governors in the 1970s saw the connection between a poor economy and a poor schooling and consequently sought to increase school finances. Later, as economic conditions tightened all state budgets, governors saw a need for supervising education in order to achieve efficiency.[19] Starting in the 1970s, Mississippi's governors also sought to improve quality in schooling. Legislation provided more finances, improved curricula, trained teachers, secured more federal funds, and so raised student achievement, which was at that time just above the lowest in the nation.

This drive for quality was matched by black leaders seeking more equity in school resources for teaching their own history. To improve the representation of blacks in history courses, black groups in Jackson did what similar groups were doing throughout the nation. They sought cultural affirmation through new state curricula requirements and new textbooks more sensitive to their concerns. Such reforms brought Jackson closer to Panola's schools, a connection matched elsewhere in the state and nation.

A 1990 summary of Mississippi's reforms for quality and equity in ethnicity, as they affected south Panola, is given in table 5.1. The state's opening "mission statement" on social studies urged that "[i]ncreased communications and mobility make it imperative that the curriculum cultivate the transmission of cultural heritage, while providing for the study of cultural diversity." These dual—and often puzzling—missions of providing both common heritage and cultural diversity created problems for teachers. But they also illustrate the increasing professionalization and centralization of many local services in America today.[20] For example, the state requirements are drawn from a professional organization, the National Council for Social Studies, that emphasizes such values as equality and respect for American diversity. To meet these dual missions, state guidelines set out required and elective courses, seen in table 5.1; south Panola in 1990 used seven required and two elective courses. From the student perspective, ethnicity is part of the curriculum in almost every semester in the high school.

Reviewing the Textbooks. In the new curriculum, elements exist to teach students about the black role, especially their role in the New South. Except in courses on the history of Mississippi and on American govern-

Table 5.1   Ethnic Topics in the Mississippi Educational Curriculum,
State Mandates and South Panola Requirements, 1990

PHILOSOPHY AND AIMS OF TEACHING SOCIAL STUDIES

Based on National Council of Social Studies (1983), includes
1. Three "democratic processes," including equal protection of the laws, rooted in eight values, including equality.
2. Interpersonal relations, including "respecting the rights of others."

INDIVIDUAL COURSE COMPONENTS

1. Topics for elementary grades include
   —Individual worth, dignity, and responsibility (grades K–1).
   —Diversity of U.S. as a nation (grades 1, 5), including ethnicity.
   —Social developments (grades 1, 5), including civil rights and the civil rights movement.
2. Individual course requirements (grades 7–12) for skills and concepts include:
   —Mississippi history:* Included in almost all the 28 components in this section is a skill called "discuss improvement in race relations," but it is not a core item for testing.
   —Mississippi state and local government:* Standard outline, including citizenship responsibilities.
   —World culture:* American history to the Civil War.
   —U.S. history, 1877 to present:* History of military and social problems to present, omitting the civil rights movement.
   —U.S. government:* Standard outline includes civil rights, omitting the civil rights movement.
   —Global studies.*
   —Geography:* Includes American values, including tolerance.
   —Ancient and medieval history, elective: Includes "know these ancient political units: Zimbabwe, Mali, Ghana, Benin, Asante."
   —Minority studies, elective: Like electives on all minorities, that on blacks includes "black role in society," and "describe treatment of blacks in the U.S."
   —Problems of American democracy, elective: A problem-oriented course, including civil liberties and civil rights.
   —World history, elective: Includes nations and movements in Africa.
   —Introduction to social studies, elective: Review of each field, none speaking specifically to ethnicity.
   —Other electives, including economics,* sociology,* law-related education, and psychology; no ethnicity component specified.

Source: Mississippi Department of Education, *Mississippi Course Offerings: Social Studies* (Jackson, 1990).

* Offered in South Panola School District.

ment, the written component, of state law for required courses do not identify a "minorities" concept, per se, which means they are not a "core item" for state testing. Rather, the new emphasis on minorities in history and government courses is provided by new textbooks in the 1980s. Often, these texts organize the course syllabus, so to see what students are learning it will be useful to summarize their coverage of minorities. What teachers offer today as a result of new political forces on the curriculum is quite different from what was offered before desegregation.

In qualitative terms, the approach of these texts range from the bland to the engaged, but blandness prevails. A ninth-grade text on civics has only two brief references to the federal government's using the Fourteenth Amendment against segregated schools and insuring votes for blacks (a task accomplished in just two sentences). There is one photograph of blacks registering, with a caption that reads, "For years, black people had met many obstacles when they tried to register as voters." Another photo shows a young black judge in Charleston, South Carolina. Another ninth-grade text on Mississippi civics and law is extraordinary for having no discussion on the blacks in that state's government. It refers to recent civil rights laws with only a one-sentence description, and there is no material on the movement that had produced them; yet their authors claim to be incensed at Republican presidents for appointing fewer blacks to federal office. It is curious that the book is silent on a major factor affecting state government in a book dedicated to that subject.[21]

But the presentation improves significantly in grades 11 through 12, where American government and history courses use texts with a much richer description of minorities. Political scientist Robert Hardgrave, author of one of these texts, provides a full chapter of twenty-one pages on equality under law with primary reference to blacks. Its contents touch on broken promises, blacks in Reconstruction government, Jim Crow laws, and school desegregation from the 1896 *Plessy v. Ferguson* case to the contemporary *Brown* and *Swann* cases.

The civil rights movement and its subsequent laws on voting rights are fully developed, but the textbook also reports the racial gap that still exists, by many measures. Scattered elsewhere are references to blacks as cowboys and lynch victims, to housing covenants, racial riots, and to southern white voting fraud against blacks. Black personalities are discussed or photographed, from W. E. B. DuBois to Reverend Martin Luther King, Jr., including long citations from King's "I Have a Dream" speech. There is a long analysis of civil disobedience discussing Thoreau, Gandhi, and King. However, another text on American government, the traditional text by Frank Abbot Magruder, then in its sixty-seventh edition, reduces these topics to one-half the pages found in Hardgrave, but it does include recent data on black voter registration and office holding. Finally, the U.S. history text, by Merle Curti, the noted Wisconsin historian, is just as complete as Hardgrave's on black roles in national events since the Civil War. There is discussion of Reconstruction (a photo and story of Hiram Revel, first black man sent to the U.S. Senate, along with another black, Blanche Bruce). Other historical black roles shown include cowboys, San Francisco Forty-niner players, artists (such as those in the Harlem movement), and soldiers from every war since 1861.[22]

Local Response in Curriculum Change. Just how these state mandates are translated into local instruction is evident in the detailed instructions drawn up by the district's curriculum office.[23] Each course is broken down into a set of concepts, and each concept is specified as to its objectives, methods, skills, learning steps, and evaluation. An example is found in table 5.2, which specifies the skill to be taught and the methodology for teaching the Declaration of Independence within a unit on "political development" for the sixth grade. The steps of teaching and learning are related to the textbook, and these in turn are tested by questions that are also provided. In short, teacher tasks and student learning are clearly specified down to the smallest details.

Instructional improvement in this and other schools is effected through a special sequence of measures. Improving the quality of the curriculum begins with requirements for general goals and missions at the state level. Textbooks provide the content, either broadly or in detail. Finally, local teachers receive highly specified instructional concepts from the state, which link up the readings for both teacher and student. Professional standards employed at higher levels are transferred to the schools, a process that also facilitates testing student achievement. Accordingly, what south Panola teachers now offer stems from new political forces, emanating in state and local professional decisions.

Clearly, what students now learn about minorities is quite different from what was taught when the ocr first turned to this district. Then, no text for either race referred positively to blacks, white teachers showed little interest in the topic, and the state was silent on the role of race.

Teacher Reactions to New Mandates

How did teachers react to these changes in south Panola? Their responses provide insight on another dimension of law's ability to change reality and cognitions. From novice to veteran, these social studies teachers were like most teachers in the country—born, raised, and trained in the same state in which they work. Like the segregated community around them, they reflected strong values about white dominance and black subordination.

Table 5.2   Illustration of State and Local Mandates for Social Science
Curriculum in South Panola

UNIT	POLITICAL DEVELOPMENT
SKILL NO.	7 (C67)
SKILL	*Identify the Declaration of Independence*
OBJECTIVE	Given 10 statements, the student will identify the Declaration of Independence by writing the correct answer in the space provided.*
METHOD	The teacher will 1. Lead discussion 2. Provide questions 3. Provide independent worksheets 4. Write notes on chalkboard
LEARNING STEPS	The learner will 1. Read from text 2. Participate in discussion 3. Answer the questions on paper 4. Read Preamble to Declaration of Independence as a group
EVALUATION	The sixth grade learner will identify the Declaration of Independence with _____% accuracy.**
MATERIALS	textbook chalkboard film projector pencil chalk film strip paper notebooks

Source: Program description provided by Dr. Dolores Barnett, curriculum supervisor, South Panola School District (n.d.).

*Multiple-choice questions are provided.
**Normally about 75%.

When desegregation began in the late 1960s, teachers reported that there was no change in instruction except, as one white noted, they had to "be careful about offending blacks in a desegregated class; I didn't want to embarrass them." In the freedom-of-choice period, familiar textbooks were still used, with their rare mention of any black hero, much less of black contributions to history. However, the books changed after 1970 due to the political pressures noted.

    In time, a process began in south Panola of selecting texts from a list approved by the state, which were then purchased on the local school budget. Teachers from across the state had produced this state list. At both local and state levels, then, professional views could be shared about the ethnic or other elements in the social studies area; these views were more supportive in stressing the role of blacks. That is, local teachers encountered professional signals about the new direction that were positive. By 1993, the state mandated a new social studies framework, meaning more race-related topics. One south Panola teacher noted there were now more courses available in the fifth grade in social studies than had existed in college when she got her degree.

Despite the professional involvement, many local teachers resent what one called the "Mickey Mouse" of meeting mandates and of staff contact with the state. Earlier, teachers had set their own core skills in the lesson plan; if they worked, they were continued. But now, the state requires "busy work that requires spending many hours of night work" to fill out state forms. Teachers dislike teaching a "skill" that is already covered in other courses. Indeed, skills in any course are now itemized in a checklist prepared for the teachers. But note that teachers' responses to the state mandates are often a reaction to having to adapt to central influences while also trying to meet local preferences. As one teacher said, "I resent being told to do what I do anyhow!"

While many white teachers think there was little benefit in adhering to state rules, the rules do nonetheless provide students with numerous black references in required courses and textbooks. In American history, teachers themselves can add to discussion from their own reading. Some discuss early black figures—Crispus Attacks, Peter Salem, Harriet Tubman, Frederick Douglass—or refer to a black regiment in the Civil War featured in a recent film, *Old Glory*. February—since it is Black History Month—provides a special focus on blacks in the United States and generates television programs or lectures often used in classes in south Panola.[24]

However, when the subject deals with civil rights and with the earlier oppression that blacks had known, teachers report a variety of approaches in their instruction—and resistance from students. One teacher has focused on barriers that blacks faced in voter registration and on the new black presence in local and state governments. Another teacher has related the movement to events in Panola County, including a visit of Reverend Martin Luther King. Typically, to teach this topic the teachers have to rely heavily on the new textbooks, which they regard as now much improved.

But the teachers find students fail to comment or to ask questions about race, rights, or politics. Teachers of both races perceive this attitude as one of diffidence that conceals "lots of bitterness by both races." That attitude explains why students would not use classes for a fuller discussion of the latent racial tension that still remains in their lives. One white teacher recalls an incident of white bitterness that also shows the school response to it:

White students don't like to hear about these changes in voting. Some will put their heads down. One white in class said I was trying to start a racial issue. I showed him the wording of the 15th Amendment. But he still complained to his mother who worked in the school and [who went] to the principal by showing this item in the book. But nothing came from it.

So I try to stay away from what happened in this county because whites don't like it; students will tell their parents and even make up lies. I didn't talk to them about King coming to this county, because it wasn't in the book. It's lots safer this way.

Reflecting on these student attitudes, some teachers found even deeper implications. While some white students resent the fact that the government changed white rights, and thereby reflect their parents' views, their resentment is only part of an underlying resentment of authority *of any kind.* What students will discuss in government courses, noted one teacher, is their legal obligations to their parents. For these students, as for others around the nation, no one they know or read about was a *local visible* figure, and so the issue seemed remote.[25] But teachers report that high school students do have an interest in two authorities—school and police—because these agents are local and can limit their actions.

Yet this lack of student interest is not as great a concern to teachers as another problem. That is the presence in their classes of dysfunctional students, aggressive males, and pregnant females. These students either overtly or by implication challenge the social values that teachers and families seek to instill. It is important to note that these comments come from some white teachers discussing black students. Their attitudes may reflect their own racial responses, their concern over maintaining order in the classroom, or both.

But deepest of all concerns expressed by teachers and administrators of both races was the limited involvement of parents in instilling in their children any respect for learning. Teachers of both races did believe that this problem was greater in the black community. One black administrator noted that there are two kinds of families in this poor county, those who "push" their children to obtain more schooling and those who do not. "The pusher families do so because, in looking at the negatives of life, they want their children to do better. The nonpushers, on the other hand, look at the same negatives and simply felt they could not do much about it because they were not equipped to do much."

This parental weakness, noted in the next chapter on north Panola and found extensively in current school research, has diluted the system's effort at schooling. There is a self-denying prophecy at work here, that is, when parents and teachers believe students cannot learn, students usually end up not learning. It has been a continuing problem in both public schools and among some teachers in this county. On the other hand, when the parents are "pushers" who influence strongly the school's efforts (as in the white North Delta academy), parents and teachers believe that students can learn, and this intellectual growth is fostered in students. In short, because adults think students can learn, they do.

Summary

This account sets out important changes in the instructional format for social sciences in the desegregated school in south Panola. In recent decades, the state has become directly involved in expanding and improving courses, topics, and books. Local teachers have resisted the details of state control but do teach the richer curriculum. But the problem is embedded in a broader one, namely, a lack of student interest in anything "political." In the 1980s, the National Assessment of Educational Progress found that the "most boring" of all courses was not algebra but civics. Indeed, the limited teacher training and the bland textbooks in this area contribute to that failing. On the other hand, professionals treat this potentially dangerous topic blandly because that is a useful strategy for school board members, teachers, and administrators alike. Blandness keeps enraged parents off their backs.[26] However, despite the lack of student interest, a changed curriculum on race and related topics is now taught to south Panola students. Together, they must deal with instructional materials that portray a new social reality and new attitudes about blacks.

If these have been important aspects of the change in schooling under desegregation, what have been the consequences of that change? Two consequences are the reallocation of resources and its effects upon student and teacher attitudes and learning. We review those consequences using information drawn from records of faculty personnel and students. Chapter 7 pursues the consequences for student attitudes about race.

Longer-Range Outcomes of Desegregation

If these have been important aspects of altering schooling under desegregation, what have been the consequences of that change, for example, in the reallocation of resources and in its effects upon student attitudes? These consequences are reviewed using another source of information, namely, records of faculty personnel, student dropout rates, and student attitudes.

Reallocation of Resources

The distribution of public resources in personnel and budget tells us much more than just numbers, for it also explains a distribution of human values; it is the satisfaction of values that drives the search for such resources.[27] In other words, this distribution of resources within a community reveals the pattern of values held by those who make these decisions. Earlier we considered the distribution of resources under traditional segregation, which reflected the values of white supremacy. Has desegregation altered this distribution in a more equitable fashion in south Panola?

The current allocation of school personnel, the largest single item in a school budget, reveals what was already noted in the previous chapter on voting. That is, equity has not been achieved. If one thinks that resources should be allocated in proportion to race, this is not happening in south Panola with respect to personnel. Despite a nearly equal racial population in this district, the proportion of school personnel who are white is much higher. In table 5.3 we can see the distribution overall and by individual schools a quarter-century after desegregation began.[28] Most of the personnel in any school are teachers, and in 1992 in south Panola 70 to 80 percent were white, overall and at each site, as were the superintendent and central office staff. However, administrators were of both races in all schools except the smallest. Coaches in junior and senior high schools were usually of both races, as were band directors in the senior school, while librarians were black only at the senior level.

How is one to evaluate these numbers in terms of the goals of desegregation? It is clear from the memories of the staff that strong efforts have been made to recruit blacks, first as teachers and later as principals. However, the difficulties in recruiting black teachers—indeed, any teachers—to rural county schools anywhere in this nation are immense. Local people who are qualified to be recruited here can find better incomes in cities and suburbs, regardless of race. Promotion to school administration has usually relied on in-district experience, but that has only yielded in Batesville the recent appointment of a black principal; there have been no black superintendents.[29]

This analysis assumes, though, a simple goal of desegregation, that is, getting the number of positions proportional to the black population in the district. This definition of representation as "symbolic" is a first objective of blacks, and, indeed, of earlier immigrant groups.[30] For the blacks in south Panola that goal still remains their test, which may account for energetic efforts by the trustees to recruit black professionals to meet that test. For other blacks, though, another goal of desegregation is whether

Table 5.3   1992 Certified School Employees in South Panola, by Position and Race

Position	Black	White	Total
Central Office			
Administration	2	5	7
High school			
Administration	1	1	2
Teachers	14	43	57
Counselors	0	3	3
Librarian	1	0	1
Coaches	1	2	3
Band directors	1	1	2
Jr. high school			
Administration	1	1	2
Teachers	11	30	41
Counselors	0	2	2
Librarians	0	1	1
Coaches	2	1	3
Band director	0	1	1
Intermediate school			
Administration	1	1	2
Teachers	14	33	47
Counselor	1	0	1
Librarian	0	1	1
Elementary school			
Administration	1	1	2
Teachers	11	40	51
Counselor	0	1	1
Librarian	0	1	1
Pope school			
Administration	0	1	1
Teachers	5	21	26
Coach	0	1	1
Child development center			
Supervisor	0	1	1
Teachers	1	2	3
Education for employment			
Supervisor	0	1	1
Teacher	1	2	3
Total	69	198	267

Source: Data provided by Bobby Carlisle, Central Office, South Panola School District.

their children have access to the educational resources that whites share. The criterion is whether one's children are in the same classroom as whites, have access to the same library, or are judged by the same criteria on their athletic talent to "make the team." In short, for many black parents their children's being in the same school as the other race means that there is an equivalent access to resources. Underlying this concept is the value of equity, namely, a sense of fairness in access to resources. It is a concept that sounds loud through our history for all kinds of groups besides blacks.

The Problem of Discipline

Whatever black goals of desegregation are, however, not all parents were happy with efforts in south Panola. Parents of both races occasionally complain that a particular teacher or administrator of the other race is either too strong or too weak in "discipline." That complaint means either the school is not demanding enough academically or is penalizing excessively those who break school rules. Black children here, as elsewhere in the nation, receive a larger proportion of school penalties; but they also receive more school services in the form of staff and student enrichment programs.

Recognizing that discipline would be a problem, the trustees and superintendent of south Panola developed remedial programs and detailed rules about discipline, both fully publicized. The provision of funds for remedial programs—like Headstart and Chapter I funds[31]—not only permit students to do better and stay longer in school (as noted later), but also fit well the desegregation goal of providing equitable access to more resources.

As for disciplinary rules, if any student breaks them and punishment ensues, then it is hard to argue that there is inequity in treatment. But the problem lies in the larger number of blacks whom teachers believe have violated the rules and whose judgments the administrators have accepted. Parents here and elsewhere do not like the result of such discipline and often have challenged such rules themselves. To deal with this problem in south Panola, the administration has trained the staff to implement a widely publicized, rule-based discipline. But from the perspective of teachers, student behavior that challenges professional control of instruction cannot be ignored; they believe that other students lose out if instruction is hampered by misbehavior. Consequently, school leadership had to adopt several measures: clearly publicized rules of discipline, teacher training on racial implications in their judgments, and stressing to parents and their children the responsibility of adhering to rules. It is this new awareness by school leaders—developed over time—that reflected the new sensitivity in a biracial environment.

Behind this formulation of discipline lay another set of rationales. Discipline was one of several principles that had to be worked out by district officials in the new reality that had been created by law. An insistence on rules had several uses for the school system; it would provide a learning focus about racial implications for school personnel, a guide to using the rules for all personnel, and a protection against legal suits if fairly used. This sensitive thinking was a success, at least from Washington's viewpoint, where there was little exception to these rules. Records of the OCR over the last quarter-century report few challenges to south Panola's actions, and even those few were in the earliest years.[32] But there was no challenge to these disciplinary rules or, indeed, to other aspects of desegregation in the district. Nevertheless, black students still receive a disproportionate amount of discipline today.

In sum, one consequence of desegregation has been the reallocation of school resources. The reallocations did not always fit a goal of desegregation based on racial proportionality, for example, in hiring or discipline. However, another goal of desegregation, that of broader access by black children to school resources, has been achieved in this district. This is seen in the wide use of state and federal grants for educational remediation that affects blacks much more, reflecting the new biracial reality of schooling.

Student Achievement

Shifting from inputs of resources into the desegregation of south Panola, to the subject of student achievement, how did this new schooling reality affect student learning? We suggest two comprehensive measures of school effectiveness, namely, student dropout rates and achievement scores. These measures tell us who lost and who won among the young in this law-inspired reality. It would be a positive result if dropouts declined over time, because more youth would obtain more time for education and opportunities that more schooling brings. A second measure is improvement in learning. Did the students learn more or less under desegregation, a serious worry among whites when it began? It takes time to develop these numbers. Estimates that are short-run, whether positive or negative, ignore long-run, or "sleeper," effects that take time to emerge. But evidence for the answers now exist from south Panola's experience of a quarter century. What is particularly illuminating is the attitudinal differences among students from these three types of schools. That larger question will be treated in chapter 7.

South Panola Dropouts over Time. Dropout rates are measured by comparing the number of students in school at the time of the survey with

Table 5.4   Dropout Rates, South Panola School District, Selected Years

Grades	NUMBER OF STUDENTS DROPPING OUT		
	1970–75	1988–92	% Decrease over Period
K–6	22	1	95
7–9	40	26	35
[9 + 10]	[87]	[28]	[68]
10–12	104	53	49
Total	166	80	54

Source: Abstracted by the author from annual data provided by the South Panola School District. Nearest whole number is used.

the number from an earlier time. While commonly used as a measure of a school's effectiveness, the measure does have a problem. It does not take into account the fact that a student counted as missing may not have dropped school; some may have moved to another school. But comparing these records over time should show if there was any effect at all.

As table 5.4 shows, over time there has indeed been a dramatic decrease in the number of dropouts. The actual number of *annual dropouts* over the two periods fell from an average of 22 in the period 1970–1975 to 1 in the period 1988–1992 in grades K through 5, dropped in grades 6 through 8 from 40 to 26, and from 104 to 53 in the senior grades. Put another way, the dropout improvement in percentage points for each set of grades was 95, 35, and 49.[33] Even in the worst grades for dropouts—9 and 10—there was a 71 percentage decrease in dropout rates. In recent years, race was not a major factor in these data; in 1991–1992 and across all grades, a total of 38 blacks and 35 whites dropped out, mostly in grade 9.

Why is this change significant? Staying in school means that today's students receive more education than did earlier generations. That increase means a chance for both races to achieve better jobs and greater incomes than their parents had. Today's generation of students have options besides farm labor, which was once the only job opportunity for blacks. Indeed, a later test will show that one-half the seniors in the early 1990s in south Panola wanted to attend college, which usually means a two-year institution in a nearby county. We have no earlier poll data, but far fewer than one-half of blacks have ever attended college in this county. Increasingly, local newspapers report blacks with a degree from a community or other college. While often these degrees were for vocational education, that accomplishment should still lead to greater income than their parents ever

Table 5.5   State Assessment Scores by Course, South Panola School
District, 1990

| Course | GRADES | | |
	3	5	8
Writing			
South Panola	384.8	573.2	877.0
State mean	386.1	573.1	875.3
Mathematics			
South Panola	378.8	570.2	877.9
State mean	382.1	576.8	871.0
Reading			
South Panola	384.2	574.1	871.8
State mean	385.1	574.4	873.0
Composite			
South Panola	382.7	575.3	875.0
State mean	384.4	572.8	872.7

Source: Abstracted from state reports, Basic Skills Assessment Program, from printouts provided by Bobby Carlisle, Central Office, South Panola School District.

knew.[34] Consequently, one result of desegregation in this district is that
young people now have a greater likelihood for a better life than their parents did.

Learning Gains among South Panola Students. Another measure of the
success of desegregation is whether students improve or weaken in their
learning. One standard measure is a district's rating on state achievement
scores. Unfortunately, since such tests have altered over a quarter century,
it is impossible to get a comparable base line. But, as noted earlier, governors have started to reform the weak condition of Mississippi schools;
one effort was to broaden the assessment of student accomplishment for
many grades. The 1990 results for south Panola appear in table 5.5, using
scores for grades 3, 5, and 8, which show an improvement across all the
grade levels.

A more useful test is to compare this district with the *state* average,
using three subjects as well as a composite score, as table 5.5 shows. Within
each pairing of district and state scores has this desegregated district improved or not in its learning outcomes? Grade 3 shows slightly below the
state average (especially on math); there is a mixed record in grade 5, but
it is still improving; and the grade 8 result is above the state level on two
subjects and overall (but not on reading). In short, the results show that

Table 5.6 Achievement Scores of South Panola School District
and National Average, Selected Courses, 1990

| Courses | GRADES | | | |
	3	7	10	11
Reading	42.7	40.4	40.0	40.6
Math	48.8	46.1	42.9	43.1
Language	49.4	45.2	50.6	50.6
Science	47.0	41.7	—	—
Basic	45.6	50.0	50.0	50.0

Source: Data from Stanford Test Series results for the district, 1990, from printouts provided by
Bobby Carlisle, Central Office, South Panola School District.

Note: The figures in the columns represent the mean percentages scored on the national test
by students in the South Panola School District; 50 percent is the national average. No data
provided for science scores in grades 10 and 11.

the desegregated district had an improving, but still middling, achievement record in south Panola.

An even larger measure compares these students with the *national*
average on certain subjects. The same result holds when they are compared nationally (table 5.6). From elementary to high school grades there
are average to below-average mean scores. Over the grades, the district's
national ranking is lower in reading and mathematics, but higher in language and basic skills. Its overall achievement range is still at or somewhat
below the national mean, even though there is still some improvement in
the higher grades. That conclusion is significant, as these tests occurred
in a period when test scores across the nation showed that achievement
in most schools in all states and regions was falling.

Summary

When desegregation began in the nation, the policy had different aims.
One was to redistribute schooling resources. In the original *Brown* case,
the maldistribution of resources under segregation were judged unconstitutional because it provided unequal services to blacks, and was thereby
unfair to students, affecting their learning and chances in later life. Subsequent challenges in courts sought to redistribute these resources by desegregation. In a school district like south Panola, which has seen over a
quarter century of desegregation, did the black students *gain* from these
new practices?

Answering that central query after some decades is complicated because there are different definitions of "gain." If the test is whether blacks

closed the learning gap with whites, then the evidence is that was not the case. This racial gap emerges elsewhere in the South and North and it is persistent and pervasive over time. On the other hand, if the test of desegregation is whether more students stay longer in schools with access to more resources, we have clear evidence that this is happening in south Panola. Dropout rates declined dramatically at all grade levels, while general achievement scores have improved overall, even in a district with limited resources. For some blacks, there were also opportunities to excel that in turn could lead to college and better jobs; these were opportunities that their parents never knew. That possibility was evident in the record of success among individuals who benefited from more schooling, such as Leonard Morris.

In interviews with residents of south Panola, one of the questions put regularly was *"Without the law, would blacks today have as many votes, as much education, and as many jobs?"* Most whites agreed, often reluctantly, that this would *not* have been the case. The new schools under desegregation, using new resources and rules, have provided a quality of schooling for black students never known before in that county's history. In short, not equal, but better, education was the result of a quarter century of work in schooling blacks.

Students' Attitudes about Life

Another test of desegregation has been whether the two races have different attitudes about themselves. South Panola serves as a crucible in which students create common notions of self, school, and community; these cognitions are drawn partly from school instruction and partly from their personal interactions. For each grade, these cognitions can exhibit common views of life, but they may vary across grades or when the nature of the community varies. Immersed in an institution for six or more hours daily and influenced by common cultural influences like the media or peers, school children at all ages have much in common.

From that general concept, then, a proposition for research in this district arises, which is to test desegregated students' attitudes and behavior, not all of which are racial. The context of desegregation may generate racial similarities or it may not. Finding similarities demonstrates the influence of institutions in shaping members' cognitions; finding differences points to external influences on students that ignore institutional concerns. Thus, we can ask, do these students have similar or different racial contacts, racial views, self-esteem, and political attitudes? We cannot compare these young people with those from the segregated years where we could reasonably test the effects of that institution. But we can

Table 5.7   South Panola School District Student Scales on Attitudes and
Behaviors

---

1. DISCUSSION OF PUBLIC PROBLEMS: in general, or with family, friends, leaders; N of
   items in questionnaire on this scale = 4.*
2. VOLUNTEER WORK: in youth groups, church, politics, hospital, school, or arts
   groups; N = 6.
3. RACE-GENDER EQUALITY: attitudes on equality in jobs, schooling, and income,
   with race and gender treated separately; N = 8.
4. RACIAL CONTACT: in school, sports, church, community, and social events; problems with race believed to exist in school, neighborhood, community, and nation;
   N = 11.
5. SELF-ESTEEM: standardized tests of how one views the self; attitudes toward one's
   school; N = 17.
6. POLITICAL EFFICACY: standardized tests of one's trust of and responsiveness to
   political systems, elections, and leaders; N = 10.
7. GOVERNMENT POLICY: support for the following:
   a. New Deal liberal: fairness in jobs, health, housing; N = 3.
   b. Populist: attitudes about big corporations and big labor; N = 2.
   c. States rights: state control over voting and schooling; N = 2.
   d. Cold-war warrior: isolationism, policy toward Communist nations, military;
      N = 3.
8. RACIAL COMPOSITE SCALE: all items on race from scales above; N = 11.

---

* For individual questions, see Appendix A.

ask whether today both races hold similar cognitions. If they do, it could
suggest that desegregation yields a common outlook. One recent event
suggests that possibility. A letter to the local paper in 1990 criticized a recent invitation for a "white-only" reunion of the class of 1980; the signers
of this criticism were a black and a white.[35]

Design of the Test. We needed to test students from grades 6, 9, and 12
on their behaviors and attitudes; these grades mark the end of elementary,
secondary, and senior schooling respectively.[36] If there was similarity in
their attitudes despite racial differences, then the school experience might
explain this commonality. In the next chapter we will search for other
explanations than just race, that is, for those found in class, occupation,
gender, and age. We can then compare south Panola students with those
from the north Panola and North Delta schools.

The data were drawn from a sample of over 1,200 students from these
three grades from all three districts in the county; they were tested within
a three-day period just before graduation in 1990.[37] The test used sixty-six
questions that form eight scales, as set out in table 5.7.[38]

Table 5.8   Differences of Means on Attitude Tests by Black and White Students, South Panola

Scale	Whites	Blacks		Significance of Race
Discussion of public problems	1.123	1.115	.800	NS
Volunteer work	.847	.845	.951	NS
Race-gender equality	1.049	1.160	.017	Blacks
Racial contact	.880	.782	.000	Whites
Self-esteem	.739	.715	.479	NS
Political efficacy	.627	.420	.000	Whites
Government policy				
New Deal liberal	.874	1.181	.000	Blacks
Populist	−.025	.001	.672	NS
States rights	.195	.079	.143	NS
Cold war warrior	.210	−.053	.000	Blacks
Racial composite scale	1.055	1.041	.369	NS

NS = not statistically significant. When race is statistically significant, students of the race specified scored higher on that scale.

Uses Anova t-tests, two-tailed, pooled variance estimate.

The question that drives use of these scales was simple. Did both races in this district hold similar attitudes and behaviors or did they differ by race? If there was biracial similarity on any scale, then race would not be a significant difference. But if the scores were significantly different, race might be the explanation, although other factors may intrude. The evidence for the question is found in table 5.8; the individual questions appear in appendix A.

Evaluating the Results. For those early reformers who thought that deseg-regation would mean not only more resources for blacks but also some weakening of racial hatred, this table is generally supportive. A striking finding appears in the scale combining measures of racial attitudes (*racial composite scale*), for there is no significant difference based on race. This is the key finding on desegregation in south Panola. The policy of deseg-regation has developed students over a quarter century whose different attitudes and behavior about many aspects of life are not based simply on race. There were differences within each racial group, but the differences between races was not significant.

One might suppose that blacks in a discouraging world might hold different attitudes and take different actions than do whites, for whom the world is better. Blacks then should hold less optimistic attitudes on their personal worth, on their chances of succeeding, and on volunteering to participate in community life. Blacks might also report feeling more powerless, be more critical of big labor and big business who do little for them, and oppose state control of voting or desegregation, which had never helped blacks in the past. However, table 5.8 does not support these suppositions; the distribution of attitudes and behavior is quite similar by race. Of course, we cannot compare these cognitive differences with students *before* desegregation appeared. But we can show that, after a quarter century, students in 1990 had a surprisingly similar racial distribution on these major measures of child development. This schooling experience, created by actions of school officials under stimulus from federal law, did not separate the outlooks of the youth of either race.

But these are not students who are all of a kind, stamped out by cookie cutters; there are differences among them. On the *race-gender equality scale* (table 5.8), blacks were more supportive than whites. That is not surprising, as the items measured here call for fair treatment of blacks and women. But this scale combines two topics, and so the results blur the racial aspect (the racial part is picked up in the racial composite scale). Also, whites report greater *racial contact* than blacks across a range of activities. There may be perceptual problems here, for these students are living in a new environment. That is, on a scale for racial contact that is measured on a more to less contact basis, whites may perceive even the small contact in school as "more" contact, for they have less contact with blacks in other aspects of community life. But blacks could interpret the same contact as "same" or "less."

Whites are also score higher on the *political efficacy scale,* namely, in their attitudes about participating in the political world and in elections, and their trust in political leaders. Other research has shown this same finding, which may be related to the higher status of whites.[39] Despite the earlier generation of blacks spurring an interest in politics through registration and voting, the new generation seems quite apathetic. As a black social studies teacher in north Panola lamented, "Today's kids don't know what we did to get the vote, and they don't care about it now." Note here though, that this sense of efficacy does increase nationally with greater age;[40] that increase is also seen in this analysis, a matter discussed in the next chapter.

Racial differences also emerged in table 5.8 when blacks claimed stronger support than whites for national *public policies* on equality on race and gender; more jobs, better housing, and higher pay; and a more aggressive stance against Communist nations and using soldiers to support American policies abroad.[41] The reason for the black support of the first two of these policies is clear, for they enhance their own resources or status, but the reason for their support on international policies is less clear and is little studied in research anywhere.

Equally important to attitudes about race and issues is the students' *self-esteem scale*, shown in table 5.8. Used widely in youth research, this scale measures one's sense of personal adequacy in understanding the world and one's place in it. Given their world of poverty and whites' racial attitudes, blacks might be expected to feel lower self-esteem than whites. However, on this scale there is very little racial variation, and none of it is significant. Overall, the students' views on the role of luck and planning, the sense of one's importance, or the chances of success lose any racial distinction in this analysis.

Similar attitudes appear also in concepts about one's own school, a segment of the self-esteem scale. One might suppose that blacks would reject their schools if they believed that racism prevailed everywhere. However, the desegregation experience might be so favorable that the two races would not differ in their evaluation. In fact, five questions found surprisingly high support among students for their schools in south Panola, with no regard to race and grade level. Focusing on just those students of either race who "agreed" or "agreed strongly" in school support, they reported that they were, in matters of school: relaxed and confident (60%); very positive (65%) and proud (75%); and schools were important to them (88%) and would help them as adults (91%).

Of critical importance is the fact that *black support exceeded white support on every question*, regardless of grade level, although these differences were not statistically significant. Whatever the furor over desegregation had been or whether racial resentment continued, students of both races, especially blacks, saw desegregated schools as a positive environment for learning. In time, going to school with one another had become one part of the new social reality that they would carry into the future.

Teacher Concepts of Self and Society

Not only students in south Panola went through the desegregation experience, but their teachers did as well. What were the teachers' attitudes about themselves and their schools?

Teachers' responses (75% of respondents were white) to the same questions provide a contrast in professional attitudes and personal beliefs. Their support of the schools is just as high as the students' for every grade level.[42] Large majorities of teachers believe that both races should receive the same school (81% support) and job (73% support) opportunities. Their attitudes, compared with students, also showed no significant racial differences, except in the category of racial contact. Black teachers have higher racial contact and racial composite scores, which indicate more liberal attitudes than white teachers. However, both races believe that racial problems exist—*but outside their own locality*. Thus, they see racial problems as being low in their neighborhood and community (3% saw problems in the neighborhood, 6% saw them in the community); but the percentages perceiving problems increase for the state and nation (26% and 37% respectively). Further, despite their positive assessment of desegregation, most white teachers believe that Washington should stay out of school desegregation (65% agree or strongly agree) and voting laws (78% agree). Also, three-quarters (mostly white teachers) report that they have friends, or closest friends, who are white.

These teacher responses suggest they do believe in equal schooling opportunities, and their own teaching, as noted earlier, supports this viewpoint. But their attitudes about, and their contact with, blacks suggest a difference. As southern culture demonstrates, both in the old and new forms, there are two worlds of racial contact. Racial contact mandated by law has gradually worked its way into the community life. There is an "inner" and "outer color line," and the latter has been penetrated recently only by law, which, in turn, brings changes in its politics.[43] However, as these surveys of teachers imply, where no compulsion rules, as in the world of friends, church, and social life, this is still a traditional society in action and belief. But still, professionalism and law have altered behavior within the realm of education. Both the Old and New South are reflected in the views of these teachers.

Summary

Student attitudes were most impressive in this test of one outcome of desegregation. Compelled by law to attend school together in south Panola, the two races have developed cognitions that are surprisingly similar but not identical. We will turn to these results later, in reviewing them alongside results from the segregated north Panola and North Delta schools. But in south Panola, where racial comparison is possible, desegregation has made a difference for schooling the young. Dropout rates have been reduced and achievement tests are closer to the state's mean scores, consequences that greatly assist the chances of students improving their quality of life. Some, but not many, significant racial differences in student and teacher attitudes do remain; but student attitudes about race, self, and schooling rarely differ as a function of race. As for teachers, their contrast of professional and personal attitudes in the workplace is a reminder that prejudice and nondiscrimination can exist together.

Leadership for Desegregation

Much of the outcome in south Panola under desegregation is clearly a function of leadership by the board of trustees and the school superintendent in adjusting to social change. If law works to change social reality, it must do so through leadership in its implementation. The positive consequences of efforts by school leaders are seen in improved achievement and attitudes among students and teachers. In approaching desegregation in this fashion, the school board and educational professionals of south Panola highlighted the cultural differences between their district and the Delta culture. As an experienced trustee of the southern district noted,

> We owe much to the community, and we acknowledge that support. Without it, we'd be like north Panola, which had support of neither black nor white communities. The influential people in this half of the county worked for us later on with school referenda issues by using the telephone, indicating to others their support. That support is a big plus for us as we developed a close and good relationship. Superintendent Cole was responsible for maintaining that relationship.

It would be impossible to relate every detail of the community conflicts in which the board and superintendent engaged. In the early days, community conflict over the outside law was overtly racial. But in time, the conflict shifted to the educational scene, that is, to questions about how to organize and use the resources, human and material, that would improve student learning. The first conflict, over attitudes about the law, has now gone, for a recalcitrant attitude among the whites has given way to a pragmatic one. But the conflict over school improvement still remains. In both cases leadership has been the key to implementing the objectives of federal law. Whether people in the community oppose that law—as they did in every state and local institution in the 1960s—or whether they support it—the norm within a decade—those results relied upon leadership.

The Study of Leadership

Much of what we know about leadership rests upon identifying leadership traits, which fall into two broad types.[44] In the classic study by James Macgregor Burns, the "transformational" leader alters the nature of an organization by redefining its goals in new directions for the followers. The "transactional" leader, on the other hand, manages and directs ongoing organizational activity. The former type appears in educational administration, where *leaders' cognitions of what they want schools to look like act to shape their own behavior within the school; this, in turn, alters that school's culture, which, finally, affects student learning.*[45] Qualities of such school leadership include defining the school mission, promoting instruction, managing curriculum and instruction, supervising teaching, and monitoring student progress.

Superintendent Cole: Leadership under Desegregation

Such concepts were illuminated in Superintendent David Cole's leadership style in south Panola desegregation. His success in leadership was the result of his personal view of schooling—or "mission"—as well as the support of his board of trustees. Earlier events in his life had helped produce his sense of mission, which, in time, would alter the reality of schooling in this area. A local person, first in his family to attend college and to teach, Cole carried values learned from a supportive mother and childhood experiences that were always positive about education and blacks. Cole had a deep belief in education, recalling that his own family's schooling had improved their quality of life. Like many others in both races, schooling had been reinforced by another personal value—a strong family life. Consequently, while many white small farmers around them in the nearby hamlet of Pope might express "redneck" attitudes, Cole grew up with different beliefs.

An early incident in 1970 when he was a beginning teacher in south Panola made him realize the importance of schooling. A racial fight began at a newly desegregated school and he suddenly decided to stop it, because he realized that the schools, not simply the students, would be hurt by a riot. He received parental support for using discipline on the antagonists; a board trustee thanked him for stopping his own boy from participating in the violence. Cole later recommended the expulsion of three "radicals" on each side, and at the end of the year he believed that students were getting along better. Amid all the local turmoil over schools and the national riots over Vietnam, he came to realize that these students simply did not know one another. To change that, he worked with racial attitudes one student at a time, even though it was "rather like moving a cemetery."

Cole clearly recalled that he had developed two missions in taking the new position as superintendent in 1974, namely:

— Move the community into accepting the new policy of attending schools together. Note that this goal was to change the social reality of both races.
— Spread to both races what he saw as the middle-class values of cooperation, of being positive about life, and of excelling in school.

In effect, Cole acted as a transformational leader by formulating a mission of what schools should look like under desegregation. That mission guided his implementation strategies with school professionals, trustees, and both races in the community. In the nearly two decades that followed, Cole emphasized to all school constituencies the need for improving instruction for both races. While he kept an eye on leadership—with supervising teaching, overseeing curriculum, and monitoring school programs—he gave priority to this first mission of the new school in this new social reality. He was guided by the board, but he also helped them to reshape their own thinking, as more than one trustee observed. In reshaping those cognitions, Cole had urged on the board his belief that the old notions they had learned early in life—like those about race—might no longer apply in a contemporary society. Born and bred in traditionalism, but without accepting that racial emphasis, Cole provided leadership for a new type of school.

Superintendents in America had once held a role as the "benign autocrat," laying down professional principles that all must accept in a nonpolitical fashion. They regarded themselves as apolitical experts, for there was no Republican or Democratic way of learning long division in schools. But that role changed as new issues and newly politicized groups came on the scene after 1960.[46] Now, all superintendents must work at being "politicians," that is, to shape the increasing demands generated by the new political turbulence. The educational issues arising from this change could vary, from desegregation to finance to curriculum. Leadership also required power sharing with teachers and parents and forming working consensuses for action amid new issues.

Cole had earlier seen the need to reach into district constituencies to build community support for a new kind of schooling. He held many meetings in towns and neighborhoods to explain new programs and their rationales, as the agenda shifted from obeying the law to improving schooling. Black leaders today recall that "he was always open to hear us." This new openness, he thought, would also stimulate families to support their children in school, not so much for discipline—which many blacks disliked—but for urging children to meet their school assignments. If the transformational leader, as Burns once noted, encourages others "to higher levels of motivation and morality," Superintendent Cole and his board did just that in adjusting to this major social change.

However, that leadership was a necessary, but not a sufficient, condition for desegregation to work. Even with that leadership, with trustee support, and with persistence, none of this would have succeeded without the authority of law. Other conditions were also necessary here and elsewhere in the South. One of these is racial balance in a particular community. A severe racial imbalance could generate intense white fears that would block change. But south Panola's leaders operated in a roughly equal racial balance in these years, as they urged the need to obey the law and to improve schooling.

The test of these outcomes is a comparison with the other two systems that emerged in Panola County, namely, a mostly black public school and another all-white private system, to which we now turn.

6 | Two Responses to Desegregation in North Panola

The responses to federal desegregation in the two sections of Panola County were as different as those of two nations. The leaders and people of the area centered on Batesville accommodated their public schools to the new reality, as the law had sought. However, across the hills and bottom lands of the Delta culture, white resistance had not only rejected any such effort, but led to creation of private schools. Left behind in the former public school system was an almost all-black student body administered first by whites, and then later by blacks. But like Mother Hubbard facing her cupboard, black leaders found a weakened system when they entered. Whites continued to vote down more school taxes to improve it, and major problems arose with teaching and administration.

The white departure raised different problems for both school systems, it generated different types of leadership, and it affected student attitudes and learning. Bluntly put, the Delta whites' flight led to the best and to the worst of county schools, but each school had to face new challenges. This chapter, reviewing these consequences, concludes with an account of one major consequence, student attitudes in all three systems a quarter century after federal law had intervened to change schools.

Delta White Response: The "Exit" Strategy

The immediate response to desegregation by affluent whites in Panola and throughout the Delta was the classic "exit" or "flight" response found in any human confrontation.[1] Even before the Department of Justice had started desegregation in Panola County, affluent whites withdrew into newly created private schools. While poor finances continued to plague their effort, the organizational identity was quickly established, and in time their private system joined other accredited private schools in the South.

The Beginnings

In 1960, there existed in north Panola a public school system that was deeply segregated, like all in the Old South, but there were also some stirrings of change. Table 6.1 surveys that year, using coverage from the local paper, the *Southern Reporter*.

Whether the issue was a bond to improve black schools in north Panola or a request for a new dictionary, all-white governing agencies were part of a too-late response in the South to the "separate but equal" challenge. The requirement of "equal" education for blacks had been widely ignored, as many studies demonstrate.[2] Table 6.1 shows that, for the county, in 1960 racial separation was embedded in traditional culture. Its own newspaper reflected that culture, as seen in its editorial on a White House conference that criticized that meeting's nontraditional themes, or the editorial supporting a loyalty oath for students taking federal funds, a conservative fear in that era.

Creating North Delta. In the early 1960s, Delta whites became ever more uncomfortable at national events that might affect them. Courts were challenging all aspects of white supremacy, a Great Society president and Congress were passing threatening laws, and state school systems were coming under court orders to desegregate. North Panola's Delta whites had met with public school officials to encourage resistance, but little help was provided, as officials faced strong federal implementation. As a consequence, a group of wealthy planters, businessmen, lawyers, and bankers met in 1965 to call for a new and private school, named North Delta. Another school, West Panola, was also created about this time in the flat fields of the county. In the hamlet of Pleasant Grove North Delta supporters purchased an old school from Work Project Administration days in the 1930s for the sum of one dollar; it was repaired by parents. In the first year, twenty-three elementary grade students were enrolled, with tuition paid by parents. It is important to stress that in this first stage of the "exit" option, not all whites joined in, primarily due to the high cost of tuition. That early problem never disappeared.

However, parents who could afford the option made no effort to work out any relationship with blacks still in the public schools. Whites repeatedly mentioned that it was completely outside their understanding of the world to have their children attend school with children whose parents were poor field hands. For whites, their sense of place, indeed, their foundation of social reality, focused only on the world of wealthy whites. It was race, but also class, that constrained white decisions here; several parents

Table 6.1   Educational Events in Segregated Schools, North Panola, 1960

JAN. 14	Board offers $700,000 bond issue for white high school.
JAN. 28	New bond issue to include also new grammar school for blacks, while expanding black high school in Sardis.
FEB. 4	Editorial supports loyalty oath for students before receiving federal student loans.
FEB. 11	Sardis city council funds unabridged dictionary for local black library, with pictures of presentations to two blacks.
FEB. 18	Editorial shows confidence in state's textbook selection process while sympathetic to aims of the state Daughters of the American Revolution in objecting to unpatriotic books. Another editorial hopes governor will hold down spending for teachers salaries.
FEB. 25	A driving school for black bus drivers to be sponsored by county school board; another for whites to be held later.
MAR. 3	Pictures of white students appearing in student Who's Who.
MAR. 10	Announcement and picture of black bus driver school course, just completed; white bus driver school course to come soon.
MAR. 31	County school trustees discuss new black high school.
APRIL 7	School bus safety patrols revived for both white and black students.
APRIL 14	County school official announces approval of $535,000 for black school buildings, one new, one addition.
APRIL 28	Editorial objects to recent White House Conference on Children and Youth because it expresses support for desegregation, arms control, and more federal aid to schools.
MAY 12	Picture of white senior graduates.
MAY 19	Drawing of new black high school in Sardis, as bidding for contracts proceeds. Two more pictures of white graduates.
JUNE 2	Separate bus driving schools, one for each race, announced (similar stories appear twice that summer).
OCT. 13	Announces new ACT tests, which "every white college in Mississippi is recommending" for freshmen.

Source: Southern Reporter, 1970 files.

interviewed used terms about black parents like "sweaty" or "ignorant." While culture shapes our expectations of reality and, by responding to it, further guides behavior, in the face of changes in the environment, culture also limits the possibilities of adapting to change.

The North Delta was run by a board of eminent men from Panola and two adjoining counties who screened the applicants. Later, an elected school board undertook the central function of administering finances. Organization and finance were tied to the school's purpose, although officials denied "doctrinal sectarian, or denominated [sic] teaching."[3] But traditional culture still insisted that the school be Christian. Consequently, administrators required that student assemblies be opened with a prayer and Bible readings, and its bylaws had students using the Lord's Prayer at least once a week. In later years, the Bible would be used in the high school as a piece of literature; its Christian-oriented schooling focused mainly on the elementary grades. To judge from local records, the Christianity was mainstream Protestant and eschewed evangelical sects. Almost all the students were white, except for a few Chinese.[4] Transportation from surrounding counties was handled by carpooling. Textbooks and funds (as noted later) were provided with public funds under a state law of 1964 for "nonsectarian" schools, one legal response by the traditional state to desegregation.

Early Growth. Signs of growth were found in North Delta annual reports and the local newspaper, the *Southern Reporter.*[5] Teachers left the public schools for the private system, even though it meant lower salaries. Some grades, such as first and second, were combined to fit limited funding, and parents bought supplies to supplement state textbooks. But it was not enough just to be white and Christian, because some parents also wanted a "quality" education and held off joining until that was assured. Signs of quality soon appeared. By the end of 1967, North Delta had been accredited by the state for certain elementary grades. The school's annual report also included ads of endorsement by local businesses; twenty-one appeared the first year and fifty-two the next.

Competition in the form of other private schools appeared around them, but North Delta continued to grow while complaints increased over the public schools.[6] A Baptist parochial school had opened in 1970 in Batesville, and in 1971 a West Panola school, deep in the Delta, opened for all grades. North Delta advertised itself in local newspapers as providing "quality education," clearly a code term that meant "white," and local papers covered its scholarly and sports events. By 1972, North Delta had added a new kindergarten and formed a junior high football team (twenty-one students and six cheerleaders); later, a senior high school appeared.

Stories were appearing about North Delta graduates who were entering colleges. By the end of 1977, then, where once there had been only a total of twenty-three students, there were now more than that in any one of the grades 7 through 12.

One sign of the maturing of this private school was the development in regulations. The first rules in 1965 were limited to the school's purposes (nonsectarian), recruitment, student conduct, curriculum, teacher responsibility, and transportation. But organization and rules grew symbiotically. For example, by 1972 the student rules covered many aspects of student life, such as excused absences, dress code (no shorts or hot pants), and boys' haircuts (must cover only half of upper ear and no sideburns). A year later, girls' dresses had to be no shorter than six inches above the knee (in the era of the mini-skirt), and no blue jeans were permitted. By then, the rules filled eight pages—single-spaced—and by 1974 they covered eighteen pages. Despite a very controlled environment for students, in 1975 in the senior yearbook students reminisced sentimentally: "We are going back to days of fun, laughter, dreams, and no worries. These were the best days of our lives, and we would like to share them with you."

Maturation: Professionalism and Finance. The instructional program had to meet some external and professional goals. In 1972, the Mississippi Private School Education Association reached about ten percent of all Mississippi students in 114 schools; for two decades thereafter, the number of schools ranged somewhat lower, from 92 to 101.[7] The association's central office in Jackson maintains standards of accreditation and teacher certification, as well as other programs for athletics, teacher needs (linked to a separate, nonunionized group of teachers), public relations, and so on. Separate state committees must check every year for each teacher's certification (using a thirty-two item form) and for other accreditation requirements. Teacher certification (requiring a bachelor's degree in secondary education) is reciprocal with other states in public and private schools.

When North Delta began, state-accredited teachers joined from local public schools, especially those who wanted their own children to escape public schools. Teachers were paid less than in public schools then and still are today (according to one estimate by about one-third), and they lacked retirement plans beyond social security. They also teach smaller classes, as the ideal of a one-to-twenty-two teacher-pupil ratio was maintained as the central standard of quality. Early teachers brought to the schools shared information drawn from existing public schools. Because they exercised this exit option, the teachers were not embroiled in the turmoil of the public school, but they paid for that peace with less income.

The weakness of all private schools, sectarian or not, lies in financing.

While North Delta was born among rich planter and merchant families, its growing costs continued to plague the school and drive away others.

North Delta began with a $500 subscription (money or promissory notes) drawn from every participating family, but in recent years the tuition had reached $1,200 to $1,400 per year. In 1965, with its twenty-three students in only a few elementary grades, this school had received funds for textbooks from the state. Under a 1964 state law, each student received a $187 book grant, to which was added $250 a year for tuition. Six years later in 1971, the North Delta board had a 2 percent surplus in the budget (mostly used for salaries); nevertheless, the board suggested that parents should provide 10 percent of their annual income before taxes. Meanwhile, Title I's federal funds had enriched the two public school systems by about $900,000.[8]

In the Delta private school, the cost problem continued to grow. Capital equipment costs rose because it was adding more grades and more students. The alternative methods of financing, a family tithe scheme and interschool cooperation (e.g., a science lab), had failed. The ever-higher tuition costs moved some Delta whites to join a private school in nearby Tate County, where there were more white residents than black, and so a larger private school market existed. However, other whites stayed with North Delta until academic quality was assured. Despite limited facilities, by the end of the 1977 school year there were 170 students and a senior high school (19 graduated that year). As a former board member noted, the school's strength was "made up by the quality of teachers and their ingenuity"; one teacher demonstrated principles in physics on levers and pulleys by using a fishing rod and reel.

But student athletics continued to be limited because of the smaller enrollment. These problems finally led after 1987 to a merger of the North Delta and West Panola schools. Neither school had a headmaster then, but a new administrator, Henry Crain, was brought in to oversee the union and to decide which teachers to hire or fire. By 1990, about 400 students were located within one building for all grades, thereby providing a fuller educational environment for academics and sports. But funding problems remain; one observer in the early 1990s estimated that the annual expenditure per student was $1,850, compared to $3,600 in the state and $4,000 nationally. By then, the headmaster, Henry Crain, managed about a half-million-dollar budget for salaries and other matters.

The Governance of North Delta. Lay groups, typically organized like similar groups in the public schools, oversee education in this private system. The emphasis is strongly upon parental control dedicated to "quality." The organizational authority consists of regular meetings of different boards.

The headmaster hires teachers using a private school salary schedule that sets the market prices; $12,000 was top pay in 1990. For teachers, there is no health care plan, but they do use workmen's compensation and self-provided hospitalization plans. A 1980s state law had changed the conditions for recertification of teachers, which once required more college courses, to in-service training only. This change was opposed by North Delta and other private schools, and the Southern Accrediting Agency, who predicted a deterioration of standards if teacher improvement was left to people with no schooling after college.

Curriculum decision making in North Delta is typically the domain of professionals; teachers recommend programs, department heads approve the final decisions, and the headmaster supports their efforts. While there is an emphasis on parental control, an external control operates over the parent committees by establishing professional standards through oversight by the MPSA, noted earlier, and the Southern Accrediting Agency.[9] For example, control over instruction and discipline always rests with teachers. Demanding curricula (some exceeding state requirements) and strong reading requirements are in effect. Discipline in the form of paddling is rare but authorized; a board member's son was expelled in the late 1980s for failing to accept this punishment.

In the academic courses, the school continues to emphasize that it is not sectarian; indeed, observers point to the presence of some Roman Catholics in school. However, in grades K through 6 a Christian education is emphasized, using a textbook that has a scriptural foundation and comes from the Pensacola Christian College. For parents, however, the Christian content is regarded as important but not sectarian because it is not identified with a particular sect. But this is clearly a Christian school. Of course, all the students are white, despite efforts made recently to recruit black students. No black student had accepted a place in the school by 1990, for it is clear that a qualified black, even with a scholarship, would be like A. E. Housman's poem, "I, alone and afraid, in a world I never made."

Consequences of the Exit Response

This quarter century of Delta response to desegregated schools is instructive. They withdrew their leadership from the public system, leaving them weakened financially and under poor leadership. Interviews with older whites in the private school leave a dual impression. They were delighted by "their" private schools for its intimacy and shared values, which they themselves supervised. But they were also bitter about the legal changes that had caused them to leave behind "their" public schools, which had trained them a generation or more earlier. A long-time board member bitterly recalled the north Panola public school as once one of the best in

Mississippi that had now become one of the worst. Interviews were filled with stories of the new teachers' incompetence in the public schools. One banker noted that in the past a question used to come up at cocktail parties: Was it an injustice to the public schools when Delta whites went to private schools, especially when the old school was severely weakened? They recognized the high financial cost involved with this option, but most said they had wanted quality education, which they could not even contemplate being available in a racially mixed school. The reality of the Old South precluded any other way of adjusting to such sharp changes in a new reality.

At the core of this option was a cultural recalcitrance to stay with the schools in order to improve them, even though that was what whites did in the south Panola district. Fearing confrontation for themselves and their children, viewing working with poor black parents as incomprehensible in their reality, the Delta whites went private. Of course, in south Panola where the racial mix was about 60 percent white, some planters did stay with public schools and even served on its school board. But the white planters of the Delta, as one noted, "could not even *contemplate* their children in such schools because they would lose out on learning." As a banker noted, "That question of [the wisdom of our] retreat is no longer talked about." These words reflect how perceptions guide action. Law cannot reach in and affect that recalcitrance when they avoid the law itself. The culture did not "contemplate" that possibility, and so the only response was exit.

What were the consequences for these students of the North Delta system? Scholastically, they have done well, as measured by college acceptance (over 90 percent recently), with a few attending high-quality institutions. But how did schooling affect their outlook on life? We will answer that query later by comparing these students with blacks in north Panola public schools and with both races in south Panola. We will find some surprises there.

Black Responses in North Panola: The Apathy Strategy

As the exit response of Delta whites led to private schools, the blacks who were left behind had no other option but to stay with public schools. In many respects, their strategy was one of "apathy," that is, neither fight nor run but put up with what you have and make little effort to change conditions. After the late 1960s, the number of white students slowly dropped, so that by 1991 only 2 percent of the school population was white.[10] For most years after desegregation, white administrators led the change; but only in the late 1980s did blacks emerge as superintendent and principals.

What they inherited, however, was the weakest educational system in the state, which is often the weakest state in the nation. New black leadership sought to address this legacy and to move the black community from apathy to a fight strategy. Only limited academic success resulted in the years following, but it was followed by financial ruin in 1995–1996. Under a new law, the state took over the district, appointed a white "conservator," and cut personnel budgets severely to overcome a deficit of over one million dollars.

The Beginning Years of Desegregation

It will be useful to provide first a sketch of what the north Panola district used to look like before desegregation. The local newspaper reported on its beginning in 1960 (see table 6.1), and on the first signs of the effects of desegregation in 1970 (see table 6.2).

As the local newspaper, the *Southern Reporter* reflected the community's traditional culture; note its regular coverage of a state senator's speeches that were hostile to desegregation. Its news coverage of public schools was standard—full reports of scholastic achievements (including awards) and sports events (so many that they are not presented in this table). Signs of both races in the public schools emerged in accounts of blacks and whites in school (e.g., parent committees encouraging academic achievement). The federal hand was clearly visible in stories of a desegregation order for students (but not the faculty) and of substantial Title I funds for educating poor children (covering most of over 3,440 students).[11] The leadership problems emerge in the story of an earlier white superintendent, for example, urging that private schools were useful as a "safety valve" by removing students and parents most likely to cause problems. If he had in mind poor whites, he failed to see they could not go to private schools because of the costs involved. However, if he had in mind the Delta whites, he had to know that white leadership was lost by those escaping the problems in his schools.

Observers agree that in north Panola there was no consistent effort to get racial leaders to deal with the public schools, unlike the early days of desegregation in south Panola. Whites saw "their" schools being degraded because the new blacks were children of farmhands. During 1970–1971, a black principal in a formerly black school was fired (southern desegregation had regularly led to such actions affecting blacks). However, this black principal's firing, despite his experience as administrator, his tenure, and his degrees, led to black students boycotting schools for a short while. On this occasion, many white parents quickly took the exit option, for three reasons. They saw violence on the school buses, the school quality was declining, and peer pressure came from like-minded whites. While

Table 6.2   Educational Events in Desegregated North Panola, 1970

JAN. I	Outside columnists continue to oppose cuts in funds by U.S. Department of Health, Education, and Welfare (HEW) to schools during desegregation.
MAR. 26	News of delays in desegregating Charlotte, N.C., prior to U.S. Supreme Court's *Swann* decision, with Mississippi Senator Stennis approving.
APRIL 2	Picture of Sardis student teachers, all white.
APRIL 9	High school student leaders attend state meeting of such officers, which is racially merging.
APRIL 16	Picture of academic achievers—all black.
APRIL 30	Federal Title I program to provide about $445,000 for education of poor children. Black parents to call for public meeting seeking information on pending desegregation plan under discussion. [No follow-up story.]
MAY 21	Picture and story of high school award winners; two blacks in photo.
MAY 28	Group picture of graduating seniors, with some blacks.
JUNE 25	HEW approves desegregation plan for one junior high, one senior high, and elementary attendance zones based on zones. No faculty changes announced. Senator Stennis hopes recent resignations of key HEW personnel will lead to less aggressive desegregation.
JULY 9	Federal Title I funds summer reading program, with picture including black teachers.
AUG. 20	Schools open, general information given with reference to upcoming biracial meeting on schools.
SEPT. 3	New busing plans announced consistent with HEW desegregation order.
SEPT. 17	Superintendent of schools (a white) condemns federal control of schools and declares that private schools serve a positive role as community safety valve.
SEPT. 24	Special parents-teachers organization committee to assist teachers and parents with studying problems.
OCT. 15	Senior high school paper receives award, with pictures of black and white coeditors and black teacher.
OCT. 22	Picture of black junior high student council with black members in majority.
OCT. 29	Senator Stennis complains that the South is treated more harshly than the North in schooling policy; also condemns a national commission on pornography's recommendation against less legislative control.

Source: Southern Reporter, 1970 files.

there were scattered cases of violence and decline, it was the new perception that drove behavior. Black critics complained that had whites stayed, better schools would have emerged; white leaders privately discussed the matter but later dropped it.[12] Also, blacks noted that many white critics of desegregation did not have children in the schools.

One final issue remains to be noted in this coverage of desegregation in the north Panola schools. By 1980, there were more news stories about students in the desegregated schools, and they were more focused on the black students (then 85 percent of the school population). A simple count of newspaper stories of public schools (excluding athletics) in 1970 compared with those in 1980 shows how education had become a larger story and that there was an increased focus on race. There were two white-only stories in 1970 but none in 1980; also, there were seven biracial stories in 1970 compared with eight in 1980, and one all-black story, compared with fourteen. That is, public schools began to loom larger in this newspaper after 1970, as its focus on blacks grew. While many black leaders were critical of its editor ("He's no friend of ours," said one) he covered this new reality as it developed locally.

Changes in Leadership—Early 1980s

What happened thereafter in north Panola education was a source of distaste for whites and a matter of concern for blacks. Student achievement scores on state tests slowly declined, as the white enrollment declined. The more experienced white teachers had left for private schools, and white leadership lacked the ability to stop this decline. Even more serious, most adult whites would not provide additional finances to the schools. Indeed, in the nearly thirty years of experience of one black educator in these schools, only a single school referendum ever passed, and that by a margin so fractional that the whole matter ended up in courts, which later supported its passage.

From the beginning, Delta whites blamed desegregation for creating poor "quality" instruction. By that word they meant not only that they supported higher standards; they were also complaining about the intrusion of blacks into their schools. Yet whites themselves made it difficult to effect any improvement when they supported a private school, when retirees feared more taxes, and when they voted down school levies designed to improve quality. Delta whites still use a collection of "war stories" about behavior by black students and teachers to enhance these judgments.

For the black parents, many (but not all) found the change to a desegregated school harrowing for their children. They had come to see the old segregated schools as "their" schools, and many of them thought the students were getting a good education in them. But the school diploma had been for many only a ticket to nowhere. As more black children attended school for longer periods, they found the existing standards were not easily met. Black parents found that their children, who had once been judged "bright," to be just average or worse. In time, under pressures from these black parents, teachers diluted standards of instruction. We should note that this "dumbing down" practice reported by black observers in north Panola also occurred in many American schools after the 1960s, regardless of race, as achievement tests have demonstrated. Whatever the causes, state achievement scores in this district did show a sharp decline that finally left it in the late 1980s at the bottom of all state districts.

Evaluation of the test results leads to questions about this district. Did those scores decline because so many of the brighter and experienced students left for private schools? Or did the black students, poorly educated in segregated schools, themselves lower the scores? Or were there intrinsic problems in schooling when there was strong parental pressure against more rigorous instruction? If so, how was it that this same process occurred for *all* districts of Mississippi, not just in north Panola where their scores hit the bottom? Or for most schools in the nation, regardless of racial proportions?

Any change in these results had to come from the largest constituency of these schools—the black community. The task required leadership, but it led only to a changing set of superintendents—all white. Until the late 1980s, white superintendents faced a political whirl in which nothing seemed to improve student learning. All superintendents in America have recently experienced a dramatic alteration in their role from educational leader to a political agent who must work amid clashing interests. And few do well, as judged by their decreasing tenure in office across the nation.[13]

In north Panola, the board of trustees and superintendent attempted few actions in the early years. Superintendent H. A. Grisham in the early 1980s seemed to withdraw from this conflict; board members noted that he kept himself from public view in both racial communities. As one result, a student boycott erupted in October 1980.[14] With about half the students absent, their public complaints provide insight into growing concerns in the black community, including

— reading program levels that unfairly prevented promotion to higher grades (cited by the local paper as "the main grievance");
— a need for preschool training;
— a ban on teachers' children going to private schools;
— some unsafe elementary school buildings; and
— a move to fire Superintendent Grisham.

The boycott was entirely black, for as *The Panolian* noted, "Most of the white students attend private schools . . . [and have done] since the early days of the school desegregation controversy." There were students marching and picketing for a week, but there were also divisions among the black adults; the Voters League and NAACP decided not to support the boycott. It all ended when the school board promised to revise the reading program, to require teachers to send their children to public schools, but not to fire the superintendent. A black spokesman said publicly there would be more protests if these promises were not kept.

Changes in Leadership—The Late 1980s

The rest of the decade was just as turbulent, involving declining records and leadership changes. The man who succeeded Grisham three years after the boycott (Paul Messer, a white) stayed for another three years, until 1986. Black leaders thought that he had given the schools little support. He was little prepared for a state site visit (pivotal to accreditation), and he had failed to report on problems as they developed. Finally, under pressure and nearing retirement, Messer resigned to be succeeded by the system's first black superintendent, James Harris, an action that itself revealed splits within the black community.

Harris was born locally, had received a master's degree in education from Ole Miss, and had worked for almost twenty years as an elementary principal in north Panola schools. Over the years, he had garnered many white supporters, including those who supported his appointment as superintendent. In this selection, three whites on the board supported him and two blacks did not. Some blacks thought he had applied too late in the selection process, but also thought that he was not the man for those times. Faced with this division, other black officials organized their community to support Harris when he came to office in 1987; the central theme was "Give him an opportunity." After over twenty years of desegregation, could black administration do better than whites in improving student achievement?

Over the next five years, Harris's leadership faced growing concerns about funding and student scores.[15] In 1986, fifteen black residents presented grievances to the school board and letters to the local paper. A year later, a report on school dropouts pointed to this as a continuing problem, but one that also existed nationally. In 1989, a black legal service attorney was appointed by three black board members (reconstituted by recent elections). For a few weeks, the attorney precipitated more confrontation with his complaints against local schools. But this challenge was opposed by leaders of both races, and he quickly resigned (the incident is reviewed later in this chapter). Yet the grave news at the end of the 1989 school year was that north Panola was put on educational probation by the state for its low achievement scores in literacy and basic skills (reviewed later in this chapter). After a year of effort by the superintendent and staff, the test scores did improve slightly in the following years for every grade and every subject; indeed, on one test, this school surpassed the results in south Panola for the first time since desegregation began.

Problems remained for leadership, though, because money was needed for building repairs and curriculum improvement. In 1991, the bond issue for repairs and renovation failed at the polls despite two referenda. As with all previous bond issues in this district, a precinct's percentage of whites equalled its percentage of referenda opposition; the reverse was true for black precincts. In July 1991, the total support in this district was just below the state-required 60 percent level (57%), as the heavily white precincts opposed it (100% in Belmont-Hebron; 89% in east Sardis; 78% in east Como).[16] In the next referendum that September, white groups publicly advertised their opposition to higher taxes, while Superintendent Harris and other black leaders publicly endorsed it as necessary to improve schools. The second bond election results edged the total up to 59.5 percent approval, still short of the margin. Thereupon, two whites and one black school board member voted to accept the result, but two black members opposed it, and that vote in turn led to litigation over the deposition of a few votes. In 1994, a higher state court approved passage of the bond issue.

In 1992, the board came into open racial conflict over another political matter—redistricting seats on the school board. A black majority supported one plan, with three of five seats to be black, each representing a district with over 75 percent blacks. A second plan modified the racial distribution to make two seats black and one seat open for either race. The racial acrimony was expressed in public meetings and in letters to the editor. A white board member indirectly accused the schools of settling for poor performance, and Superintendent Harris countered with records of the newly improving schools. In the end, though, the two plans went to the Civil Rights Division of the U.S. Department of Justice. Amid this conflict, however, south Panola had sent a single and unanimous plan to Washington after the Office of Civil Rights criticized an earlier plan.

Climbing up the Ladder: Improvement Programs

Amid this racial turbulence, there are other aspects of schooling in north Panola that point to some success in the classroom. The gains by 1995 were not major, but they resulted from the superintendent's efforts to improve them.

Program Improvement

During 1989, Superintendent Harris instituted a set of changes in instruction and curriculum that were designed to improve the weak test scores condemned by the state. In public statements and private talks, he saw improvement as the primary goal of the school system; mission definition is one of the major tasks of transforming systems, as noted in chapter 5.[17] While state mandates called for certain levels of proficiency in each grade, implementing them was left to the local district and its administrators. Here is where leadership can be effective if it exists. But there is another kind of leadership needed at local levels, namely, securing resources for the tasks of any mission. That effort involved not simply finding money or equipment, but securing community support. In none of these tasks had there been any success prior to the late 1980s, an omission that helped account for the lowest scores in the state. In this change, Harris secured staff and community support over five years, reflecting the new political skills of the modern superintendent.[18]

To improve student skills in taking tests, Harris set out to meet several objectives, many involving technical assistance obtained from the state's department of education. First, the staff had to believe in the meaning of those tests. Accordingly, collaborative methods between administrators and teachers helped them to analyze the tests and the data themselves, and to suggest how instruction might be better shaped. For each grade, an "instructional management plan" was then devised that involved a detailed set of curricula, along with numerous skills that the students must master. In the classroom, every day the teacher would

— explain to the class the learning objectives;
— make the lessons relevant to student experience;
— check on their learning throughout the lesson;
— provide closure on what was learned; and
— provide the principal a check-list of teacher efforts.

Such activities as these are not new in many schools, but here they were. Leadership from the superintendent to the principals involved joint efforts with each teacher in creating "joint improvement targets." Typically, a target for improving teaching would be to help those who had failed to meet deadlines, or to have principal and teacher work jointly to improve this weakness. Or the regular use of lesson plans was now emphasized for all teachers—standard behavior in most schools—with the principal checking their progress weekly. In the first year, staff objections arose over filling out forms or structuring learning; but in time these tasks became the way in which each teacher came to define the job. Of course,

Table 6.3   Mean Achievement Scores of State and North Panola, by
Grade and Subject, 1990

	TOTAL SCORES			
Grade Level	Writing	Math	Reading	Composite
3	0.6*	4.3	−2.6	0.5
5	6.6	7.9	5.1	8.2
8	12.8	15.8	9.7	13.9

Source: Computed from North Panola's summary tables in Mississippi Basic Skills Assessment Program, May 1990. Data provided by Superintendent James Harris.

*This number indicates that the state mean score is greater than the local mean. A negative sign indicates that the local mean is greater than the state mean.

improvement on test scores through the early 1990s also reinforced these administrative efforts. Also helpful were programs of curriculum enrichment in foreign language (none had existed before), in advanced placement in math and science, and in academically gifted students.

Changes in Test Results

Note the improvements in test scores after Harris took office; even so, when viewed nationally, they are still less than even middling. But the results also show how effective leadership, even in poor schools, can be significant in starting changes in curriculum, teaching, and learning. For example, across twelve substantive and skill tests in 1990 that were applied to grades 2 through 10, north Panola students ranked at 35 to 45 percent of the *national* norm of 50 percent, which it rarely met on any test. Large percentages of students came in the "below average" rating.[19] By another measure, however, there was some improvement. On the state's functional literacy test for 1990, students had improved on three of six items in reading, six of eight items in math, and all four items in writing.

Something important was also appearing when these results were compared with the state means. As noted in table 6.3, the younger children were improving quite well on the state averages, but the older students had a much poorer record. That consistent improvement by younger students existed for three subject tests and a composite score. On one test—mathematics—younger students in north Panola were actually surpassing the state average. One can read this trend as evidence that the program improvements had begun to show positive effects, particularly for the youngest, who had less experience in the earlier and inferior school known by older students.

Administrators and staff often judge their own progress by comparing test results with nearby schools that they regard as equivalent, for example in racial proportions. North Panola's comparison was with south Panola (about 60% white) and Senatobia to the north (about 60% black). In 1988, students in north Panola had failed most state tests and were the lowest scores in Mississippi; but by the end of 1991, on seventeen of eighteen tests there were passing grades. When compared with the equivalent school systems, these results were better on half and worse on another half. That is, for black administrators, staff, and board, these results were seen as an improvement by their own standards of judgment. However, more recent reports on college-bound SAT scores shows this district still near the bottom.[20]

Community Leadership

Even this effort at improvement, no matter how effective, met some community opposition to Harris's leadership; it is here, outside the schools, where leadership is just as vital as inside it. Professional influence over the community has weakened throughout the United States, as other groups have arisen to claim their own agendas. No longer is the superintendent the professional who had once provided the "correct" ideas about schooling and had done so without much challenge.[21] In the local context of north Panola, one finds the same trend affecting efforts by Harris to manage that conflict.

One community group is composed of whites who often have no children in the public schools. Their existence as voters, however, creates white opposition to tax referenda for public schools. But even with these test improvements, white leaders in interviews regularly expressed their concern over the schools, which they saw as a barrier to greater economic development. Sardis alderman Jimmy McClure, member of a distinguished white family, said on the record in 1992 that competition with nearby towns for new business was being weakened. "There is no way around it. They have better schools than we do. Until our schools improve we have problems." He was pointing to the need for "better teachers," as he saw the problem to be in "the instruction."

A white board member, Robert Haynes, complained that school leaders were satisfied by improving test results, which produced only an average school instead of trying for the best. Superintendent Harris countered with reports from the schools, such as a state award for a local principal and new test results that showed sixteen improvements in grades and curriculum.[22] But in recent years, large-scale support by whites on a matter of great interest for the schools—referenda—is still absent.

Harris regularly worked hard in selling the schools outside the school buildings. He was interviewed in the local press and appeared at local meetings to explain new developments. Typically, he described new state curriculum mandates, or noted new state resources like computers in elementary schools to facilitate early literacy. This public relations effort is another indicator of the expanded roles of the newly politicized superintendents in America.[23]

In addition to problems originating in the white community, there is also a community problem that arises among some blacks. Selling this program had required Harris to convince black families to accept higher standards and to deal with failing students. While agreeing that the schools had been poor before, black leaders thought that a new approach would have to be taken slowly. But here was the superintendent pushing for much change in a hurry. Ironically, the change to black leadership, often sought in the past, was too much when it came. More serious, though, was the problem of lack of parental support, a problem that was complained about in all interviews with school people in both districts. It is a familiar complaint, heard throughout the nation, not just of black parents. In north Panola, black professionals noted that the community rarely supported any school activity, not even football, when its members were all black. This lack of support focused especially on the high school, which had been the target of serious complaints in the late 1980s, when a favorite principal was removed. Even more difficult are the continuing divisions among the blacks themselves (as noted later in this chapter) which diluted community support of new programs and instruction.

One visible sign of this problem among blacks lies in student discipline, a phenomenon also noted in south Panola. Enforcement of discipline throughout the nation has normally antagonized black parents because their children receive more of it. In an almost all-black school like north Panola, enforcement in the past had not been focused or publicized very well.

Harris sought to deal with this problem by developing a detailed sequence for using discipline. Referrals for discipline first begin with a teacher applying to a school committee; if it agrees, there is a parental conference; then tests are provided for learning disabilities and—if parents fail to give consent—for further testing. This procedure can lead to a student's dismissal by action of the school board. The emphasis is on an open approach that seeks remedies, not punishment.[24] The school people interviewed believed that this publicized procedure, with widespread parent involvement, works to acquaint parents with their children's problems and possible penalties. Black parents today still complain, as do those elsewhere in the nation, saying that their children are always "right" and the school "wrong." But the publicized presence of clear rules, public stages, and equal enforcement provide a professional procedure that informs students and may avoid later litigation.

Financial Deficit in the District

A further and unsuspected problem underlay all the problems of this district, namely, insufficient financial control by the superintendent. When Harris retired in mid-1995, his replacement, another black, found after some months that revenue was not available for ongoing costs of the current year. Weak auditing controls by outside agencies and by Harris had failed to note the hiring of many noncertified staff whose wages ate into the salaries of teachers.[25] It looked at first as if the teachers would not be paid for the last part of the year.

A state review at the end of 1995 said the district's finances were in deficit, but there was no state law to provide additional funds. A local representative urged the legislature to pass a law requiring any district with a deficit to borrow state money to fulfill revenue needs, but the district had to pay it back. Moreover, a state-appointed "conservator" would control finances until a balanced budget was in hand.

When all that was carried out, including a meeting of Governor Kirk Fordice in March 1996 with the local board (which promptly resigned), the conservator put a notice in the press of the budget cuts and revenue additions. These came primarily from:

— eliminating positions such as janitors (8), assistant teachers (3), elementary teachers (2), special education teachers (2), assistant principals (3), and teachers in driver education and general arts (1 each);
— reducing the number of work days by staffs in noncertified, maintenance, secretarial, vocational education, and other positions;
— eliminating band and athletic programs; and
— raising additional revenue from small increases to local property taxes.

There was no suggestion of corruption in all this by Superintendent Harris, but the state's action was a clear sign of his inability to supervise the planning and execution of a large budget. It is also noteworthy that Harris was replaced by a black whose first action was to find and identify the problems that led to the state action. Also, the state response was novel here, but it set a standard of control found in many states today; for the first time local districts were required to be accountable and report deficits to a state authority.

Whatever Harris's success in improving student test scores, it is likely that this financial problem will feature most in later accounts of his tenure. But even solving this problem will have little to do with the greater problem of student achievement. That has deep roots in the Old South and will continue to plague the New South.

Summary

In an environment of unsupportive whites (particularly the older ones) and of apathetic blacks, school improvement in north Panola needed strong leadership, new programs, and supportive faculty. By 1994, those conditions had been achieved, and so it was not surprising that test results improved. But all agreed there was still much to be done. The considerable debate across the nation on the utility of such achievement tests had passed over this district because the tests had deep meaning for both races locally. With the improvement in scores, black parents strongly supported school referenda. Despite the budget deficit of 1995–96, the local newspaper reported that student scores in that year had continued improving. Further, successful black students had greater interest in attending college. All this change flows from a black and white administration and staff that had developed a stronger sense of mission.[26]

These efforts flow from a quarter century of struggling with desegregation. From their early descent into an educational pit to the gradual improvement of recent years, the north Panola schools show a new pattern of response to law. Without white support, the picture was drastically different from that in south Panola. The task of leadership was primarily to awaken a black community to support professional programs provided by administrators and staff. As a group, whites did little in the past and do little now to improve black education, whether in leadership or funding. Whether for reasons of race or cost, the Old South continues to dominate their outlook, in a modern version of the traditional culture. Regardless of whites, though, school leadership must deal with a community of blacks. Altering the attitudes of the staff and the community are major tasks that are still under way in a district that, comparatively, is new to adaptation. At the core of these efforts is a political task of conflict resolution, to which we now turn.

Political Leadership: Source of Division

The record of limited improvement within these schools was not matched by improvement in the elected school board of trustees. Turnover on the board became high, always a sign of political unrest; in the 1993 election only one member was returned to office. Turnover continued high until the state takeover in 1996.

Racial Divisions on School Matters

In 1993 there were three blacks and two whites on the board, but black members did not think that race divided the board very much. Major issues did, however, find the two races opposed, as noted in the discussion earlier on the two proposals for district representation. A similar division arose over representing community interests. At one point, black members called for an advisory committee to the board that was to represent different segments of this community. The committee was to visit local schools (but not enter school rooms) and recommend matters to the board. But it did not get a chance to function. First, the board removed its attorney after only a one-month appointment. He was replaced by another (immediately termed a "radical" by a white member), who appointed an advisory committee but insisted that it be all black. Some black board members came to dislike his habit of talking at length and disagreeing harshly with blacks. Meetings in which he was involved were long and left little time for the board's own agenda. In all interviews, including those with at least two of his supporters, he was criticized for disrespectful language to both races. Black opponents were "Uncle Toms" who "sold [blacks] out to whites," and a white was a "racist."[27] Blacks were angered even more by the remarks of one white board member, and so the rancor continued for a few weeks.

These details are significant because they reflect an underlying conflict over different meanings of "representation."[28] Were board members to represent "all" the community? Even those not participating in these schools, such as most whites and the aged—both groups fearful of more taxes? If members were to be "trustees" for interests of all constituents, they would suffer criticism from those whose views were ignored. But should one represent a clear group in the community, in this case whites or blacks? Even if it meant ignoring the interests of the unrepresented? If members were to be "errand people," votes would then be easy to determine—do what one's constituency wants—and expect reelection from them. But a third representational role is possible, namely, balancing narrow interests against one another to adopt policies that may benefit one group less than it wants.

Reviewing this board in recent years, it is clear that all three roles were adopted at one time or another. Some blacks, supporting an outside attorney who was recruited to reflect broader interests, found later that his concerns were too "radical" for other black constituents. The superintendent's effort to improve education became a matter that board members of both races could support as both sides agreed on change. But even then, issues arose, which representation could do little to resolve. Members could ignore issues on which they lacked awareness or expertise, like the 1995 financial failure.

This disagreement over representational roles was not simply racial. We can see, in table 6.4, the trustees' responses in 1989 on major problems facing their schools; the cells in this table are condensations of longer interviews. Thus, whites saw low test scores as constituting their major criticism of the schools, while blacks saw the low scores as racial problems. In this disagreement, whites focused on outcomes of educational substance and blacks on outcomes of race.

That distinction is not accidental. While neither group is blind to the role of race in schools or in many other public matters, there were some leadership differences in handling them. Many white leaders in both sections of the county sought public policies that were results-oriented. That outcome was achieved by using accepted procedures within an organization, such as obtaining better grades, satisfactorily completing governmental forms, securing government grants, or recruiting new industries.

On the other hand, some, but not all, black leaders fastened on procedures that lay outside the organization and focused on racial relationships. This is clearly understandable. Blacks for generations have defined their world in the public—and often private—life by racial relationships. This consideration may have underlain Harris's hirings of so many blacks for noncertified jobs, but the evidence is not clear. Whether they harbor a continuing and generalized suspicion of whites or a particular fear that whites get more public resources, these black leaders approach public policy with attitudes drawn from their own history. What is important to them is to focus on how attitudes of race will affect particular processes, and not just on what the processes are. Whites approach the issues with another concern, the need to adhere to processes. But as we have noted, whites reflect a new racism, rarely manifest in public but often covert, which is one aspect of the New South.

This racial division was not always evident on other issues (table 6.4). Often, reality principles overcame racial attitudes and created common positions regardless of race, sometimes even achieving racial agreement. Thus, both races agreed that desegregation had improved black schooling, that the superintendent and staff were the school's strengths, and that the need for more money was the first problem in the district. Judgments summarized in table 6.4 on which were the first and second most important problems confronting the district were widely split, but with little racial division. Both groups agreed that greater school improvement was indeed possible and that there was a need for more state financial support.

Table 6.4   Policy Perceptions among North Panola School Board Members, 1989

Question	MEMBERS' RESPONSES				
	White	Black	White	Black	Black
Why did north Panola become desegregated?	Federal law. No strong leader in either race.	Long story of whites ignoring blacks.	Whites fled for fear.	No answer	No answer
What criticisms can be made of north Panola schools?	Low test scores and weakness in both races.	Lack of white support.	Low test scores but now improving.	Division between within races.	Advisory unit.*
After money, what is the biggest problem?	Advisory unit.*	Poor parent support by both races.	Teachers don't use discipline enough.	Students moving to south Panola.**	Fear of consolidation.
What is the second worst problem?	Need finance skills.	Need more state money.	No answer	Problems with our staff.	Fear of consolidation.
What are north Panola's strengths?	Supt. moving on new ideas.	Blacks are just surviving. Old seg. was better due to parent support.	Better facilities and Supt. Harris's ideas.	No answer	Teacher care for students. Respect for improving schools.
Can north Panola improve on its own?	Already did so— student scores.	No! No discipline. State & feds have abandoned us.	Yes, but state should monitor us.	No. State must help us.	Yes, if Supt. Harris supervises teaching.
Were student scores improved by desegregation?	Yes, without any doubt.	It opened students' eyes. Lost their false confidence in old schools.	Yes. Created higher expectations for both races.	Yes. Kids like other race now.	No evidence of it.

* = reference to a black group whose disputatious attorney advising the school board; the attorney was dropped shortly after these interviews.
** = this practice was blocked later by state law strongly enforced by south Panola.

Summary

In these details of a quarter century of change, we can find the difficult problems that emerged with improving schooling in a once segregated system. Leadership is critically relevant in north Panola, as it was in south Panola. As leadership was abandoned by one group of white leaders, including administrators, the context and outcomes of schooling were weakened. It reached the point that these schools became the worst in a state that is often the worst in the nation. Here, leadership had failed, and the exit option used by whites had generated special costs for both races. Delta whites paid in higher school costs (they also paid public school taxes), but blacks paid in ineffective instruction; adults paid the first bill, but the young paid the second one.

But leadership can make a difference in administering the law, as noted in the case of Superintendent Harris and the faculty involved in improving learning. We have noted some details of what implementation meant in terms of new programs and enlisting community support. But white animosity to public school taxes, and some black parents' indifference or resistance to improving schooling, can dilute such leadership. State support over the last decade has helped greatly to improve the planning and materials for instruction and curricula. It also helped in the financial crisis of 1995–1996. But as the next millennium approaches, both state and local units must work even harder, and together, in the face of a racially split constituency and a limited supply of funds. On the other hand, without leadership, not even state support can help, as the recent financial crisis shows.

7 | The Results for Students in Different Systems

The reactions of the two school systems in north Panola to federal desegregation have highlighted two basic strategies—flight and apathy. The word "strategy" implies an element of "game" in this effort. Like all games, flight and apathy involve strategies, rewards and penalties, and rules. In these two schools the game is ostensibly played only among adults, as they focus in the organization and management of schooling; for them, the students are only indirect objects of this game. The reward in the adult game—control over the values that schooling reflects—is less educational than political. Whites had dominated such rewards in the Old South when segregated schools perfectly matched the rewards of the system. But federal law had changed the rules in a way so fundamental that the old political control had vanished except in "seg academies." In south Panola and north Panola there were actually two different games being played, one of desegregation and the other of black control over the schools.

The time has come to review the consequences of these games, not for adults, but for the children. In this "children's game," the focus is on their cognitions in the three institutions that evolved over the quarter century after desegregation began. Our interest is less in standardized scores of student tests than in how students view themselves, their schools, other races, and the larger political system. To provide a useful framework, we should understand how the students performed in these cognitive worlds by employing the concept of culture to review the results.

Schools as Cultures

The context that surrounds any system can influence those who operate within it, and so it is that the school's context, sketched in these two chapters, influences what students learn about the social world. Three fundamental types of context exist, each having variations that also shape different school cultures. These contexts are *mission, resources,* and *community quality.*

"Mission" refers to preexisting goals set by school leaders and reflected in their institutions. The goals may differ with respect to the purpose of education and to the behavior and information needed to achieve them. For example, a Christian school has a different ideational orientation to learning from a public school. Or one school may emphasize student behavior and have numerous rules of conduct that reflect a control model of learning, while another school may be remarkably loose about student activity, which is yet another model of learning. Also, the kinds of information that are needed may vary to meet the expectations of students, say, in an elementary school in a widely scattered rural population compared with a school in a wealthy suburb.

"Resources," constitute a second contextual influence that forms a school culture. The word means, loosely, anything you use to get what you need, for example, money, leadership, numbers of persons, and so on. This dimension has a long empirical tradition in political science, which relates variations in resources to those who participate in politics or policy making. Put briefly, studies show that there is a "more-more" syndrome at work, that is, those with more resources get more of what a political system offers. At the individual level we find more political activities among those with higher status and income, who report they get more from this behavior.[2] In the South, this understanding is expressed colloquially as "Them as has, gets."

The opposite of this syndrome is "less-less." In public policies designed to redistribute public revenue among different groups—policies that are often thought to help the poor at a cost for other groups—there is a quite different pattern. As one analyst of the kinds of American policy noted, "[T]he total mix of U.S. domestic policy is only mildly redistributive toward the less advantaged in a few areas and is fairly strongly redistributive in favor of the already advantaged in a number of other areas."[3] As for education policy, the evidence shows clearly that schools with few resources of money, personnel, or materials perform less well than those with more of them.

Finally, the "role of community" helps shape school performance and that in turn affects student achievement. Implicit in this concept are the driving expectations of those who shape and are served by an institution. Thus, the community leaders' expectations of teachers over a century ago included a long list of forbidden actions (no smoking, drinking, or dating) that shaped their rather narrow world. Theoretically, then, we would expect that among differing communities there would be differing expectations that shape different cultures. Another element of community quality lies in political expectations, that is, in the degree of political consensus, conflict, or apathy within which school leaders must work out policy problems. Again, those variations of consensus should reflect differently upon school cultures.

In short, these three contextual influences of mission, resource, and community exist in various combinations that have different effects on school cultures. I have described in detail in earlier chapters the two white cultures of the Delta and the Hills of large and small agriculture, of plantocracy and yeomanry. Despite the state mandate that local administrations must provide a uniform education, considerable variation exists in the three types of schools in Panola County in their missions (private versus public, Christian versus secular), resources (a range of parental income and resultant provision of qualified personnel and adequate materials), and community qualities (the two white and one black cultures). Given these variations, we should expect to find three school cultures, in which student cognitions should also vary.

Student Cognitions

Given the context of north Panola, what were the consequences for student cognitions in that part of the county? The student cognitions reviewed in chapter 5 for south Panola relate to behavior and attitudes, and we will use those categories again here (see appendix A for the questionnaire used to measure cognitions). We wished, then, to see how much difference there was in student *behavior*, such as, discussing public problems (four items on the questionnaire), volunteer activity in school and community (six items), and racial contact in school and community (eleven items).[4] Also there were differences in five sets of *attitudes:*

- Race-gender equality (eight items), expectations about the equity of gender and race in providing jobs, schooling, and income; for example, "Men and women should be paid the same money if they do the same work."
- Self-esteem (seventeen items), standardized items[5] from other research on how one views the self, with new scales about local schools; for example, "This school gives me very positive feelings."
- Political efficacy (nine items), standardized items, testing trust of and responsiveness to the political system, elections and leaders; for example, "People like me don't have any say about what the government does."
- Public Policy (ten items), federal policies on welfare, international policies, and state oversight of desegregation and voting; for example, government should "Help people get doctors and hospitals at low cost."[6]

— Racial composite scale (sixteen items), derived from preceding behavior and attitudes that touch on race. If this racial factor underlies
community life, even in the New South, then this scale can demonstrate it in several dimensions.[7]

This instrument tested 1,240 students in grades 6, 9, and 12 in May 1991
in all three school systems. With this author, administrators and teachers
oversaw the testing of hundreds of squirming students on the last days of
school. The cooperation of these school professionals was characteristic of
the New South, a response quite unknown a quarter century ago.

Alternatives to the Cultural Explanation

There are several theoretical explanations for variations in student responses that we can test. The different school cultures might explain
them, but these students have diverse characteristics which may also
shape their views, such as race, class, age, gender, and schooling interest.
Any explanation must take into account the possibility that either culture
or demographic qualities can shape cognitive variations. Hence a test for
multiple explanations was devised.

If *school cultures* do affect cognitions, then a minimum test would show
that each of the three types of school systems has its distinctive set of student attitudes. The three types of schools will be the measure we use to
reflect different school cultures.

Race is a traditional alternative explanation of differing attitudes. Some
studies, however, find racial differences to be less important to political action than differences in status, but that finding has been sharply
challenged.[8] Nevertheless, in the closed racial world of Panola County,
where racial differences in life have been stark indeed, the proposition
that race may shape student attitudes independently of the school culture
is certainly testable. In one sense, though, race is a surrogate measure for
another kind of cultural difference that leads whites and blacks to different cognitions.

Class or *status* is another indicator that has traditionally been used to
explain many differences in political behavior and attitudes.[9] This explanation invariably rests upon indicators of occupation, income, or education, all highly correlated. But in this study, the measure of status can only
be suggested because of two difficulties when using children as respondents. They often don't possess such information, and the younger they
are the more likely it is that this is so; recall that sixth-graders were a crucial cohort in this study. Consequently, by adopting the approach of "Keep
it simple," we asked students only about their parents' occupations. These

answers were then categorized into a range of occupations by status, from the professional to the unemployed; if two occupations were given, the higher status was selected.[10]

Maturation in the child's mental outlook is linked to age, and this factor also may account for variations in student attitudes. Developmental psychology has contributed greatly to our theoretical understanding of the evolving nature of young people's political socialization, as their awareness, information, and feeling expand through time.[11] Consequently, we can test for differing maturation levels by using as a scale of age the students' grade levels of 6, 9, or 12.

A subtle and rarely studied aspect of students' outlook is the degree to which there is an *interest* in *schooling* itself. This measure of interest gauges how useful the school seems to be for one's effort to shape life and seek more schooling. Of course, the two attitudes—the role of school and the effort to secure more schooling—may be related. This view about the efficacy of schools may rise either from the family or the self, but reflects the intrinsic value of learning that a student sometimes finds. This explanation is a surrogate for the familiar finding that education shapes many qualities of life, including political orientation.[12] To measure it, we employ two student answers: success in schooling (self-reports of one's overall letter grade[13]) and plans to enter college.

Finally, regarding the significant and increasingly studied role of *gender* in the political system, it would be useful to test political cognitions drawn from earlier studies.[14] There may be some aspect of gender learning that generates a special view of one's role in society. This attitude may be reflected in one's self-image, or views on political efficacy and racial contact, or one's government policy preferences, which could suggest differences between the genders.

Having set out the theoretical possibilities for understanding attitudinal differences, we now turn to testing them with respect to cognitive differences about self, race, community, and the larger world. The first question is the crucial one: Are there indeed differences among the three educational institutions that emerged in Panola County after desegregation?

School Culture versus Individual Influences

The explanation is clarified by a regression analysis, which is summarized in table 7.1 (exact numbers are given in appendix B). The plus and minus signs indicate that a correlation exists—positive or negative—and an absence of signs indicates no significant correlation was found. The first analysis tests the significance of school culture and the second that of personal variables.

Table 7.1   Regression of Effects of School and Personal Variables on Student Behaviors and Attitudes

	BEHAVIOR			ATTITUDE			
	Public Discussion	Volunteer Work	Racial Contact	Race/ Gender	Political Efficacy	Self-Esteem	Public Policy
Segregated blacks		+	−	−	−		
Desegregated blacks		+	−			−	
Desegregated whites		+	+			−	
Parents' occupation		+					+
Female		−	−	+	+		+
Age	+	−*	−	+	+	+	+
Interest in school College plans	+	+		+	+	+	+
Grades	+	+		+	+	+	

Notes: The regressions for the first three rows were obtained by comparing responses of segregated blacks and desegregated blacks and whites with the responses of segregated whites.

Beta significance at least +.05. A plus sign indicates a positive correlation; negative signs indicate negative correlation; empty cells indicate no significant correlation.

* = significance is .514.

For full description of variables, see Appendix B.

School Culture Explanations. Table 7.1 shows that the student's school and race play some role in explaining differences among these scales of behavior and attitudes. Four types of student groups were analyzed, that is, segregated blacks (north Panola), both desegregated blacks and whites (south Panola), and segregated whites (North Delta school). In the analysis, the first three types were compared with the fourth.

In this comparison, we first find that blacks in either public school seem similar; on many matters, the school culture explains little. That is, they are separated from the segregated whites of the North Delta school both physically (on issues of racial contact) and psychologically (on efficacy, self-esteem). Segregated whites—surprisingly—report more often that they had frequent racial contact although clearly it did not occur in school. Black scores show that they do not share these attitudes and behaviors. One would have thought that desegregated blacks in south Panola would report frequent contact, but both black groups imply that regardless of school culture, they live in a world of less white contact. Curiously, the scores for both black groups indicate more volunteer activity than do the segregated whites; one inference is that the latter group lives in a more secluded world than blacks.

One effect of desegregation emerges here, though. If one supposes that blacks feel better about themselves due to legal advances or to integrating with whites, that is clearly not supported by this table. That is, these scores indicate lower self-esteem for blacks in desegregated schools than in segregated ones, a finding that is familiar from other research efforts.[15] It seems that black students' views of themselves are enhanced under the modern segregation possibly because there are no whites to challenge their self-esteem.

But desegregation does have an effect on white students. Desegregated whites in south Panola report that significantly more aspects of their lives are related to race than do segregated whites in North Delta. The former group reports greater racial contact and—as shown in table 7.2—are more supportive of some attitudes involving blacks. However, like the black students in south Panola, south Panola whites report lower self-esteem than do North Delta whites. The explanation may lie in the class distinctions between the two school districts, North Delta with its affluent parents and south Panola with its working-class and welfare parents. Students in the more affluent constituency, like those elsewhere in the nation, score themselves higher on self-esteem than any other type of student. Family influence is thus important in both schools. In the affluent group, students aspire to more in life, as their parents provide more options and resources for self-improvement; for the other group, both options and resources are limited by their families. We will return shortly to these school and race distinctions.

Demographic Explanations

The major explanations of student attitudes lie in age, gender, and interest in school, as shown in table 7.1. Note that these age and gender variable are independent of the school itself.

Overall, the influence of age is extraordinary. It predicts positively for every scale of behavior and attitude (albeit marginally on one item). This finding demonstrates clearly that psychological maturation carries with it a growing contact, political or otherwise, with the larger political world of discussion, efficacy, and policy preferences. Sixth-graders may well have a dim idea, if any, of public policy—and certainly their self-esteem is lower —than do twelfth-graders, who have read more and had more courses on such topics. In contrast, volunteer work and racial contact are more frequent among the younger students. The inference is that by the time students reach the middle or high school, the child has withdrawn so much into the peer world of other youths that this relationship detracts from work in the community and contact with the other race.[16] Whether desegregation affects this attitude will be noted later.

Of striking interest is the role of gender among these students. The pattern for female students shown in table 7.1 matches that for age, as quite a strong indicator of behavior and attitudes. Females report more liberal attitudes in race-gender issues and public policies and a higher sense of their political efficacy. On the other hand, females report less volunteer activity and racial contact than do males. Young males appear the repository of the traditional culture in their less liberal views on many policies. They have more significant contact with the blacks—suggestive of sports involvement—and they engage more in volunteer activity. But there is no gender difference found on self-esteem.

The third striking finding is the influence of an interest in school. Whether it means having college plans or holding higher grades, there is a positive correlation for every scale but frequency of racial contact. A separate analysis shows that interest in schooling is not affected by more education, for it seems to exist at all levels of schooling. Whatever influence the family or teaching has on some students to make them aspire to good work at school, it also brings about more positive political and personal attributes, as found in these scales.

In contrast to its showing on the strong influence of personal attributes, table 7.1 shows limited influence for class, indicated here by parents' occupation. It does show that higher-level occupations predict more volunteer activity (clearly a middle-class preoccupation) and more liberal attitudes on public policies; but its limited correlation with other student behaviors and attitudes is significant.[17] Indeed, the finding that students with higher-occupation parents predict more liberal attitudes about public policies runs contrary to the popular view that those with resources have little sympathy for government help. It also suggests a curious fact when matched with previous findings. That is, older female students with more interest in schooling seem to emerge as a liberal bloc in this community. Does the recent debate about women's rights move these students to support policies improving race and gender status or to use government to provide common social services? Is this a modern effort by females to break out of the traditional culture by expressing a political self? Recall that historically this was the last region of the nation to support the Eighteenth Amendment on women's votes (indeed, Mississippi ratified it only after World War II); no state in this region supported the Equal Rights Amendment decades later.

Summary. The preceding analysis suggests the role of school culture and personal qualities in the complex consequences of desegregation. The findings about the effects of school culture and of age, gender, and schooling interest inform us that these factors do influence student attitudes and behavior. But there remains a problem. Identifying a desegregated school like south Panola as a group confuses its racial identity, as there are two races there. We must separate the effects of race upon the same scales.

Types of Students in Type of Schools

Can we relate differences in attitudes to schooling experiences? There are six pairings of students that we may compare:

— desegregated whites versus (1) desegregated blacks, (2) segregated whites, and (3) segregated blacks;
— desegregated blacks versus (4) segregated whites and (5) segregated blacks;
— segregated whites versus (6) segregated blacks.

We can use a differences of means test on the scales (shown in table 7.2). There, the student population type with the largest score on each scale is placed above a student population type with lower scores. Thus, in the first column of this table, "Desegregated whites/Desegregated Blacks," means that the scores of desegregated whites (i.e., those in south Panola) were higher on these scales than the scores of desegregated blacks. With children of Delta whites and poor farm blacks schooled in two segregated institutions, and with both races together in the desegregated school, we can test almost experimentally the long-range results of the federal law among the youth of this county.

Explaining Individual Variations

Racial Contact and Attitudes. Propositions to explain these six pairings focus, first, on race. The simplest theory is that desegregated schooling, due to its biracial interactions and newer instruction on race, will produce more racial contact and more liberal ideas on race issues. Note that the *Brown* decision of the U.S. Supreme Court in 1954 aimed to desegregate in order to redistribute resources to improve the schooling of blacks. Here, however, we look at the long-run consequence of that decision's implementation, namely, that desegregated students think differently about themselves and society than those who are segregated. Here we may test

Table 7.2 Student Responses by Type of School Population

	SCHOOL POPULATION TYPE					
Student Scale	DesW DesB	DesW SegW	DesW SegB	DesB SegW	DesB SegB	SegW SegB
Race						
Racial contact	.000***	.000***	.000***		.000***	.000***
Racial composite scale		.002***	.000***	.010**	.000***	
Attitude						
Political Efficacy	.000***	.008**	.000***	.000***		.000***
Self-esteem		.000***		.005**		.000***
Race gender	.017**	.061?			.017**	.051?
Public Policy						
New Deal liberal	.000***	.024*	.005**		.026	
Populist			.040*			
States rights						
Cold War Warrior	.000***	.005**	.000***			
Political behaviors						
Public Discussion						
Volunteer work						

Notes: In each row, the group named first in the column head has the higher scale score compared with the group named second. DesW = desegregated whites; DesB = desegregated blacks; SegW = segregated whites; SegB = segregated blacks

In difference of means tests, empty cells lack significance; others are significant as: * = .05; ** = .01; *** = .000; or ? = just above acceptable level.

directly my major thesis, that law changes reality, which in time changes perceptions that change attitudes. *The evidence that follows overwhelmingly supports this explanation.*

In table 7.2, desegregated whites report more racial contact than do segregated blacks and whites, at a statistically more significant rate, and the same is true of desegregated blacks versus segregated blacks. Indeed, south Panola's whites report greater racial contact than do their black classmates. That same finding applies as well to a more comprehensive scale—the racial composite scale—which combines numerous racial contact and race-gender responses. In short, judging from the outlooks of these different students the striking finding is the importance of desegregation for both races, compared to outlooks among the segregated whites or blacks. A generation earlier, such frequency of racial contact in different circles of community life, and such willingness to support race-gender issues, would simply not have existed. This finding provides empirical support for the frequent comments found in all adult interviews in this county that the law had made a difference in the community life. That influence in shaping attitudes cannot be better demonstrated than in this finding, even when both race and school type are held constant.

Attitudes about Politics and Self. As to the race of individuals and their schools and other attitudes, we find again a much greater difference in the desegregated whites, as shown in table 7.2. For example, *political efficacy* measures how highly students regard their role in the world of politics. The different school structures in this county do demonstrate differences on this scale. Thus, the two kinds of black students are not significantly different from each other, but in a comparison with whites, the results are mixed. The desegregated blacks of south Panola regard themselves as *more* efficacious than segregated whites of North Delta do, while blacks in north Panola rank themselves as *less* efficacious than whites do in either type of school; in no comparison do north Panola segregated blacks show a higher score. Despite a generation of government improving black life, desegregation has not, for some black students, increased their belief that politicians are concerned about them or that one can trust the government. The basic distrust in the larger institutions that is found among those at the bottom of life's opportunities also appears here.

Other attitude scales show a less strong association. There are some distinctions on self-esteem, where only those with an interest in schooling interest rated very high (see table 7.1). The segregated whites' sense of self is weaker than that of both races in south Panola; but the desegregated populations score is significantly higher than the segregated blacks. One expects the families of segregated whites, with greater resources of all kinds and more insistence on better schools, to have children with higher scores on efficacy and self-esteem.[18] That does not always occur, however, because in desegregated schools, children representing a range of affluence (albeit heavily dominated by the poor) are higher on these scales. Even the desegregated blacks are strong on these scales; it is only against the segregated blacks that the segregated whites can dominate. Again, the context of desegregation seems to have influences that reach even into the student's concept of self, as found in south Panola.

A final personal attribute arises in the *race-gender scale*, that is, how women and blacks should be treated with respect to their opportunities in the economy and education. The association found is less regular than that noted for race, but again the desegregation context is important. Only two of three pairs of student population types show significant differences, and another two are marginal. But in two of the three in that set, we again see the desegregated students taking more liberal stands. Surprisingly, such liberalism for desegregated whites in south Panola is greater than even that for their black classmates; but even the latter group scores higher on this scale than the segregated north Panola blacks. If one argues that desegregated students of either race are more liberal than segregated students of either race, and that difference is traceable to desegregation, the evidence provided here is marginally supportive, but not very significant.

Attitudes on Public Policies. As for student preferences for state and national public policy, we see in table 7.2 that only two issues loom large.[19] Those wishing Washington to provide jobs and medical care for all, and fair treatment for blacks—policies labeled "New Deal Liberalist"—score significantly higher among both races in south Panola, compared to the two racially segregated schools populations. Earlier we saw how the south Panola school, with its roots in the Hill culture, had shown traces of the populist influence in its distaste for the influence of big business and labor unions in government. That view of government finds support among black students. In short, the desegregation experience seems to have produced a more positive view of Washington as remedying life's inequities, about which the poor farm and town children must know well. Both races thus have perceptions about the world that have been altered by the intervention of federal law.

Two unsuspected findings emerge in table 7.2, though. The New Deal liberal views held by both types of blacks are not significantly different from those of North Delta whites. Why would two cohorts at different ends of the social scale not be opposed? There is a rational assumption that in public life, each group supports or opposes government for the benefits or regulation it brings them. Thus, Delta whites should be firmly opposed to government intervention, given the traditional culture, while both black groups should be supportive of policies that enhance their position in life. However, the absence of significance in both cases points to a randomness within each student cohort that add up to a lack of significance. In this policy matter, then, theory is not sufficient to explain cognitions.

The other policy stances are moderately helpful in explaining racial attitudes. Students' views on states rights reveal no racial difference at all. It might be expected, though, that the races would differ on this score, particularly the segregated whites. They should approve with a significant margin that government should not interfere "with whether white and black children go to the same school," and should support "letting the state set its own rules on who can vote." But not only did this difference not emerge in this cohort, it failed to do so for any other student type. One inference can be derived from this finding. The ideology of the Old South holds no special dominance in the thinking of this younger generation of Panolians of either race. The earlier generational differences that led to more acceptance of blacks voting and to introducing a more progressive local government have persisted into this generation.

Another public policy preference listed in table 7.2 is the populist stance, that is, a preference for preventing trade unions and big business from running government. But a preference for populism was weak in predicting racial differences, as only one comparison proved significant, namely, desegregated whites over segregated blacks. That might be explained as the last trace of the political movement of populism in this region, persisting among the young whites. Historically, this outlook, particularly among poor whites, had opposed large business, like the railroads, and Mississippi leaders like Benjamin Tillman had made a political career out of this ideology earlier in the century.[20] But if that is an explanation of modern youth's differences, it is quite weak, for populism seems to have faded for both races.

Finally, in international attitudes about the United States and the Soviet Union (these views were polled just before the Soviet Union broke up), or about using military force abroad, we find a classic cold war orientation among some students. In three cases, the scores of desegregated whites of south Panola were significantly higher than those of their black classmates or those of students in either segregated school. Given the dramatic changes in the Soviet Union, and given the United States' overseas military action in recent years, this is the one aspect of the study that might well change in future research. Yet the finding parallels the traditional white support for a strong military stance against external threats. That stance was reflected historically in large southern representation in military recruitment, officer commissions, and military bases, a situation that has persisted for well over a century. The irony here is that in any future war the whites of south Panola, supporting this view, would end up in the ranks, while those of Delta, who were not consistently supportive, would be their officers.

While these attitudes about race, self, and the political world have demonstrated significance, especially for south Panola, very little of it led to much political action by students. That might be expected among twelfth-graders, but their efforts to discuss political issues or to volunteer in the community were also limited; these were among the few actions they could take before they reached the voting age of eighteen.[21] No group of students scored significantly on these two scales because their involvement was minimal and race was irrelevant.

Summary. This review of student thinking about the self and the world discusses two important findings about the changes in this county. First, there is the structural finding: institutions do matter. Thus, the attitudinal scores of blacks and whites in the desegregated schools of south Panola are significantly higher than those for the segregated students of either race. The finding applies to significant aspects of life—racial contact and attitudes, trust in the political system, appreciation of the developing self, and positive views of federal policy, domestic and foreign. The second finding is that variations in the personal attributes of these students act as screens that help fill in their views on such matter. Thus, older students, female students, and those interested in schooling score significantly higher on these scales than those who are younger, or male, or less interested in school.

Behind these differences lie the local cultures to which the black and white students belong. Looking from a passing car on the interstate highway that bisects parts of the county, one might think the people look or think alike. But those who think that blacks think alike should note their differences of opinion on racial contact, political efficacy, and self-esteem. Also, those who believe that whites think alike should note similar differences on the same scales or on those regarding federal policies.

Reflections on Law and Schooling

From the last three chapters on desegregation, we can understand how the outside intervention of federal law was diffused into the schools. Nothing in law itself encourages self-enforcement when it challenges economic or moral purposes. However, strong implementation of the law can create possibilities for changing the reality of life, even among recalcitrants. Locally, both races in the county witnessed an early and strong implementation, which was the source of hope for one race and fear for the other in earlier years.

Cultural limitations shaped local responses to that law. South Panola schools adopted the "fight" strategy. Its earlier fight against desegregation gave way to a fight to secure support by local leaders in both races in the Hill culture. In north Panola, the Delta whites adopted the "exit" strategy, making a grand retreat to private schools because they could afford the costs. Their culture made it incomprehensible for them to send their children to schools with the children of black fieldhands whom they had derogated for generations.

That decision left behind the blacks of north Panola, who for so long had adopted the "apathy" strategy. Community and leadership did little to support effective schooling for them in a system totally abandoned by whites. The chronic opposition of whites to supporting taxes for black schools still works today against any improvement; indeed, to correct the school district's finances required an unprecedented state intervention. Even then, though, a white leader objected to using funds for consultants on improving financial procedures before a 1996 meeting on budgets. In short, good advice is too costly for black schools. For two decades white administration of the ever-larger black schools had the same effect, leaving the black community helpless to effect change even had it wished it. Only recently has that picture altered, with black leadership mobilizing school programs, with considerable state help, to improve somewhat student results. However, the district's 1995–1996 financial failure and the state intervention that followed show that administrative ability in other areas than instruction is vital to the schools' continued health. The failure of white voters to support the schools and of black leadership to act makes the outlook very dim.

These three cultural responses suggest that citizen concepts can work to refract the law. Where strong implementation of law did occur, as in south Panola, and where both races were involved, important changes took place. Community support of schools through tax levies remained high, and student results, in learning and attitudes, improved for both races. When this school's football team won the state championship in 1993, both races contributed to the celebrations, which took on the air of a Mardi Gras in the quiet streets of Batesville. For both races, in the words of poet James Wright,

> Their sons grow suddenly beautiful
>   at the beginning of October,
> And gallop terribly against each other's body.

The reaction of both was one of support for "our" team, even though the team was mostly black. In short, under conditions of implementation and local leadership, the purposes of the law were realized.

In north Panola, where Delta whites fleeing the law had created their own private garden, the costs to the schools were considerable, not simply in terms of money but in the loss of leadership in the schools they left behind. In north Panola, finally, black students received doubtful benefits from a law whose purposes were irrelevant here, because there was no desegregation. Left with a one-race school, there was little to help students besides federal grants; without community and leadership support, such money only underwrote failure.

In previous chapters, we have seen the positive results of federal law on voting and the mixed results of law on education, all occurring over the last quarter century. Next we will trace the law's impact upon a third aspect of life in Panola County—job opportunities. Once again, we will see cultural differences among whites in response to the new demands of the outside factors of law and the economy.

8 | The Local Economy and Political Regimes

The currents of federal law in Panola County that altered local politics and schools have also influenced the local economy. But here again, the whites of the Delta and Hill cultures responded differently, while the black culture fully supported the effort to find jobs in a sea of poverty. In Batesville, new white leaders took advantage of an altering national economy and a new federal law and adjusted to meet local needs. As a result, many blacks got jobs as more small plants expanded within the new local political system, as we have earlier seen. However, the story in the Delta is familiar; it followed its traditional culture and resisted economic change until recently.

The local economy for blacks in the early days after the civil rights laws came into effect had rested upon two federal instruments—subsidy and regulation. That is, blacks received income supplements from subsidies in the form of different welfare programs, and Panola County was a natural recipient with its high figures of poverty. Also, regulations in the form of affirmative action on hiring benefited blacks, after a slow start. By the 1990s there were many blacks in local industries, mostly in entry-level jobs, that had been generated by leaders in a new political system. We must first understand this local economy and its political links, which will give us a picture of jobs and power in the different cultures of the county.

Theory and the Local Political Economy

Even the casual viewer of American local business is struck by its diversity. Local enterprise also emphasizes a decentralized control of the economy. Local government can influence it, but the political and economic systems at all levels have not been that separate, as each system needs the other. The national government provides a degree of protection and subsidy to business that is found from early on in our history. Recall the colonial settlements of the nation, many of which were basically commercial organizations; recall also Alexander Hamilton's *Report on Manufactures*, road and canal building in the east in the 1830s, free land to farmers and railroads in the 1870s in the west, and tariff laws throughout our history.[1] The state governments have also provided some support to business. Most often that has meant letting business go unregulated for much of our history; but more recently, the states have provided funds to attract new industries.[2]

Local governments today seek developmental policies that support existing business or attract new ones. These policies attract wide support from business, labor, political parties, and local taxpayers. Clearly they generate far less conflict than policies for allocating public services or redistributing services to the poor.[3] Local officials support business because they are persuaded by a theory of political economy that businessmen see as "practical." This theory proposes that local government can create favorable business climates by promoting existing business or attracting new plants by offering land-use programs, more public services, or tax deferrals. If successful, such developmental policy brings in more business, more jobs, more dollars to tax for more revenue, and public services that, in turn, attract even more businesses. However, without such a policy, business contracts or moves elsewhere, with a consequent local loss in jobs, taxes, and services.[4] This theory of local business is supported by considerable evidence in regional development,[5] in suburban competition, and in state efforts, as may be seen in Mississippi.

The Economy in the State and County

The days when King Cotton ruled the economy of Mississippi have gone. Cotton has been overtaken by income from many sources—tourism, federal programs, and new kinds of farming (e.g., catfish or cattle). Of greater importance, though, has been the growth of a small-plant industry that is widely scattered among its small towns. The roots of this effort lie in a state program from the mid-1930s, "Balance Agriculture with Industry."

But one element of that old economy remains, the striking and widespread poverty. Table 8.1 sets out starkly the indexes of poverty found within the state, the county, and its communities. Whatever the measure employed, this is truly a poor state.[6] In 1990, despite all federal programs, one in three Mississippians was still beneath the poverty level. Panola County is a bit better off in comparison than other counties—it has higher income and a lower percentage of poor. Still, one in four Panolians lives in poverty. A few towns in the county do somewhat better, especially Pope, a hamlet south of Batesville in the Hill culture and the source of many Batesville leaders. But it is Panola's black population that is hit so

Table 8.1   Indexes of Poverty, State of Mississippi and Panola County, 1990

Index	Panola County	Missis- sippi	Bates- ville	Sardis	Como	Pope
Median income (in dollars)	7,537	9,648	9,338	8,395	6,995	9,007
% in poverty	25.2	33.8	28.1	31.8	32.7	10.5
% families in poverty	20.2	25.7	17.7	23.4	29.3	6.5
% in poverty:						
White	13.2	14.8				
Black1	46.4	53.6				
% unemployed	8.4	9.5				
% of households with no plumbing	5.5	21.2				

Sources: Drawn from the Mississippi volumes of Bureau of the Census, *1990 Summary Social, Economic, and Housing Characteristics*; *1990 Summary Population and Housing Characteristics*; and *1990 General Housing Characteristics* (Washington, D.C.: U.S. Department of Commerce, 1992).

much harder than whites in this countryside of poverty. Almost one in two blacks lives in poverty, while only one in eight whites does.

It is not surprising, then, that local officials have aggressively pursued expanding the local economy by seeking new industries. So much of this state effort was diverted to small towns that by 1960 a curious situation emerged; industrial activity among these towns was closely and positively correlated to agricultural activity. But how Panola communities sought new plants was modified by differences within the white culture. Most observers believed that leaders in the Delta culture had rejected development, fearing it would raise the wages of farmhands through competition. Even today, when agricultural work is done less by farmhands than by giant machines, this Delta reluctance to encourage industrialism has blocked efforts to expand the local economy. Among Delta whites in Panola County, industrialism was associated with the "money-grubbing culture," meaning Batesville. But outside the Delta, other communities had worked hard to attract small plants, each with its scores of jobs. It is this cultural difference that emerged once again in Batesville and Sardis.

The cultural shift was imposed over a political shift in how decisions were to be made. For one thing, outside forces came to play a larger role, in the form of governmental mandates, economic pressures, and a new professionalism.[7] Not simply mandates from the national government— actually, far more came from Jackson than Washington—but changes in the national economy had local influence. For example there was the job market shift away from cotton to small plants, as we will see. Professionals became more important, as school superintendents, police chiefs, or city planners operated under increasing pressures from state mandates. In their work, these new actors introduced a special set of values—quality, efficiency, and honesty. We have seen earlier the significant role of a new superintendent in Batesville's schools; similarly, a new police chief came to Batesville in the late 1980s to deal with the drugs and violence that were spinning out from the big cities.

These new actors are important because they alter the local agenda. At any time, local politicians and businessmen act in response to their perceptions of what problems are and what solutions should be used. This distinctive "set of solutions"[8] incorporates ideas about reality that will shape their behavior and that of the community. Of course, these ideas can change over time, which can also shift the old set of solutions. And new actors, inside and outside the community, can introduce new ideas and new solutions. These concepts suggest that social change in Panola County has created new possibilities about the control of power. The vision of the old culture, bound to that of the small and large farms of whites, has changed. As one scholar has noted: "[A]t times, urban regimes are poised for relatively rapid change—because old ways of doing things have become glaringly dysfunctional, or because new problems press in, demanding resolution, or because new political actors clamor for incorporation, or for a myriad of other reasons."[9]

In this county, as in the Old South, outside forces impelled changes in many familiar aspects of local decision making. Existing visions of local power still remain and hold influence; however, these newer and "out of equilibrium systems generate considerable positive feedback when pushed."[10] The older system could resist where its supporters were numerous and powerful, as in the Delta culture. But where the system could be altered by a new generation with new solutions to community problems, then law could provide the opportunity for more local change. This theoretical framework explains how the two local economies of Panola adapted to economic change when it was accompanied by new laws.

Panola's Local Economy in the Old South

The term "King Cotton" tells us much about the considerable economic and political power that was rooted in that narrow base.[11] Since the history of the plantocracy of Panola County lies with that older culture, we will take a closer look at how it developed.

The Basis of Cultural Divisions

The roots of the state's economy lie in the pre–Civil War origins of cotton in and around Natchez. That culture, primarily French, had used state authority to subsidize and regulate its economy. As one historian notes:[12]

> State government rarely interfered in the lives of its citizens, concerning itself primarily with the problems and maintenance of the cotton economy. Keeping credit fluid, easing transportation difficulties, and regulating and protecting slavery were the accepted functions of the legislative and administrative branches of the state. . . . When the state became involved in the lives of Mississippians, however, it did so to uphold law and the existing social order rather than to effect social change.

Clearly, black slaves had no economic power for themselves; and slavery may have driven away white immigrants who would have been needed for any new industry.

The post–Civil War's Black Codes used law to reinstitute the old system of labor and farming, coming close to redefining slavery in legal terms.[13] For example, blacks could not lease or rent land or sign labor contracts, and apprenticeship systems tied black laborers to their white former owners. Those codes were abolished in the Reconstruction era by the Republican federal government. Contrary to old southern legend, this government was exceptionally progressive; for example, it provided laws on civil rights and local services for blacks. But the white planter reaction to Reconstruction was to erect a new plan to control blacks, using intimidation, deceitful business practices, and miscounting of votes—all of which helped to elect conservative Democrats to office.[14] In the repressive era that followed, blacks were denied the ballot, and segregation became entrenched in states' constitutions and laws until the present era.

But there were also major divisions within the white culture of this state.[15] The economy was based on large plantations and poor small farms. As noted earlier, Delta whites came to see themselves as an aristocracy, with values of honor, dignity, and fairness, one that opposed the Hill whites, or "rednecks," for their greedy and devious nature. From today's perspective it is clear that both groups were protecting their own culture earnestly and eagerly. William Faulkner's novels of Yopknowha County paints both groups with exquisite detail.[16] Delta culture looked at the other group with disgust, and the Hill whites looked back at them with envy.

The two white groups differed on all matters except race, but setting that aside, they split on most economic matters, including government policy. In the 1930s, Delta whites rejected New Deal social policies but supported better health care and schooling for blacks; they also disdained campaigns based on racism. The new "progressive" movement of the Hill whites, using racism in their campaigns, also supported New Deal measures for supporting poor whites, while campaigning against corporations and bankers.[17] Federal laws controlling banks and businesses had introduced protections for poor whites in the areas of health, education, and the workplace. One historian notes that this cultural division had jump-started Mississippi in its economic development by "[b]attering some of the bulwarks of conservatism in an agricultural state which had become static."[18] However, both cultures also opposed trade unions. On this stance, conservative elements in this progressive Hill culture joined with plantocrats who feared that unions would raise wages for field hands. Both groups' opposition to unions, as one scholar has noted, acted to inhibit industrial development of this state.[19]

Caste and Class in Northern Panola

Panola's history was influenced by cotton for most of the period from Appomattox to recent decades. From Natchez up through the Delta, white wealth dominated all local institutions, and along with it the characteristic racial attitudes of white supremacy.[20] In northern Panola, wealth accumulated among a few families with established homes in Como (once termed "the richest small town" in America). The farmland they owned lay to the west, over the Chickasaw Bluff and down to the Delta that stretched on west to the Mississippi River across several counties. Sardis was the government center for this culture in Panola County, while the small scattered hamlets surrounding it supplied the culture's religious and commercial needs. Few blacks owned land in this region, as most of them worked directly for the plantations.

The Delta white culture created not only a caste society but one based on class.[21] Caste made the whites dominant; social relations between the races was forbidden (but overlooked white men's desire for black women). This caste division was maintained by violence. Class divisions overlapped those of caste, with a thin layer of plantocrats, merchants, and lawyers on top, and a large mass of poor people—black and white—at the bottom. Caste and class pyramids were maintained not only by violence or economic sanctions but by dominance in social circles, by religion, and by control in the public schools—all of which were segregated, of course.

Northern Panola and the Traditional Culture

The plantocrats of northern Panola belonged to this culture of caste and class. Historical records show that in 1860 there were 8,557 slaves and

5,237 whites, a racial imbalance that did not change until 1980; the ratio went as high as 2 to 1 in 1910. Sardis had outnumbered Batesville for all its history until 1950, but by 1980 its numbers were only one-half those of Batesville.[22] The planters at the top of the pyramid were not simply "locals," for they had strong influence in the banking circles in Memphis, at the state capitol in Jackson, and in Washington and New York. They traveled often and well to major cities in the United States and in Europe. Their children went to college, the University of Mississippi (affectionately known as Ole Miss) if average, to Vanderbilt if more knowledgeable, and to Princeton if gifted. They returned to pick up family business in farming and banking and to hold together the caste and class systems they had inherited. Their social circles reached to similar families in Delta counties to the west, and their marriages were often with the scions of those families.

Racial Relationships. The planters' crops were produced by blacks and supported by banks that the planters often owned. Whites were always in a dependent relationship with blacks both personally and economically. However, as many whites relate, these relationships sometimes felt close, even warm, a personal tie that was neither dependent nor independent. Such ties were formed with small children on the plantation or with what were once called "house Negroes"—cooks, nurses, and other staff of the main house. These connections—almost familial—were rooted in a white paternalism that had reached back through generations. But it was an attitude so strong that whites could not understand why blacks would want desegregation when it came, as noted in chapter 3.

While Delta whites' perceptions of blacks were clouded by this relationship of dependency, blacks regularly masked their feelings of frustration and anger at such paternalism, even to white friends. As the black poet, Paul Laurence Dunbar, noted years ago:

> We wear the mask that grins and lies,
> It hides our cheeks and shades our eyes,
> This debt we pay to human guile;
> With torn and bleeding hearts we smile,
> And mouth with myriad subtleties.

Whites interviewed in Panola often did not understand such black perceptions; they judged relationships based on contact only with fieldhands, who were less educated and less close to them than house servants were. For plantocrats, these hands were simply necessary tools for producing cotton, and their economic concern was to maximize production and reduce costs. Many blacks were tied to the plantation by direct hiring and a few by sharecropping. White methods of bookkeeping often left blacks dependent on whites for future goods.[23] Consequently, the economic control exercised by whites was for the blacks direct, inescapable, and confining.

The only release for blacks was emigration to the North. In the decades before civil rights law came to the South, blacks left this county by the thousands and the region by the millions. But, for the blacks who remained at home, sustenance came not from the economy but from religion, which was often an evangelistic outpouring of hopes and fears, a dream of a better life beyond Jordan.

Consequently, until 1965 what Delta whites saw were institutions that they dominated, economic rewards that they generated, and a black way of life that was remote from their own. These "white families"—a commonly used term of reference—controlled all nominations for city and county offices; thus elections became superfluous in the then Solid South.[24] They controlled the main—if not only—banks in their region. Local white merchants owed these banks for mortgages, rents, or goods, and they shared the racial views of their customers. School systems relied on property taxes, of which these families paid the most, although greatly diluted,[25] and the schools were as a result run by them. Two generations of one family had sat on the North Panola School Board when its last representative, Carlton Hays, left because of desegregation. White ministers in the leading churches of Baptists and Methodists were clearly picked for their accordance with local values.[26]

The linkage of caste and class thus formed overlapping circles of influence reaching every element of life, affecting blacks and whites alike. All in all, north Panola was a close imitation of medieval feudalism, a traditional system that worked for these families well into the twentieth century.

Small Farm Culture in South Panola

The Tallahatchie River ambling across the county contributed to a divided white culture. To the north of it were plantations and wealth, and to the south were small farms and town merchants living amid rolling hills. In both sections of the county, however, there were large numbers of poor of both races. Awareness of this distinction based on this line of the river seems long-rooted. Before World War II, there had been opposition to consolidating the schools of the two sections of the county or to using TVA electricity; there were also raucous conflicts over school sports. Those in the south resented the wealth and dominance in the north; when the TVA was eventually accepted, it created a large recreational lake, located in the north and named Sardis Lake. The division may have gone back even earlier to the political division that had led to creating two county seats, one in Sardis and the other in Batesville.[27] Or maybe it originated even earlier, when the regularly flooding river cut the two rural societies off from each other almost every year.

Whatever the source of division, both black and white today talk about it as a real element in their perceptions of reality. A question to all interviewees about such differences found unanimous agreement in both races and both sections; interviewees provided many examples. Generally speaking, Sardis sees Batesville as too commercial, while Batesville sees Sardis as "stuck in the past."

In south Panola, farms were much smaller, but it is crucial to note that both races owned land. Black leadership here in the civil rights era of the 1960s had rested in part on one black farm owner. Throughout the South many of these black landowners had been created by a mid-1930s New Deal program that underwrote farm ownership, until powerful southern congressmen cut it off after one year.[28] In south Panola, other blacks and whites worked as sharecroppers, and a few were artisans in the small towns. A scattering of merchants and lawyers, active in the Baptist church, dominated Batesville's public schools and limited social circles.

Power in Batesville before 1965

Political power rested, however, in other hands. Like many local political systems of that time[29] — and today — a "courthouse circle" of whites, led by a mayor or supportive members of the county board of supervisors, dominated all public authority. In the case of Panola County, the power rested in the hands of Mayor Daniel Ferguson of Batesville, whom we noted in chapter 3. Like his colleagues, he was not too well educated, but he knew how to control local power. Before the state's later reforms, a mayor could combine functions that were judicial (levying fines on misdemeanors), executive (controlling local services to the town), administrative (appointing personnel for those services), and political (controlling all oversight of voting through appointments). As federal law began to invade the South, including Panola County, Ferguson's response was typical of white supremacists in positions of local authority. As chapter 3 shows, he worked vigorously against voter registration using his legal authority.[30]

Ferguson was also adamant against other kinds of change. Through his support on the county board of Batesville aldermen, he was resistant to any idea of bringing in small plants.[31] Ferguson feared economic change, partly because he shared the fears of town merchants that plants would bring in higher wages to hurt local business. That view also matched those of plantocrats up across the river who feared the effects of industry on field hands. But these opponents were also concerned about the organization of local workers. Not that there was any threat of unions, here or elsewhere in the South. But Ferguson believed that groups of workers, first white and later black, might share views critical of local power holders that could result in election opposition. In short, he controlled all the marbles in this game, and any small intrusion by outsiders was regarded as a crucial threat. Given his support from the white community and the placement of his officials, he was regularly returned to office.

As elsewhere in the rural South, then, small elites in both sections of the county had dominated society. Without any outside interference, that structure would remain. So also would the white supremacy viewpoint and the diminished opportunities for blacks in the economic sector.

Batesville Development: Resistance and "Progressivism"

In the South, adjustments to major social change ran the gamut from re-sistance to adaptation, and Panola County was no exception. One sign of adaptation was the enhancement of black economic status, although only for a small number. The widespread poverty in the county meant that those without jobs were sustained by the federal government. But for some blacks, industrial jobs became available when the Hill culture turned to economic development against Delta resistance.

Emergence of Industrialism in Batesville

After World War II, Batesville's local businessmen lacked the great wealth of the planters around them, and they also found it hard to secure bank loans for expansion.[32] The traditional Bank of Batesville, like others in Sardis and Como, did not lend much for business expansion. Their invest-ment philosophy was extremely conservative—actually rock-like—for its own economic security rested not on a public seeking risk capital, but on massive deposits of plantation profits. The constant complaint back at that time was that those banks thrived by doing nothing more than pay-ing 3 percent interest on savings deposits, and charging 6 percent for their loans. One Batesville banker noted wryly that their work was so slow they left work by noon.

In economic theory, this local constraint on lending should have stimu-lated other outlets in a market economy. And indeed, a few men did orga-nize, in the early 1950s, to create a new Batesville Security Bank in order to attract deposits that could be used to encourage loans that would expand small businesses, although charging a somewhat larger lending rate. This bank also encouraged its officers to be active in the chamber of commerce and to seek new business (the earlier chamber had collapsed before World War II). Consequently, before the emergence of the civil rights movement, a new group of white men, usually of a younger generation, were seeking to expand local business and to move the job market from farming to industry. Profit making was in their mind, of course. But there was also a realization that the only way to relieve local poverty was to create more jobs, especially when farm jobs were declining.[33]

The new men termed this approach "progressivism."[34] This word is usually defined, as a business leader noted, as "putting the community before one's own business; in the long run, that business will be stimulated. Local government is to encourage what is necessary to make the business go, but it must be on the outside, giving support to local businessmen." Here is the essential ideology of an emerging political regime in this rural town.

However, this expansion needed support from city and county officials who could open up land uses and revenues that would attract new industry. The state was also in a position to help by publicizing the community's interest to industries, but it could not provide revenue. Unfortunately, in this early period after 1965, the support from local officials was negligible. The Batesville merchants needed new ordinances or community referenda to expand locally. But to do that, they also required officeholders with a progressive attitude, which in turn meant removing the old-time, antiexpansion incumbents. The challengers were younger and college educated, had served in the military, were often Baptist (typical in this county), and were sometimes from nearby towns.[35] They agreed that the old school of political dominance that had discouraged new business was now outdated. Consequently, a grand strategy emerged in the mid-1970s to attract new industries. The tactics were first to replace the political incumbents, then to find new land and facilities for new business, and, later, to adjust to the new civil rights laws by hiring blacks. This new "set of solutions" was created by local whites who responded to the market and to mandate requirements arising outside the community.

The Political Challenge of Progressivism

The first tactic was to overthrow the established town boss, Mayor Ferguson. His successful "friends and neighbors" approach of attracting votes in return for favors, and the network of support and patronage linked to local and higher officials, were tough barriers to change. In this early period, the county board had helped defeat a new industrial park (as discussed in the next section), and Ferguson may have purposefully delayed by not meeting deadlines for it. Accordingly, the Batesville progressives had to organize to remove—one by one—the mayor, the city board of aldermen, and the board of supervisors using the electoral process. A long campaign was called for, but it worked surprisingly well.

First Moves toward Development. Changes in local business began with the support of wealthy individuals. For example, Jack Dunlap, a tire distributor, gave land for a new state highway department building from his large land holdings.[36] David Still mobilized merchants to provide $20,000 to buy a hill south of Batesville to fund the Panola Industrial Foundation. When industrial prospects came along, the town could then provide private land and did not need the support of Ferguson. For example, in one case a firm needing ten thousand square feet got the land with much local cooperation. Local officials provided surplus federal bulldozers to clear the land, and a local contractor volunteered a black driver and fuel costs out of his pocket. Dunlap privately provided tires for earth movers and trucks. In the process, the contractor leveled a twenty- or thirty-foot hill in order to create a level site. With the site in place, the business next got a water tower with a public referendum of approval. That project was at first defeated by Ferguson, who alleged that this project was a "play park for Batesville." But a second referendum passed once the factory was built. This effort took about two to three years and led to about seventy-five new jobs.

But job creation by private effort alone could not be used for much expansion. Consequently, a legal authority was organized (as discussed later) that operated across the county under the board of supervisors. But in keeping with part of the Old South traditions, its promise to new prospects was an agreement not to attract new businesses with unions.[37] By the early 1970s Batesville leaders had reached out also to other levels of government; for example, they helped create a federal job corps center training workers from across the state.

In short, development began with a small group of younger business leaders mobilizing private resources to generate new industry. Later, with their successful campaign to remove political old-timers, the progressives would establish a public authority that would attract new industry. This process closely parallels the economic development model noted earlier. That is, by promoting business there would be more jobs, revenues, and public services that would attract even more business. This was clearly a new solution for Panolians, and they set about providing a new local politics to make it work.

First Electoral Changes. The first change in the political system was to find new candidates for office who would accept the new "solution set" and beat the incumbents from the older tradition. The first task was to beat Mayor Ferguson. Progressives selected a promising candidate in Bobby Baker, a realtor, who succeeded Ferguson in 1976, and has since won in every election. City aldermen were subsequently elected who were also open to development (e.g., in the 1990s, Hudson Still, James Yelton, and Bobby Carlisle). There were also some "firsts" in the elections of Willie King and Bobbie Pounders, the first black and female members respectively of the Batesville board of aldermen. Finally, the old guard president of the county board of supervisors, James Travis, a former sheriff, was beaten by David Craig; and another supervisor resigned under indictment for embezzlement during the state's challenge to local corruption (see chapter 2). These changes brought new faces into county offices — like Mack Benson, John Cooper, and William Knox (a banker). Later in the 1980s, two blacks were elected, Robert Avant and Jesse Lyons.

Changes in Governmental Capacity. Later changes occurred in line with this progressive thinking to improve the community's ability to govern itself more efficiently. Much of this change paralleled "modernization events" that were occurring throughout state government.[38] In Batesville, local courts had changed due to state law, as the mayor could no longer act as judge; justice was now overseen not by a merchant in a business suit but by a lawyer in robes. Special favors that had gone to Ferguson's friends were suspended, such as city insurance, which local aldermen contracted to a firm in nearby Clarksdale, where rates were more competitive. City spending was logged into a master computer that dealt with an annual budget that reached $10–$11 million by 1990. The budget process was centralized through a new Department of Public Works that covers all service utilities, and which reports to the city aldermen every five to six weeks.

In the county, as well, a new manager was appointed who illustrates the progressive outlook. David Chandler became county manager in 1987, the first one from outside the county; he had a CPA degree and experience in the state audit department. After this appointment, an election to the county board overturned two white incumbents who were replaced by two blacks (Avant and Lyons) who also supported development. Driven by the state to remove corruption from county government, Panola County — like about forty-five others — was reorganized into a "county unit system" that made two basic changes.

First, there was central purchasing for the whole county for supplies used in each department of government, with weekly requisitions for supplies from stock that had been obtained by competitive bids. The introduction of bids had reduced the cost of bulk goods by 30 to 35 percent in the first year, thereby saving revenue and preventing tax raises. Second, the older system of one "beat" supervisor who controlled all services within his jurisdiction (the most notable example is the supervisor of road services) was abandoned. The board now made general policies applying to all beats, which were then administered through individual departments by its manager.

But for years thereafter, these men still sought to control road services, a rural form of patronage for supporters. Like all changes that seek efficiency, it was opposed by those who preferred favoritism; citizens could no longer get their roads improved by promising bribes or votes. But when this reform came up for renewal in the early 1990s, citizens again supported it, albeit narrowly. Before and after that date, complaints by supervisors and citizens that their roads were poorly maintained exposed the new system to wide criticism. Nevertheless, the traditional culture of patronage politics had been effectively replaced by the more modern, needs-based, and rational system of policy making. In this change, the community moved into the modern age of urban administration.[39]

The New Political Regime of Batesville

These changes in local government created a new kind of political regime, one that is often found in big cities. Major political and economic decisions received informal input from leaders of both races. A local black observer, in comparing these changes, suggested that power had changed from "command to persuasion," as in Atlanta.[40] The individual's power of persuasion in this new climate was strengthened by easier access to government at different levels. When the progressives first met for dinner at the country club or in their homes, they were few in number; but in time these meetings were attended by aldermen, supervisors, and black leaders, whose continuing agenda focused on capital improvements. Their first reach of influence was local, but by 1994, the state and federal officials were involved. In Batesville, the governor helped dig foundations for a large mall, and a U.S. senator helped local businessmen remove the threat of an environmental constraint on an existing business.[41]

Ironically, the new political regime is a mirror image of the Ferguson organization. It differed from the older regime in local goals, in public responsibility, and in the new reality it found itself in as the community changed around it. But both systems were political regimes; one froze existing assets, and the second adapted to social change. It is important to see the details of this new regime, as they are reflected in observations by those involved.

The Progressive Team at Work

By the 1970s, Batesville was slipping economically. Jobs on the farms were down, and there was need for job replacement. "No one liked the idea of

displaced farmhands coming to town, finding no jobs, and going on to welfare," as one businessman noted. But this town did have potential industrial assets. Batesville was served by a good transportation network, two
roads bisecting the county and the Illinois Central railroad.

With the elections of Bobby Baker as mayor in 1976 and, later, of David
Craig as president of the board of supervisors, new political leaders could
now seek industrial growth. A state highway department office was con-
structed. Voters joined in by approving bonds for an industrial park with
access to truck and train routes. After five years of hard work, state senator
Charles Ray Nix secured a bill from the state legislature to construct an
off-ramp from the interstate into the industrial park. The success was due
to strong efforts by local wealthy figures. A similar sign of modernization
was the Batesville city staff learning to prepare applications for state and
federal grants for roads, rail spurs, water, and sewer services. After President Reagan in 1982 turned community block development grants over to
the states, small towns like Batesville could apply and did so successfully.

Recruiting Teams Display the Town

By the late 1980s the industrial recruitment strategies from this new political regime had produced positive effects.[42] In the years ending in 1988,
Batesville had achieved nearly $75 million in investment for local indus-
trial development, doubled its income from industry in eight years to
almost $1 million, and secured 3,256 industrial jobs in a population that
totaled 5,522 in 1980. By the early 1990s, as we will see, these numbers
had increased even more. All these results stemmed from a Batesville "recruitment team" designed to demonstrate to prospective investors that
the town was a good prospect.

The local funding for this operation reveals how local and private sectors
could be combined to achieve success. In 1980–1981 the county Economic
Development Authority was created when state senator Nix successfully
proposed a state law to allow the board of supervisors to appoint one person from each county beat to this authority. This group could issue bonds
to buy, own, sell, and aid property by using the power of eminent domain;
all its actions were backed by county authority. With later amendments,
that law became the legal basis for later development.

Moreover, in 1985, the local chamber of commerce and the Economic
Development Authority were combined, thereby attracting businessmen
who did not like some of the chamber's activities. The Authority held
dinners with state legislators and partially paid the chamber director's
salary. Another venture was a special fund, the Industrial Development
Authority, that could invest funds on a rotating basis.[43] Joining the banker
who created the concept were the mayor, the president of the board of

supervisors, and head of the chamber of commerce and the development director. Later in the 1990s, the Public Improvement Corporation, a non-profit city agency, was used to help build a new public library through a special assessment, and was seeking to help build a new post office away from downtown.[44]

When plant representatives came to see the town, the local recruitment team used members from both public and private sectors, and their tasks are illuminating. Mayor Baker, an ebullient spokesman for the community, was a politician with contacts beyond the city, but his local resources were even better. He had a staff that prepared grants, he enjoyed the support of the city aldermen, and he had the ability to encourage the general public to support referenda for getting new money without using local funds.[45] Another recruiter, David Craig, president of the board of supervisors, was skilled in administration and assisting industrial needs. Charles Nix, over ten years the chamber director into the 1990s, knew his state government could help with development efforts, like arranging visitations. Local banker, J. C. Burns, president of the Industrial Development Authority, was the "detail man" for linking specific local services to plant needs. Add to this team some specialized figures to present favorable community aspects, such as the school superintendent, or the two black leaders, Willie King, city alderman, and Leonard Morris, now state representative. The impression was clearly made that this was an open community that welcomed business by providing land, infrastructure, and even bond support.

Many other Mississippi towns were making a similar effort at this time, as the outside influences were also altering their economic bases. But Batesville's success is seen in the large number of plants that settled there (as shown later), and by state reports of its economic growth. But to achieve such a transformation, a change in politics was required.

The New Political Regime

Note the connections between the public and private sectors in this political regime. Heads of the two governmental bodies, city and county, provide local cooperation to potential investors that are sent by the state's economic development agency. The chamber director gets state help on certain local proposals and arranges a local team for business visits. Such officials are driven not simply by attachment to business but by the idea that *outside* investment multiplies *local* resources. As one noted, "A dollar spent here turns over six or seven times before it leaves the town."[46] The banker makes sure that the new development is legally and financially correct.

Others had similar tasks in bridging local and outside agencies. The school superintendent, David Cole, was highly commended by the state development agency for his work here. His successor, Tommy Wren, explains how well integrated and effective the local schools are, claiming they are in the top 10 percent in the state.[47] Black leaders speak enthusiastically of their community's support of new plants and of their steady work habits. When the occasion arises, voters endorse necessary bond issues. Not surprisingly, then, the state office on federal-state programs has commended Batesville as "one of the boom communities in Mississippi"; it notes that its three state grants had created even more jobs than the applicants anticipated. Moreover, the regional Delta Council also commended the county as a whole for its increase over the last decade in manufacturing employment, tax revenues, and farm production; the first two gains were focused in Batesville.[48]

Other elements contributed their support, especially some wealthy men who first stimulated this development and later donated thousands of dollars privately to help the community. As one merchant noted, "As long as economic development for others goes on, I can sell my goods." Another businessman noted that he and others did not seek personal favors from local government but rather sought an expanded local economic base from which they themselves would thrive. For example, Bob Dunlap, son of the man who was among the first to adopt progressivism after World War II, gave much to the schools and even supported annexing his business location into the town. Well supported by both state parties even though nominally Republican, Dunlap, along with Henry Heafner, a leading car dealer, could bring local problems to the state's attention, including the governor, when help was needed. From one such effort came the new interstate ramp that fed into a new industrial park in the 1980s; by 1994 another governor had approved location signs near the interstate advertising a new outlet mall in Batesville.

One feature of a political regime is its ability to adapt to a changing local context, and that is clearly seen in Batesville. But adaptation was also necessary to deal with the impact of federal laws affecting blacks in schools, voting, and jobs. When black voting was strongly implemented by federal law, the progressives realized that a black alderman would have to join the board of aldermen. After a review, they supported Willie King, as did most blacks from his community on the west side of town. An activist in that community, King was also a supporter of plants because they would secure jobs that he was certain that his neighborhood would need. The same business support was accorded to Leonard Morris in the school district; he had been the key in securing federal grants before being elected to the state legislature in 1993. When blacks were elected to the county board of supervisors in the 1980s, they also agreed to seek plants for jobs.

Indeed, all black leaders interviewed were enthusiastic about the job program, although they wished there were more of them and better ones. Many whites in Batesville, however, were suspicious of these new black supervisors, partly because they were from north Panola and partly over fear of county jobs moving to that race.[49]

This agreement in Batesville on development, regardless of race or position, established common ideas for economic growth, including city-county cooperation over land use and tax programs and consolidated the enthusiastic community support for referenda issues during elections. The leaders of Batesville accepted a certain definition of what problems existed and what solutions were necessary, clearly creating a "solution set."[50] In coming to this acceptance, public officials and private merchants could satisfy both the community's concerns and their own business and professional needs. Clearly, such solution sets "enhance the value of their fixed assets by attracting mobile capital to the city."[51] The word "enhance" had real meaning in Batesville. As a local banker noted, someone putting $20,000 in his own bank in the 1950s would have been worth $750,000 in 1990.

Black Perspectives on Economic Change

While whites in the new political regime sought and approved the changes, what were the perspectives of blacks? Their views present a more complex picture, although it is widely accepted that the new laws brought favorable changes for them. Blacks, too, accepted the ideology and solutions of development policy. Some of their views are illuminating.

A black leader noted the back-room nature of deals that had once existed under the earlier white-dominated regime. But now the new leaders had created a relatively open regime that actually sought black input and provided benefits for blacks. They agreed that the new regime recognized the need for more jobs and better education in order to deal with the poverty of whites and blacks. However, they know well that they are still slighted socially; for example, no black has been invited to join the country club and no black was admitted to the Rotary Club until 1994 (when Leonard Morris became a member).

However, there now exist open meetings enforced by state law that allow public participation for inputs and decision making. In the private sector, blacks regularly report that the local economy treats them differently from before the appearance of federal laws. Banks now treat them much better; "There you are called by name with titles of 'Mr.' or 'Mrs.'— no 'boy' or 'girl' label nowadays!" However, few blacks get positions in the Batesville Security Bank, although one is a loan officer. But almost all black leaders interviewed did use this bank for their own accounts.

As one black leader noted, the progressive leaders did make changes in the economy and did ameliorate racial relationships in order to fit the new reality. On racial matters, one noted, "Early on, they told me informally that they wanted to change things and they did." Now, many matters are first "run by" black leaders to get their approval, for example, in public appointments. But they believe that behind this change were not only new men but also new law that had changed the context for whites as well as for them.

Another black professional emphasized, as did many, how this difference distinguishes the two sections of the county, and the positive consequences for blacks living below the Tallahatchie River. On the other hand, he noted, both white and black leaders "have a way of squashing things that would hurt the community. They have networks that can effectively do this. They would go to those local people directly involved, get someone who can talk to him—no use for a gun in the head for all of this—and show how their problem can be worked out another way."

Law's Effects on Jobs

It is clear that job discrimination was dramatically reduced by federal laws. Affirmative action opened the door for many blacks, who took advantage of their new opportunities. One Batesville plant (Parker Hannifin) employs about 70 percent blacks, and Panola Mills also had a high percentage until it folded in 1996. Black leaders now are aware of a curious contradiction about these new jobs. Their people have shown they can handle them, but nevertheless there is still great poverty. A large minority of blacks, almost half in the county, can do no better than live on the welfare rolls.

There are some exceptions to all this change. A black merchant noted how newcomers to the community seeking jobs had also brought in more crime. This is a local version of the "outside agitator" story, the outsider is blamed as the source of local problems. More important, though, there were widespread complaints of white discrimination in the local plants, not in hiring but in promotion. A common complaint was that "whites are hired alongside experienced blacks, but then the whites move on up over that of the blacks." There are a few black supervisors in these plants, but two plants (Parker Hannifin and Thermos) have black personnel directors.

Black concerns over promotions face the reality principle of organizational hierarchy. Not every one can be chief in an organization, for the specialization of labor keeps most personnel at the bottom. But if there is prejudice in the plants, blacks now know how to approach it. One black professional noted a case of a northern firm with a plant in Batesville where blacks had complained of "racist" attitudes among the other workers (i.e., blacks were being implied as inferior). But there were enough complaints from local leaders to move the company to educate its personnel.

Another exception to racial harmony in jobs lies in the distribution of public employment; in county jobs, as before, patronage still operates. When the first black supervisor was elected in the mid-1980s, he found all the courthouse jobs were white. In opening those positions to blacks, despite some whites' opposition, he was nevertheless encouraged by a white board president, David Craig, an early candidate of the progressives. However, as noted, some whites on either side of the river still fear that a black majority on the board of supervisors would replace white jobs in the two county courthouses. Black leaders deny that possibility. But in other southern counties where blacks came to dominate, such racial patronage has occurred, as it did earlier for all ethnic groups in big cities when they finally came to power. The small number of public jobs may well reduce the size of the problem for blacks, but it also is evident their leaders know how to manipulate the system to seek even more opportunities.

Another form of discrimination reported by blacks lies in some merchants' treatment of consumers. A federal program of the Legal Services Corporation, headed by a Batesville black lawyer and staff, handle such consumer complaints. A staff member estimated that 60 to 65 percent of their work involves claims of whites cheating blacks. This result may stem from the white misperception that this agency is just for blacks (i.e., white consumers would not turn to it for help), or from the fact that there are more white businesses than black. The same staff member noted, though, some of the white businessmen's attitudes when they call in response to consumer complaints:

> Whites resent this effort when called to task. I handle much work on the phone and many don't know I'm black. They will rant on about "nigger," and then suddenly ask if I'm black. Finding this, the white often says, "Didn't mean any harm." But their real feelings had emerged earlier, when thinking the caller was equal.
>
> But I understand this as they are the product of their culture. If your lives are dependent on racial contact, you must cover up racism. *Without such law, without dependent relationship between races, you would see it like it was twenty-five to thirty years ago.* By acting out another reality, like being "progressive," they can make real a new perception. Twenty years from now, when the kids are

coming up, they will say, "That child is my friend regardless of race." We work together now, but we are not there yet.

Clearly, this is a sophisticated view of change, but one that is quite understanding of prejudice. This view was also often heard among both races in evaluating change, that is, as another black noted, "Things are never right, but they're getting better."

Hirings and Affirmative Action

The shift in local employment from agriculture to industrialism is visible in the hiring of many blacks in the county's new plants. In 1968, only one black—a woman—had gone to court over job discrimination, as whites dominated the local job market. Twenty years later when this research began, blacks dominated hiring in the many new local plants; we have noted the numbers. The question is, did law bring this change about?

One finding that is clear from the last quarter-century is that federal law was *not* a direct instrument of such change. Records of the U.S. Civil Rights Division show that it was not called on to deal with discrimination in jobs in this county. Personal recollections of local business leaders do not recall federal involvement, something they would be certain to recall, given the tight little economic islands of small towns. And yet, massive change took place.

A study by James Button, which provides a careful explanation of economic and other changes in six Florida small towns, points to varying rates of change among Old South and New South types of communities. He found that "the vast majority of business in the communities studied have employed blacks, and they have done so since the mid-1960s."[52] But who got what kinds of jobs is significant. Proportional racial representation in jobs was achieved or exceeded *only* in unskilled or menial positions in business; in the hiring of professional or skilled labor, it took affirmative action to increase black representation. Leaders of bigger businesses in Button's study reported that "they were going out of their way to hire blacks and therefore had a formal or informal affirmative action program." Curiously, the Old South community in these Florida towns hired even more than the New South communities, a finding true for all types of work. That is, once the barrier was broken, other businesses joined in, as many believed that "it was good for business" to hire blacks. As Button concludes, "economic incentives may have finally superseded certain racial fears."

Batesville and Sardis fit the distinction of New South and Old South communities that Button found in Florida. When plant directors in both places were asked for the reasons behind the change in black employment in recent decades, they sound much like their Florida counterparts. They reported that desegregation had been a "bitter pill." But they also underwent rather quickly a change in their cognition of the economic reality around them; that is, they felt they had to "buckle up" to face these changes. In Batesville the "progressive" businessmen, noted earlier, sought to bring new plants to the area to provide jobs that, in turn, would hire more blacks. Some managers interviewed reported they had received word from higher up in the corporation to hire blacks, and they did so by creating black "human resources" directors to advise them on such change.

As the town's economic development plan expanded and as more plants arrived, there was a great need for such labor. One of the largest plants in 1984 had about 700 total employees, but hired only a few blacks; under corporate pressure the total workforce increased five years later to about 1,200 employees, 55 percent of them black. By the early 1990s, major businesses—and even a few small ones to judge from observations—were hiring large numbers of blacks; one large plant had 65 percent blacks hired by the 1990s. The explanation was that, as the "application flow" became more black, plants hired them. Similarly, managers sought to employ more women for jobs traditionally done by men; but late-night shifts did not suit women with families and children. Yet, said one manager, "We encouraged blacks and women to apply, and we hired many. We deliberatly tried to do what was right, and not be in violation of any law."

Summary

The record of race and the economy in Panola County is mixed, but clearly the mix is different from that of a quarter century ago. As a black leader noted about federal law, speaking for almost all blacks interviewed, *"I wouldn't have my present job if it weren't for that law."* All agreed that with the development stimulated by the progressives there came more jobs for them and other blacks. While few made it very high in the hierarchy of work, figures show (see later this chapter) that hundreds do have jobs amid a sea of poverty.

Moreover, other kinds of jobs became open to blacks. Today they include car salesperson, cleaner, house painter, garage owner, and even doctor, lawyer, nurse, and pharmacist. Newspaper accounts feature such blacks in their stories. As a white outsider noted, after living around the state where he had seen many towns like this, "A middle-class society had developed in Batesville since I arrived fifteen years ago." That condition compares starkly with Clarksdale to the west, deep in the Delta, where the poverty is even greater, with little industry to provide work opportunities. In Batesville, though, many find jobs in the private sector, and their income generates a healthy economy that is the pride of townspeople and the envy of Sardis. All know that this change would not have been possible were it not for the leadership of progressives of both races following new federal laws with job opportunities. Quite often, the largely white leadership of Batesville attracted the new plants, and the largely black workers filled the new jobs. Here again we see that law worked to create a new reality that, in turn, created new possibilities for viewing race in new ways.

The Local Economy of Sardis

No clearer proof of differing realities can be seen than by comparing the rational boosterism of Batesville with the sluggish economy of Sardis, two towns separated by fifteen miles. The comparison also shows how a once-dominant reality can delay the emergence of a new political regime. Here again, the lack of a solution set to fit the new reality prevented white leaders from adapting to change.

Decline and Indifference

The earlier ideology of Sardis had once created a strong agricultural economy, but circumstances had changed around it. New ideas were needed but were unwelcome, yet without them the political economy declined. However, some recent efforts to emulate Batesville in development means that the local economy now looks much like Batesville did twenty-five years ago.

Towns in this section of the county look abandoned. In Sardis, as one white leader recalls, when he was young there were three grocery stores thriving on the main street, with one open late in the evening. But in 1994, only one still exists. Crenshaw, in the west of the county and down on the Delta, still has one bank, but closed stores dominate its downtown. In the east of the county, Como, once the richest town, has had only one new business firm appear since 1975 (bringing over seventy-five jobs); a recent and fine restaurant was also backed by local businessmen. This withering away of these small towns in Panola County has also happened across the rest of rural America. But it was exacerbated here by the reluctance of leaders in the Delta culture to change with changing times. Some still criticize Batesville's efforts and are critical of development. However, new leaders are now appearing who seem more open to change.

Interviews confirm this point, but there is one notable indicator of these lingering attitudes in the local newspaper's coverage of economic development, in which it contrasts with Batesville's paper. We should expect that a city that favors development would have a paper that runs more stories on the economy than a city that did not. A content analysis of stories and editorials featuring the state economy, state-local economic analyses, and

Table 8.2 Number of Items on Economic News in Two County
Weeklies, Panola County, Selected Decades

Topic	1960		1970		1980		1990	
	TP	SR	TP	SR	TP	SR	TP	SR
Economic data	12	3			23	23	1	3
New plants	7	5	18	6	10	9	4	2
Local business	6	2	2	1	2	1	9	14
State business	5	4	11	1	6	3	1	2
Other	—	—	—	—	—	—	15	4
Total	30	12	31	8	41	36	30	25

Note: Content analysis totals for each issue in each year. TP is *The Panolian*, based in Batesville, and SR is the *Southern Reporter*, based in Sardis. The item measured is the story, regardless of length, or size and number of photographs (usually found in pp. 1–2 of each issue). 1990 data are derived from a sample of issues; others are a census of all issues.

new local plants and local business shows that this is indeed the case. The years covered in the analysis were 1960, 1970, 1980, and 1990, and the differences are quite clearly shown in table 8.2.

In 1960 and 1970 *The Panolian* in Batesville exceeded the *Southern Reporter* in the number of stories it printed on all types of economic news. From early on, when Hunt Howell was editor, and more recently with his sons, Rupert and John, *The Panolian* has consistently supported development. The number of local plants was to increase greatly after 1980, yet even before that the Batesville newspaper was giving more attention to many aspects of the economy. This Hill culture paper also gave space to other stories related to the economy (not shown in the table). Thus in 1960, there were more stories in this paper than in the *Southern Reporter* on the need for land-use controls (14 to 3), and in 1970 on a concern for environmental problems (14 to 0). Meanwhile, the *Southern Reporter* gave not only less space to economic development generally, it also focused on different economic issues. Thus in 1960, it published more stories on trade unions (14 items, always highly critical) than on local businesses (7 items). *The Panolian* ran no stories on unions, either for or against.

One measure of the growing influence of economic development in this county is reflected in newspaper space devoted to the topic at the end of the next decade as seen in table 8.2. By 1980 both newspapers gave close to equal space (41 in the *Reporter*, 36 in *The Panolian*), whether dealing with local and state economic data, new plants (rumored or in place), or local business activity. Another decade later, in 1990, both papers gave almost the same space to economic development (30 in the *Reporter*, 25 in *The Panolian*), but their distribution was different by topic, as the *South-*

ern Reporter wrote more about local business. In short, a quarter century after the advent of federal law, the newspapers were clearly featuring the significance of business in their coverage, mirroring what was happening in the county.

New Response to Decline

Regardless of race, current leaders in north Panola now see their relative decline as linked to the earlier white leaders whose traditionalist culture was unable to adapt to changing times. The earlier leaders, witnessing all the changes in their world, expressed bitterness and frustration in their interviews. The universe had moved but they had not, and so they had lost mastery of society. Their control of local life had dissipated, not simply by blacks getting the vote or attending desegregated schools ("our schools," said several). They complained that farming was no longer as profitable, their children were uninterested in farming, and persons of both races were coming to political power who had new ideas about local society. Many older people see society in acute decay, if not outright perdition, but this sense of decline expressed by the older plantocrats was shot through with deeply bitter feelings.

Other criticisms came from newer holders of local office in north Panola. Until the late 1980s, there had been no aggressive chamber of commerce in Sardis and no plans for economic development. There were complaints about the timidity of Sardis and Como banks in lending money for new businesses. Critics say that while the local population has not grown, their problems are mounting. Thus, Sardis has the same population today as in earlier decades, when it had only a marshal and night watchman, but the range of local crime has grown even without population change.

Changes did occur in north Panola. They emerged slowly in the 1980s and involved both races. The political role of blacks had greatly increased with a majority on the school board and a near majority on the county board of supervisors.[53] Another change was that a new generation of leaders of both races agreed on the need for more development. A turning point was the election in Sardis in 1989 of a new white mayor, Richard Darby, who energetically sought more industry. He met with black leaders, both political and religious, to discuss this need; they then formed recruiting teams to meet with plant representatives. Mayor Darby energized the chamber of commerce in the late 1980s, even though its director works only part-time and has a tiny office.

What could the city offer to prospective investors? Darby could show them a new industrial park with a railroad spur to the Illinois Central line, easy access to the interstate, the nearby Memphis airport, and the fact that Sardis is a small community regarded as good for bringing up families. But there were other local conditions that were difficult to surmount, especially its poor schools. Batesville had the same economic benefits, a stronger record of accomplishment, and better schools.

However, Sardis was slowly changing as development found support among local officials, some businessmen, and black leaders. No "old family" names are found in the local government; the last "old family" member had left the town's aldermen in the early 1990s. One early example of success in Sardis's effort to develop came early in Darby's administration. Sardis had lost its hospital, despite a campaign involving important local people. But that loss was overcome when the Methodist Health System of Memphis was recruited to construct a $400,000 health care facility on five acres near the interstate highway. It opened in 1994. The result was due to a community effort that helped overcome many local differences.

In short, we see in Sardis the tentative emergence of a new political regime and the creation of a solution set for crucial local problems, a pattern set earlier in Batesville. There is an energetic leader in the mayor; in 1993, he converted the office to full-time with a larger salary commensurate to that of other area mayors.[54] Significantly, leaders of both races agree that the area needs jobs, and that jobs that are best obtained from new plants. There are two other opportunities for local job growth. One is to provide for retirees from nearby Memphis and its suburbs (more than half the adults in east Sardis are white retirees). Another is to cater to the growing recreational facilities in nearby Sardis Lake, a program that Darby led in its planning stages with state and federal officials in the mid-1990s. But Sardis is still well behind Batesville in development. One reason may be that there is little wealth behind the Sardis change, compared with Batesville. There are serious problems in recruiting plants, such as the weak schools, limited housing, and a downtown that looks abandoned, despite the personal efforts of citizens to clear up areas.

As the community alters its economic base, Sardis is filled with fears as well as hopes about these changes. By attracting more blacks as workers, new industry might upset the 60 to 40 percent ratio of white and black voters in Sardis by which a white majority of aldermen is maintained. Many whites in east Sardis are elderly people or out-of-towners who do not favor the new taxes that would be needed to support change (including badly needed school bonds). Local businessmen feared that any excessive competition from nearby towns would leave Sardis the loser, especially with its reputation of weak schools.

But those fears seem to have faded in the early 1990s as Darby and his supporters sought more plants. In 1989, the first citizens' biracial committee of women was appointed by the mayor to improve both white and black sections of the Sardis cemetery. Blacks and whites also cooperated to stop others from creating a new landfill near Sardis. Finally, Darby was planning, with the U.S. Army Corps of Engineers, to create a complex arrangement of annexation and new sewers near Sardis Lake designed to attract new housing. Nevertheless, little else appeared throughout this section of the county. In Como, some changes appeared when the town, with its 70 percent black population, elected a white mayor who led small changes until his defeat in 1993. His emphasis was upon developing the community through citizen involvement activities, like the neighborhood watch. Plants are still being sought, of course, but the prospects for Como are weak. No other community in either section of the county has made a concerted effort to adapt to economic change except Batesville and Sardis.

A Sketch of Economic Developments in Sardis and Batesville

Drawing on newspaper reports in these two towns, we can summarize what emerged in the 1990s.[55]

In 1989, employment had been weak in the state but was improving in the county. In Sardis, there was a new chamber of commerce office and a new factory making wooden pallets. In Batesville, the governor twice appeared to open two new firms (manufacturing caskets and pipes). There was news of a forthcoming Wal-Mart store; an editorial worried that this addition was a "mixed blessing."[56] Also, photographs were published of blacks in local plants who had won employee awards.

In 1990, Sardis reported formation of its Main Street Business Association of downtown merchants and property owners to improve business.

In 1991, Sardis reported some gains; bids were solicited for a city marina at nearby Sardis Lake, a new playhouse arrived, the interstate ramp was built, and local streets were cleaned up.[57] But a review of this year finds no new plants, although some local businesses did change hands.

In Batesville, 1991 was a year of planning for new changes. A new upscale housing development of $2.4 million to house 2,600 was announced, and local government clearance for it was sought. Partners owning the division included Bob Dunlap and Henry Heafner, leading businessmen and early leaders of the progressives. Hopes for creating a new trade union in the casket company were dashed when only 31 percent of its workers supported it. *The Panolian* reported that its paper was the largest weekly in the state. And with respect to the farms surrounding these communities, reports showed that commodities in their county had the highest value in the state, but for the third year in a row there were fewer farmers and they were earning less.

Plans for Batesville appeared in 1991 in a two-volume report on the town for the year 2010. It was prepared by a city planner; the local paper covered it in three weekly editions. The projections reflect optimism about local growth based on past efforts. Town population, industry, and commerce would grow, it predicted, even though the county's population and farm jobs would drop. Industry would be the biggest provider of jobs in Batesville and the county, followed closely by professional and related services, like sales. The first industrial park would be filled, while a second would require more planning.

In 1992, Sardis reported a new industry (plastics, 175 jobs); the chamber of commerce noted that five firms had produced almost a thousand jobs, even though one had closed that summer. A few small businesses opened in Sardis: a restaurant, a skating rink, antique and appliance shops, rental storage units, and a new primary care diagnostic center. Business was even better in Batesville, especially for local building. Despite a national recession, over $4.8 million was spent on building (one-sixth more than in the previous year); one-half was in new homes and commercial buildings. Batesville aldermen approved a road bond for the new housing division, as well as local money for its sewers and roads. The taxes would help the town, supporters claimed, but black alderman Willie King opposed it because new sewers were not yet paid for in some places, namely, his neighborhood. The Wal-Mart did open, with ten of sixty-one employees black and the manager a white woman.

By 1994 then, a new land project was created east of Batesville and along the interstate. It set aside 251 acres for a second industrial park, and six major industrial prospects were under consideration. These changes would create a housing crunch (only 320 homes were built in Batesville the previous decade); many commuters might live here if housing were more available (e.g., professionals). Consequently, a second land development was undertaken privately, with 420 acres for housing of middle- to high-income ranges. There is still a need for more schools and firehouses in that development.

The year 1994 also saw the first signs of a bridge between the cultural divisions of Panola County in the common need for business and employment. A 1993 study reflects the satisfaction of businessmen with workers in the county. A biracial county team (consisting of a white banker, a white realtor, a black plant superintendent, and a black school teacher) from both towns organized a fifteen-month study to revitalize their economy; the study was funded privately and managed by the University of Mississippi. Its first report, based on a poll of local businessmen, reported that workers had excellent attitudes toward productivity but problems still existed in recruiting any but unskilled labor. Typically, businessmen were dissatisfied most with welfare and worker compensation programs at the state level, and with roads and schooling at the local level. Still, they felt it was an excellent place to do business both for work activity and the quality of life.[58]

This search for common programs cannot override the long-term effects of differing cultural responses to development in these two towns. Table 8.3 shows the consequences for Batesville, with its longer adaptation to change, and for Sardis. Yet these job totals should also be tied to the population size. Sardis's population in 1990 was about one-third that of Batesville (2,128 compared to 6,403), but it has about the same ratio of jobs to population as Batesville does. Other influences overriding local cultural effects lie in the tides of the marketplace. Shifts in the national economy can move these plants in and out of town with little control by locals. Consequently, estimating differences between the towns is not something that can be done with precision. In Sardis, one large plant entered in mid-1994, but another left in 1995. The largest plant in Batesville (Panola Mills) left in 1995, with a loss of about 1,200 jobs.

Economic development in this county, then, has followed the great shift in the county's job base from farming to manufacturing. As Figure 8.1 shows, changes in the economy and federal laws transformed Panola from an agricultural community to an industrial one, especially for blacks. Where whites once had a few more of the limited manufacturing jobs than blacks, blacks now dominate that occupation; about one-half of the black workforce worked in plants in 1990 compared to about one-quarter of the white workforce. Farm jobs had nearly vanished in that year for both races, so that 5 percent or less of the jobs in Panola were in farming; three-quarters of the blacks and over 40 percent of the jobs had been in farming forty years earlier.

Economic development policy in this county has clearly had great impact on jobs and business for over the last quarter century, particularly in the last dozen years. Cultural differences between the two cities should not mask the important consequences of this policy. One may simply compare conditions in places that did not make this effort, as in some Delta towns. The policy's success is seen in the praises that state agencies gave to Panola's effort. But for local people, getting these jobs marked a transformation in their lives from farming to industrial. Whatever the limits imposed on them by the new industrialism, they also enjoyed the income and status of full-time workers, unlike many others in the county. These others were the large proportion of the poor who lived across the county.

For amid the benefits of development policy, where new jobs helped many, there was still widespread poverty, which affected many more. The poverty data shown in table 8.1 provided a clear sign of the problem in the Panola towns and in Mississippi in general. In Panola County in 1990,

Table 8.3   Industries Located in Batesville and Sardis, Panola County, 1994

Name	Product	Workers
	Batesville	
Panola Mills, Inc.	Briefs, T-shirts	1,200
Thermos Co.	Vacuum bottles, ice chests	500
Parker-Hannifin	Car air conditioner parts	315
Crown Cork & Seal	Aluminum cans, crowns	280
Framed Picture Enterprise	Wall decorations	280
Batesville Casket Co.	Caskets	246
Moog Batesville	Car engine parts	218
Dunlap & Kyle Co.	Rubber strip stock	150
ACI Building Systems	Metal buildings	139
Batesville American Mfg.	Metal stampings	100
Air Kontrol, Inc.	Air filters	95
Insituform Technologies	Replacement piping	81
Custom Sign Co.	Signs, contracting	50
Kroger/Delta Frozen Food	Frozen food distribution	50
Plaspros, Inc.	Injection molding	42
Accu-Tech Plastics	Injection molding	30
Med-Service, Inc.	Hospital furniture	30
Muscle Shoals Rubber Co.	Molded rubber products	30
Tucker Mfg. Co.	Football equipment	30
Total		3,486
	Sardis	
Dawson Home Fashion, Inc.	Shower curtains	390
ArmorBond Building Products	Vinyl siding	200
Irwin Schwabe	Men's work shirts	130
Lawn-Boy, Inc.	Lawn motors, heaters	100
Mini Systems, Inc.	Metal buildings	30
Coca Cola/Dr. Pepper Bottling Co.	Bottled soft drinks	27
Pulsar Plastics, Inc.	Injection moldings	25
Inca Presswood Pallets, Ltd.	Wooden pallets	25
M-2 Corporation	Wood products	15
Martin Brothers	Scrap metal	12
Total		954

Source: Chamber of commerce reports from both towns, mid-1994.

Note: Excludes newspaper employment. Panola Mills, of Batesville, closed in 1995.

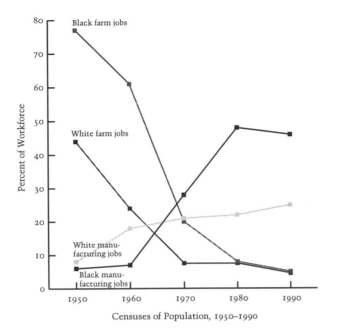

Figure 8.1. Shift in Employment Base by Race, Panola County, 1950–1990

one person in four and one family in five were below the poverty level. In most of its towns, the level of individual poverty was somewhat higher. The county itself was somewhat better off than Mississippi as a whole in measures of poverty, employment, and housing condition.

A stark differentiation by race is evident in these figures. One in eight whites was poor in 1990, but so were almost one in two blacks. Poverty is a regular element of black reality here and elsewhere in the South. Without the jobs for blacks that are found in these small plants, the poverty rate for Panola's blacks would approach 75 percent. As a historical comparison, about 25 percent were jobless in the Great Depression in the 1930s. Today's figures for the county and state suggest that economic depression is still pervasive and widespread among both races.

Washington as Subsidizer of All Classes

For the poor, assistance for the spirit is provided by the local churches, but for the body, much comes from afar—from Washington. While that linkage is the subject of much white criticism, what is not understood is that relationship also exists not only for the poor but also for the middle and wealthy classes. In the form of benefits paid out of tax revenues, both the rich and the poor receive "welfare" from the government, in accordance with its distributive or regulatory policies.[59] To complete this picture of Panola County's economy, and of local economies elsewhere in the nation, let us look at these more closely.

Distributive Policies

By using public funds to advance private goals, governmental subsidies are used to undertake an action that government wishes to reward. Subsidies include payments in kind, grants, low-interest loans, provisions in the tax code (that is, forgiven or lowered taxation), and licenses or franchises. Rural Mississippians have known federal subsidies for six decades in the form of farm subsidies for parity payments or of loan programs for agricultural development. In 1954, a committee of the Republican Eisenhower administration noted that Mississippi had received a gamut of federal services without which its economy would not have thrived. As a state legislator told that committee, "States rights is a shibboleth."

Today, federal subsidies provide Mississippians with more income than any other single source in that state. The amount of federal funds for this state is impressive: $1.5 million in 1930 had grown to $8 million after World War II and to $40 million by the mid-1950s. Twelve years later, the total was an astounding $454 million. Federal expenditures on defense, veterans, social programs, and farmers were estimated at $1.4 billion—about 30 percent of all the state's receipts. By 1967, federal subsidy was the state's second largest source of income (manufacturing was first, tourism third, and farming a weak fourth). Amid all that cascade of dollars, Panola County in that year had received $12.5 million, half as much again as the entire state had received after World War II.[60]

These distributive funds helped create an economy for Mississippi that enabled it to survive by posting a modest growth in business and agriculture. Moreover, in the next quarter century after 1967, more funds were added, not only for farming but for such items as hospitals, mass transportation, water and sewage plants, revenue sharing, university grants, and deferred taxes for certain investments. Many other groups benefited from the growth in distributive programs, which created more jobs in home construction and greater health benefits from hospitals. It is no overstatement that Mississippi's economy grew primarily from this single source, even though its total economy is still below that of other states.

Redistributive Policies

Another type of financial policy is redistributive, in which the government shifts income from one group to another in order to meet approved goals. This policy is popularly and politically viewed as one in which one group gains public funds and another loses it, through taxes. Most think of this as a shift of funds to benefit the poor; however, across all these exchanges of benefits and taxes, the middle class or wealthy benefit more. The classic examples in federal tax policy are, first, the mortgage deduction for home ownership, widely available to the middle class, and second, tax advantages to aid investment for those with capital. I noted earlier that the total federal mix of policies strongly favors the already advantaged.

But for the poor of the South, there has been a long history of blacks seeking racial economic justice through redistributive policies. One survey of this "pursuit of racial justice" in five southern counties finds an impressive record of blacks pursuing a "politics of hope" that was relatively successful, but only in recent years.[61] In Panola County, these redistributive programs included

- prohibition of racial or gender discrimination in employment (perhaps coupled with affirmative action requirements);
- government-sponsored health care for the indigent;
- income maintenance (e.g., welfare and tax credits);
- employment and training programs; and
- food stamps[62]

It is this matrix of supportive redistributive policy that marks the lives of a large majority of the blacks in Panola County.

Law and Economic Benefits

An economy is not simply a matter of exchanging goods and services; rather, it involves altering options to improve one's life. Clearly, the provisions of jobs in this county meant a better quality of life for job holders. Economic rights, then, refer to both this exchange and to the options available to the rights holder. Those rights may exist within the private economy, arrived at through market negotiations between buyer and seller. But they may also be regulated or subsidized by laws designed to defend or rearrange benefits in the interest of buyer or seller. By subsidy or regulation, then, law acts to change the distribution of life options.[63]

This was the situation a quarter century ago in Panola County. As the civil rights movement was first descending upon the county in the mid-1960s, economic rights were also being established. There were twenty-two new programs during that Great Society era, created under thirteen federal agencies that provided close to $8 million dollars to many Panolians. These included Medicare and Medicaid, hospital and industrial park construction, city planning, farm worker training, promotion of economic growth, recreation, a new library, a new bridge, a munitions firm, and five water systems.[64] Alongside existing support programs for farmers, there was also "welfare" aid to senior citizens and to the blind, to dependent children, and to the disabled. All these subsidies touched two-thirds or more of the black citizens of Panola.

While such programs are highly criticized by many whites across the nation, this degree of assistance demonstrates that redistribution is hardly possible to achieve by any government except the national one. That is, the local community is limited in power, will, and resources to redistribute to this extent. This means that local values, resources, and power systems will block local effort to correct social and economic problems. However, at the national level, there are more resources and greater will to do the job, at least until the conservative reaction of the mid-1990s began to challenge this arrangement.[65] Washington has thus been a major contributor to the local economy and to its life options. The siren song of federal money was eagerly accepted in the South despite a rhetoric of "states' rights." Clearly, southerners did not let ideology stand in the way of a good thing when it came to receiving benefits. Nor did they let their ideology blind them to a good bet when they saw redistributive policies that relieved state and local governments from addressing economic ills generated by the Old South's view of reality.

As for the use of federal regulation to enhance economic rights, in the early period racial policies on employment were weakly enforced. But that stance has given way to a much fuller compliance in hiring, due first to court and congressional actions outside county borders, and then to local business people needing black labor. Consequently, by 1990 black complaints to Washington were not about obstacles to hiring, but about promotion to higher positions. Blacks fear that this current form of discrimination can be little affected by federal law. Yet the law did make it possible to get such jobs and make such appeals. And of course, the occasional black does make it up to the supervisor level. The problem of "oneness," as one black leader noted, lets only a single black rise in any local system, despite the presence of a large black population. That limit, demonstrated in this book, limits opportunities in the political and economic aspirations of this group.

Political Economy, Power, and Culture

This chapter has demonstrated the important links between the local economy and the public arena. Through the influence of federal law, distributive policies have brought Mississippi and Panola County into the industrial age. But the influence of these external factors was mediated by the local factor of cultural divisions among whites. Those divisions rested on differences in attitudes about the quality of life and about solutions for problems; indeed, these were actually differences in reality itself. The differences in culture revealed themselves in the community's practical approaches to development, seen in local leaders' cognitions, in commercial development, and in local newspapers' articles.

But that difference is slowly fading. Batesville's leadership in economic development is being copied in Sardis, as the Delta culture gradually adopts this "solution set." In both towns there has emerged a new generation with new ideas about the economy that flow from a new political regime. Indeed, by mid-1994 the progressive bank of Batesville was considering consolidation with a leading bank in Sardis, an unusual merger, given the county's divisive history. Industrialism, feared by some early in this century, is now eagerly sought for the jobs and business it brings. Without it, the local economy weakens and the local community declines into bitter despair; other Delta towns know well that reality. Evidence from towns in many regions shows that the failure to seek a new local economy must weaken the old reality. The development approach, as demonstrated in Panola County, can contribute to the larger cultural sense that forms the New South today.

Part III | Internal and External Concepts of Race and Law

We noted in the previous section that the interactions of law and local institutions in politics, education, and the economy provide evidence of the book's thesis on how law creates a new reality. It is time now to trace evidence of this reality in the cognitions of Panolians. We find them reflected in the newspapers that reflect changes in the new reality, in changes in the language of race, and in black and white observations on change in local life.

These changes have consequences for both local institutions and local persons through the progressive enforcement of the law. Thus we may ask, how did institutions and persons alter over time such that they ended up in a new social reality with new cognitions? As we trace these changes, we can reconstruct the nature of local life, noting what law accomplished—and what it did not—in the New South.

9 | Local Perspectives on Race and Law

In Panola County, we have witnessed changes of individual and institutional behavior that also imply a change in the attitudes that lie behind them. For example, bloc voting still occurs when candidates are black and white, yet there was a strong minority of white votes for an accomplished black legislator. We have noted that the presence of black voters has sensitized white officials to respond to some of their needs. In education, we have noted that desegregated white students have different attitudes from segregated whites. Further, amid the mushrooming industrialism of Batesville, managers have opened entry-level jobs to many blacks that had been denied them a quarter century ago; but only a few blacks have risen above entry-level jobs. We see not only change, but a complex set of racial attitudes that has emerged.

Recall that there are two important considerations that underlie these changes. First, a new generation is now in the positions of institutional power. In this generation, only a few whites support the violence that was once the hallmark of race relations in the Old South. It is indicative of how far the South has come that in a review of fifteen types of racial hatred in 1993 (bombings, arson, assaults) in 156 incidents across the nation none occurred in Mississippi.[1] Of course, other aspects of traditional racism have not fully vanished, as both races now disagree over the meaning of "racism." The relevant point is that both now can talk about the issue. The second consideration that is relevant here is the availability of federal and state law to empower blacks against the uglier aspects of racism and poverty. But, as we will see, it was not only law that empowered the blacks; some whites themselves moved to support black objectives.

To explore these points, this chapter uses two types of analysis to review a quite complex set of attitudes in this county's version of the New South. First, we will look for evidence in local newspaper reports of that new reality, and second, we present reports from both races of what they saw and felt about these changes. The first reflects large-scale events that shaped the new reality, and the second provides the personal dimension of these events.

Newspaper Shifts in Racial Views

Throughout this book we have used the two county weeklies because they reflect white viewpoints of important events in community life over a quarter century. Of course, not every locally important issue makes it to these pages, for example, gossip, scandal, or discussion of motivations. But it is the events they cover that are important to our analysis. We have found that the two newspapers reflect two white positions, the traditional culture of the Old South versus the new attitudes on race and economic progressivism of the New South.

A Twenty-Year Perspective of Coverage

The *Southern Reporter* of north Panola and *The Panolian* of south Panola are more than just business enterprises. Of course, as businesses they seek to expand their market to increase profits, but how they define "market" has until recently been confined to the white community. Moreover, we have noted that in recent decades *The Panolian* did not follow the traditional line in dealing with black issues like voting and desegregation, and it was clearly more open to economic development that would provide more jobs for both races. Consequently, it seems likely that if a paper is theoretically more open to a new market, such as the black community, then, over time, it would cover more stories of interest to that market. From what we have noted throughout the book, however, we should expect the two papers to differ in their openness to market interest. This analysis is incomplete, however, because not all stories identify the races involved. For example, if a news item from a hamlet like Pope does not identify any race, we cannot include it in the total count of newspaper coverage, unless there are accompanying photographs that do identify blacks.

Such data enable us to ask a key question: In market terms, how much and what aspects of black life were presented before civil rights in the old reality, as compared with the new? To answer that question, we analyzed the coverage in every issue for three separate census years. In 1960 we observe the traditional scene of the Old South, in 1970 there is a transitional period, and in 1980 the law had been in force for some time. Of course, this is only a sampling of these papers' responses to markets, but the trend is suggestive of whether their editors sense a new market among the blacks. Table 9.1 provides the data for those three years on selected topics.

In the traditional culture of 1960, blacks were rarely featured in any aspect of their lives. The stories that were published focused mainly on farm

Table 9.1   Number of Stories/Photos Featuring Blacks in Panola's
Newspapers, by Topics, Selected Years

Topic	1960		1970		1980	
	TP	SR	TP	SR	TP	SR
Professionals	0	0	0	1	10	8
School students	0	0	3	0	19	7
College students	0	0	2	0	9	4
Human interest*	0	0	2	6	7	8
Military	1	0	5	4	1	2
Farm awards	5	5	1	0	0	3
Clubs	2	0	0	0	4	1
Weddings	0	0	0	0	7	2
Anniversaries	0	0	0	0	3	2
Total	8	5	13	11	60	37

Note: TP = *The Panolian*, SR = *Southern Reporter*.

*Stories about big fishes, special anniversaries, odd plants, etc.

achievements, like the prizes won by young 4-H members; one implication is that among whites the blacks were seen as no more than farmers.
There is no reference in any story about blacks in the professions or
schools, and no notice of personal lives such as black weddings or anniversaries. Clearly, those persons and events did exist in the black community.
However, a decade later, in 1970, the newspapers have begun to respond
more to aspects of black life. There were signs in stories of blacks in education and the military (a Vietnam War year), and human interest stories
appeared, while stories of farm awards fell off. Only below the river, in *The
Panolian*, did stories emerge about blacks in education in those early days
of desegregation or when blacks first started to attend college; no educational story on blacks appeared in the *Southern Reporter* of the Delta culture. In mid-1970 there appears (in this sample) the first photo of a black
worker in *The Panolian* and of a Sardis black fireman in the *Southern Reporter*. Where sports sections once covered all-white teams, in 1970 several stories and photos appeared about blacks in both papers. Thereafter,
sports news was biracial; in 1993, when the South Panolas High School
football team won the state championship, there was full coverage for the
almost-all black team and a large gala parade—also covered in both papers.

Another decade passes, though, during which blacks voted, attended
desegregated schools, and took on plant jobs in large numbers. By 1980,
then, these two papers reveal a new racial reality in which blacks are of
interest to editors as new markets and as newly empowered citizens. Of

special interest in table 9.1 are the many 1980 news stories about black professionals, while black farm awards are quite few. Personal achievement stories also appeared in articles or photos featuring blacks in public schools and college, or celebrating weddings or anniversaries. Human interest stories showed that blacks, too, could catch big fish or live a century or more. All this coverage showed whites some aspects of black life that had been unknown to them.[2] These accomplishments were truly "news," even though many whites may not have liked such news. But for our purposes, this table helps show how white editors could see the emergence of a new reality in race relations and respond to it professionally.

Cultural differences between these two weeklies also emerged during these years. As table 9.1 shows, for over three years the Batesville paper carried over 50 percent more black stories than did the Sardis paper. But market considerations, had they prevailed, would have called for the reverse, because north Panola has a larger proportion of blacks than south Panola, where the races are about even. The Sardis paper reported less black news in every decade than did the Batesville paper; in 1980, indeed, Sardis had over sixty percent less black news than Batesville. The explanation seems to lie less in market theory than in the old cultural divisions of the county; in that view, black news was not sufficiently acceptable to appear in the Sardis paper.

While these data provide only a blunt indicator of the attitudes of white editors, they also reinforce what has been shown throughout this book. Where law had created a new reality about blacks in voting, schooling, and jobs, the New South whites reacted differently from the Old South whites. While whites in both eras were nominally committed to free enterprise (even though backed by large federal subsidies for farming), the *Southern Reporter* was slower in adjusting its market for black news than was *The Panolian.* The latter, moreover, used other techniques for expansion of coverage; thus, new sections appeared for the young and the elderly, and there was a section on local personalities. As a result, by the early 1990s it had the leading circulation for a weekly in Mississippi.

In the years after 1980, the newspapers brought even more aspects of black life into their columns. Some stories were biracial, that is, photographs or articles featured both races, for example, stories about black and white award winners in local plants or elected officials. Nevertheless, more whites than blacks appeared for almost any story that these papers recorded. Other stories dealt exclusively with one race or the other; typical were stories about schools in north Panola, whether public or private. By the 1990s, black coverage was proportionately greater in Batesville than in Sardis; that is, while both papers were more open to black stories, it was at a different rate.

Another indicator of the newspapers operating in a market is to examine individual stories for details of the reporter's perceptions of local activities, especially those that were not bulletin-board-type stories. A special review of the period from mid-1991 to mid-1992 uses both stories and photos. In that period, *The Panolian* carried ten stories of blacks to the *Southern Reporter*'s four, the same ratio noted in 1980; only one story was carried by both papers. Two themes emerged in this coverage; the stories focused on black achievement and racial conflict.

Blacks stories of achievement in *The Panolian* featured the retirement of a black school principal, the promotion of a black police captain, the local acting company's award to a black man (in a theater production of "Driving Miss Daisy"), and a school lecture by the state's teacher association president, a black woman. The paper also gave recognition to both races in stories about a state award to the local school student counselors and about a black competitor among nine whites in the chamber of commerce's Miss Hospitality award, which was won by a white. The Sardis paper had a lengthy interview with Como's black police chief; but it also presented a state health report on a syphilis epidemic in the Delta in which "95 percent of the cases are African-American."

Conflict between the races over access to public rights had shifted by 1990 to access to public services. Not many of these conflicts emerged in the newspapers, but three were prominent in this period. Here, conflict resolution had been at work before the stories developed. One story in *The Panolian* involved the unanimous action of Batesville's city council to block construction of low-rent housing near a more affluent addition. The black councilman, Willie King, had joined the opposition, as did the more affluent residents; the new police chief noted that he had seen more crime in low-rent housing in previous jobs. In this case, there was unspoken racial conflict, for—despite King—no one spoke for poorer blacks, for whom better housing was a prime need.

A second story over racial conflict had both papers covering the event. Three whites on the county board of supervisors voted against two blacks to oppose one black road supervisor, Robert Avant, in his use of an office in his beat for an activity not connected with the roads. A black minister, to whose church Avant belonged, complained strongly, and a petition with many names also objected to the loss. A state official present at the meeting reported that such a building could indeed be used for other purposes, but then all supervisors should have them (and only Avant did). The racial overtone of this meeting was stated in the Sardis paper but only implied in Batesville's. Avant, noting also that his recommendations for appointments had been rejected while white members had theirs accepted, asked, "If that's not racism, what is?"[3]

The third story about racial conflict appeared in *The Panolian* over the shooting of a black man by two Batesville police. The black had confronted the police with a gun on his lawn and had rejected efforts by police of both races to calm down and drop his gun; when he turned it toward the police, however, the shooting occurred. Local blacks organized to express great concern to town officials, but then they were asked by the police chief to review the evidence themselves. A video camera had covered the event, and its tape supported the official account. Local officials even asked an outside team to review that tape and comment on their stand; the team consisted of a newsman, a black photographer, and several state troopers. The hubbub quickly died down. Looking back a quarter century ago in this or any other Delta town, it was never conceivable that a policeman shooting a black would need such justification, much less have the technology to support his action.

Newspapers and the New Reality

This analysis suggests that newspapers can reflect at least the surface of the modern complexity of racial relations. On the one hand, the transition from traditionalism had left behind some traces of the old ideas, but there have also been obvious changes. Both appear in this content analysis. While there was recognition of black gains in newspaper coverage, the extent of coverage was not proportionate to race population in both sections of the county.

Once again there were familiar differences between the two parts of the county, almost as if there were two different realities. For example, the south Panola paper carried two state columnists who were the New South type; the north Panola paper did not. These columnists disparaged the old violence, pointed out new racial developments, and criticized state leaders of either race. One columnist noted that so-called "red-neck" counties in east Mississippi were voting in support of one black candidate in the 1991 election, namely, the state supreme court. This black candidate had received 50.8 percent of the votes in this region even though there were only 16.8 percent black voters.[4] This story in *The Panolian* provides evidence of the newer culture, while its absence in the *Southern Reporter* points to the older culture.

This new reality reflected in the county's newspapers shows the influence of external forces, for example, law enforcement. Black-on-black crime was pervasive in this rural area, just as it is in the black ghettos of the big cities. By the late 1980s, these two papers were filled with far more stories than before about drugs, burglaries, and homicides by both races. For example, in early 1992, law officers from town, county, and state agencies assembled to seek, arrest, and jail thirty people in Batesville over

Table 9.2   Range of State Methods of Administrative Oversight

PERSUASION
▲ Informal conferences: political, professional, and social
  Advice and technical assistance
  Requirement of reports
  Inspection
  Grant-in-aid requirements
  Review of local action
  Orders
  Rule-making
  Removal of local officials
  Appointment of local officials
▼ Substitute for local administration
COERCION

Source: Parris Glendening and Mavis Reeves, *Pragmatic Federalism*, 2d ed. (Pacific Palisades, Calif.: Palisades, 1984), 153.

drug sales; of the ten pictured in a front-page story, seven were blacks.[5] In crime, as in poverty, localities can only cope—not solve—growing problems and increasingly must require state and federal resources. But these aspects of community life were also part of the new reality that was created not by law but by other social change.

Federal laws still operated to protect civil rights, even in recent years. For example, *The Panolian* covered Batesville's city council effort in the early 1990s to redistrict its seats in response to a new annexation. But its first redistricting plan was rejected by the U.S. Office of Civil Rights because it had diluted black votes in that area. The city council then produced a second plan acceptable to Washington.

Other outside governmental influence on Panola comes from the state, in increasing amounts, and the papers regularly reported on this. In all American states, there have been more state mandates that affect all communities; these deal with the kind and quality of public services, the publicizing of decision making, civil service requirements, environmental protection, and so on. It is a list that seems endless to the minds of local officials. A multistate study in 1978 found that state officials contacted local officials regularly; one in five local officials were contacted weekly and another 25 percent monthly.[6] There are many methods of state oversight. Table 9.2 sets out these methods, which range along a continuum from persuasion to coercion. Most state interactions are persuasive, including reporting requirements, while relatively few are coercive. One reason for this pattern is the political linkage of local systems to legislative power that can protest state intrusion.

In short, the growth of a new reality was created by the external influence of government, which was reported in local newspapers that roughly mirrored this new reality. That the editors could respond to social change suggests their independence in carrying out their professional concerns.

Change In Racial Language

Amid these cultural changes reported in the press and observed in one's life, what were the individual reactions of blacks and whites to the new reality? How did they perceive and judge these events? And did they understand the role of law in these changes? In the late 1960s, with new federal civil rights laws just under way in Panola County, most black observers noted that it had achieved one goal almost immediately.[7] That was the reduction of violence between the races. In the traditional culture, some whites regularly used intimidation and even violence, while many more whites condoned these actions by acquiescence. Consequently, the reduction of violence against blacks, even by 1970, was dramatic evidence of change affecting the life of every black in this county and elsewhere.

A quarter century later, yet other changes are widely seen by Panolians. Blacks see improvements in official relations with whites, but believe that it is overlain by what one terms a "veneer" of white acceptance. Whites, however, see enormous changes that they believe were imposed on them by outsiders; nonetheless, that view is overlain by a less violent response in dealing with change. Both races report that aside from official contacts between the races in which law intrudes, there are other social relationships where law does not reach, as in social or religious institutions. Yet many blacks are encouraged at the changes in behavior and attitudes reported here. One sign is the change in racial language that provides insights into new perceptions of race.

Changes in Language: Theory

One of the common attributes of any culture is the labeling of "outgroups," that is, those who are not "us." The terms used for these others express our emotions, codify our relations with them, and even constrain our understanding of them. Language that expresses disrespect can categorize the other's status, express our dislike or fear, and form the basis for interacting with them. Language is thus a screen that both shapes expectations and brings emotional order to life. That screening behavior is not genetic, of course, because, as with an old song, "You have to be carefully taught," through early and intimate contact with family and friends. By the time children are ten years old, they have a battery of language to separate insiders and outsiders and to express their feelings about them.[8]

How does law influence this seemingly personal quality of life, rooted in language? Despite earlier learning, changes may come in a person's language when new experiences challenge the familiar learning. Language terms may also be confirmed by continuing contact with like-minded persons who form a reinforcing subculture. For example, social clubs (ranging from country to bowling) will reward those using familiar terms about out-groups. However, changes can occur in our language when we are confronted by contact from outside the supporting culture.

In short, the role of law in this change is that it alters the reality both inside and outside the confirming culture. As persons move into new areas of life where law may not fit what they had already known, a changed reality becomes possible. As persons see their familiar ideas and terms challenged by the law, it is especially upsetting, for now "the natural order of life" is fundamentally questioned. Law's act of defining new legal objects, backed by the authority of sanctions, makes possible a new perception that challenges the old and familiar.

Individual responses to this change may take the form of opposition, acceptance, or indifference. Opposition may range from the violent to the passive, but one sign of it is retaining the familiar language and attitudes with respect to out-groups. Acceptance may not be immediate, and, indeed, may take generations; but the changed response will show in language used for out-groups. Finally, indifference to the law is possible only when contact with other groups is avoided; in such circumstances, also, one can retain the familiar language used within one's group. In all responses, though, language reflects basic attitudes; if attitude changes, then so should the language.

Just as the decline of a small owl can signal that a change has occurred in the larger ecosystem, so a change in language implies a change in a cognitive environment. For persons, though, change may involve making decisions by a rough kind of cost-benefit analysis; that is, one judges what will be lost against what will be gained by opposing, accepting, or ignoring the law. In any decision, these terms refer to judgments not simply about material aspects of life but also about the symbolic and emotional aspects that are rooted in values. Such decisions are crude and may well alter over time when new circumstances refigure the judgment of costs and benefits. One of those changed circumstances is the way in which a new vision of reality can recast one's estimate of old values. If, while running a bar during Prohibition, one estimates that the implementation of law is weak, and the benefits of ignoring it exceed costs of punishments, then one can ignore the law. But if implementation is estimated as much stronger, then costs exceed benefits, and so it is time to sell the bar or turn it into a coffee house.

Changes in Language: Panola County

These theoretical propositions can be illustrated by events in Panola County, where the language of racial discourse has altered over a quarter century of legal enforcement. In all interviews with whites, the term "black" was employed (with one exception, followed by a quick apology); in the research for an earlier book, the common white term had been "nigra" (for "Negro") that quickly slid into "nigger." Similarly, in public discourse today in local reports by governments or newspapers, the regular term employed is "black." "African American" had still not made its way into the white culture at the time of these interviews because it had not done so in the black culture. In fact, among older blacks, using "black" was criticized as bigoted; "Negro" was used consistently.

One clear inference about this language shift among whites is the realization that using older terms, like "nigger" with its implied racial hostility, would find a quick and public response by blacks; for whites, public politeness has become the norm. These changes among the whites in Panola County parallel the New South's awareness that the old terms for blacks had carried overtones of intimidation and discrimination that are not acceptable today.

Blacks' comments about the old language are clear. A black teacher in north Panola observed, "In the old days I thought the white use of "nigger" was not too demeaning to me, but most blacks did [think that]. I thought it was only descriptive, just the way you call a dog a "dog." That's what I was, a "nigger." But what I hated, and what has disappeared, was the use of "boy" by whites talking to me. It was intentionally demeaning, and both of us knew it." This complexity is caught in one black leader's comments:

> Back then, black attitudes were hostile. Blacks were afraid to comment in public on race relations, and we used "Sir" and "Ma'am" in talking with whites. If a white was murdered, for example, you'd go up to whites, and they'd stop talking and not mention it. Now though, it is part of a discussion by the whole community; we'll ask, "What did you think about it?" and "Sir" and "Ma'am" are not used much by blacks. I think about 75 percent of the whites stopped using "nigger"; I can even joke with a few whites about that term.
>
> But *there is a polite veneer over racism today.* Scratch the surface, and there's the same racism. But if economic and political lives today depend upon racial contact, then the whites will cover up that racism. But without this dependence and the laws, it would be like twenty-five to thirty years ago, and you'd see racism like it was then.

All blacks agree that violence is no longer used and "nigger" and "boy" have gone from public discourse, but they are also suspicious of what whites say in private. For them, the past is filled with memories of old hurts and fears. Thus, a black teacher noted that the county sheriff had earlier treated blacks cruelly; he once witnessed him shoving a black's head through the police car window and hitting him with a night stick. Another noted that the biggest change came in being able to take clothes on approval from a store. "Back then, you took it or left it, and could never return it." One black teacher, commenting on the fact that black women could not wear short pants or makeup in 1955 on the streets of Batesville, said it was "a personal insult." Personal incidents like this came up frequently in conversations among blacks who had accepted it as the reality shaping their lives.

Curiously, another teacher reports that today's black students could not believe that blacks failed to fight back against such discrimination; "They say, 'That's fiction!'" White students are disbelieving, but on other grounds, they say "Why would whites do such things?" as their parents had never told them about these events. Indeed, teachers in both public school systems report there is massive lack of student interest in accounts of the "old days" or the civil rights revolution, even in Panola. That outcome reflects the sad truth that what panics adults today will be boring to students tomorrow; it shows how completely the new reality is accepted by both races.

Some whites report that they learned from blacks themselves about changes they hoped to see. One white lawyer noted that he finds a greater intelligence on public matters in biracial boards where he works today than under the earlier traditional culture. Ironically, he believes that "law does not change morality," and then smiled, adding "except for civil rights in Panola County." He said in an interview,

> As a younger member of an old family, I recall talking with William Black [pseudonym], then in the NAACP—a very daring man!—who was working on my farm. He was himself among the first to enter his children in a former white school. Now, he was ignorant [illiterate], but he was also an instigator of progress, and he taught me lots about how blacks wanted what he called "independence." I remember talking to him in the fields when these demonstrations all began, discussing integration when it was new and learning that they wanted to be free.

The blacks, while agreeing that change has occurred, also believe that change did little to remove some—maybe many—whites' dislike of their race. They regularly report that they believe the white attitude is "much better than it used to be." But they also see signs that reflect a hidden agenda of dislike. They can recount little stories in which whites inadvertently reveal racial dislike. One such incident was witnessed by the author during the field trips.

Invited to dinner by some leading merchants and officials and their wives, I joined them and their wives in a lovely home. The men had regularly used the term "black" in interviews and had expressed great hope for improved race relations. The dinner was elegantly presented and delicious, and the conversation was quite cosmopolitan (e.g., shopping at Harrod's in London). But later, one wife observed to another that tomorrow was the birthday of Rev. Martin Luther King, Jr. That comment set all the wives off in a diatribe against him, using Old South racist language to describe his alleged shortcomings ("Martin Luther Coon"). The men's faces promptly fell at this turn in the conversation; after much frowning, one finally reminded them that the author would quote them by name for using such language. Of course, I denied this, but the account is fascinating, as it is evidence of a widespread continuing suspicion of blacks.

Why did the husbands and wives use different language? The answer may lie in how many blacks they contacted regularly and in what relationship. White merchants have frequent contacts with blacks in a relationship where both are necessarily dependent on the other. The wives, however, have black contacts only with their servants, a relationship where blacks are dependent upon whites. This linkage created in the wives' minds the same dependency that had characterized race in the Old South. Not surprisingly, the white husbands had used the new language, and wives the old, both responding to different cognitive realities of race.

These accounts suggest how changes brought by law had produced a new racial reality, one part of which is the change in language in public discourse. But in the private world of many whites, another language is maintained that stands against these changes, as this incident indicates. There are also other whites who insist that they work on changing their children's use of racial terms; as one noted, "Those words hurt and we've been at it too long." There is probably another way of analyzing the two uses of language. If private language is still racist, as many blacks believe, what difference does it make if law cannot reach it? Probably not much, because if public behavior were to reflect that private racist language, it would be open to attack by other whites and blacks in the community.

Black and White Observations on Change

What were the judgments of both races about this new racial reality created by law? How did they experience it? To answer these questions, we turn from leaders in politics, schools, and the economy, to others active in institutions at a middle level; while not leaders, they observe clearly and speak well about events. These persons are not a representative sample, but rather are drawn from diverse positions in community life to comment on that life. The questions used in these interviews were from an open-ended set, enabling us to abstract common concepts.[9] Black and white views are separated for analysis below, although in reality the two are intermeshed by the fact that both responded to the effects of law. We will find that many of their judgments agree—although not always—about the new reality in which they live.

Black Reflections on Change

Black responses reflected the most widespread view, that law had caused whites to change their behavior. Typically, a young black man noted, "Blacks seem to be saying, if I give you respect, you will try to help me and feel goodness toward me. But if there was no law, there would be no change, and the whites would go back to the old views." Like whites, blacks observe the results but are unclear on how law actually effected this. That is most likely true to anyone living amid great social change, but what they can judge is the difference between then and now.

One common black response is rooted in attitudes about their own race. Many blacks simply distrust other blacks who might try to help them. A historical analysis appeared often in their comments.

> Black distrust rests on the difference between house and field slaves from the old days because they distrusted one another back then. Still do. When blacks move up today, other blacks see them like the old days, calling them "Uncle Toms" or "White Man's Negroes." Blacks who do no more than hold up a building while drinking all day complain that they're held down by whites. They see a successful black as an enemy, saying "You've got my job!"

Black criticism about racial matters is widespread. Some blame themselves, especially for their lack of interest in what is happening. A farmer noted that a younger man, who had failed at junior college, had complained that the teacher did not like him, "But I told him, 'No, you didn't study, and weren't prepared for tests.'" Others noted, "Blacks aren't afraid but are just politically uneducated. They only want to talk. They are more involved outside of public life" and "Blacks are bothered by too many factions based on different generations. Young blacks forget the past, and so they are inactive about problems today."

A second common theme in black responses is that many of their problems come not from themselves but from whites. They believe that whites engage in sniping about race, often by making rather sly remarks. One black professional noted this incident:

> I didn't face blatant racism over at Ole Miss where I expected it. Here in Batesville, though, it keeps coming up, maybe because of my work. I recently met a white in a store, a man I had once worked with, and he said, "See you've got a nice shirt there, and you're gaining weight, so you must be doing good. Why aren't you up at Sardis getting free food at the commodity center?" [i.e., getting welfare food for poor blacks].

A continuing theme in black life is judging how to relate to whites on important matters. Some use sophisticated judgments, while others adopt the simplest approach, for example, in politics, asking "What have you done for me lately?" Two statements from older and younger generations show this diversity. In the early days of voting, blacks evaluated the history of violence in each white candidate's background; even today, the principle of personal treatment is still important. The rule for judging whites was, how did he treat blacks? One observed:

> To judge whites, you need to know the history of the state, the town, as well as the white man. How had he talked to the board [of supervisors] about race? How had he treated you or others who had contact with him in any public capacity? Some whites have a record of mistreatment. One sheriff in the early days had a record of stopping blacks from the North when visiting relatives. Once he asked such a black driver, "Boy, where did you steal that car?" and he then put a $500 fine on him. So when a white candidate came along with a different attitude, such as wanting to hire blacks, he was well received.

Another black used a more sophisticated approach to move whites in organizations to respond to black concerns. A black management specialist in the county noted:

> Blacks seem accepted by whites as long as the black doesn't go too far against the grain. For example, in my department if I decided an action was based on discrimination [I could] then picket the department for it. However, if I worked within the system and wrote to a superior about this problem and asked for a meeting with him, this fits their rules and would not be against the grain. I got this approach from Ole Miss, especially in learning from role models. [Asked whether whites would face the same problem if they went outside the rules to complain, he replied,] Yes, I guess so.

Probably the most thorough analysis of white and black reactions today came from a black retiree from another state who has closely observed the local scene. His observations, like many comments from blacks, involved mixed emotions in judging racial relations.

> When blacks got power here or elsewhere, the white strategies were to fight, flee, or modify black entry to power. Whites have adapted to change across the South by building institutions to control change. For example, Batesville government does little to deal with black problems. But they can lend $200,000 for a local hospital or $3 million for roads when they want to. So they can fix problems if whites want to. But there is nothing big for treating black problems after the failure in Washington to continue the general revenue sharing funds.
>
> However, you can work with whites on a black problem. Recently, a black was shot by Batesville police. Black ministers and others had a dialogue with white officials at their offices or homes. We provided a good reaction and saw some changes made in use of guns. My stance is: Show whites the blacks' concerns, they will check them out, and then seek to change if found correct.
>
> But there are problems with blacks, too. There is much apathy among them in both north and south Panola. The reason is that they often tried to get things done for black [problems], but they failed. So the blacks' biggest problem is the suspicion of their leaders; they will say, "They got our hopes up, and then they throw us down."
>
> There are really two types of blacks in Batesville. First, those who came through the system and made it, for example, Leonard Morris or school teachers. Second, those who never tasted their dream of America. For many of the second group, welfare is all they have, but I still object to it. It hinders the development of families. If people don't work, they can't help themselves. There are very few black bourgeoisie in this area, but even they have their own problems.

These remarks demonstrate that while blacks perceive considerable change, they also recognize their own problems in working through new relationships with whites.

White Perceptions of Change

As for whites, though, how do they perceive such change? They seem to operate in a new perception shared by the blacks; that is, they see the racism and discrimination of the Old South as bad and in need of overturning by the law. However, whites differ from blacks in their outlook because they believe that blacks have been granted too many civil rights and live now without much discrimination. This view of whites in Panola is to be compared with the findings of a national survey of attitudes reviewed in the next chapter. Among well-educated whites it is ideology, not bigotry, that influences their views of blacks and public policy (they support blacks who follow certain ideas about work); but among the less-educated whites, prejudice and discrimination prevails.[10] In this county, white leaders speak favorably about blacks who adhere to the work ethic and family values. But the white judgment that there is no discrimination distinguishes the views of white and black here and in the South. Blacks do see discrimination, though it is not like the old type, rather, a blocking out of opportunities "to taste their dream of America," as one noted.

Many whites reported a similar life story about race and changing views. When young, they became aware that there was something different about the way blacks were treated, and many were bothered by it (at least, many Hill whites were; Delta whites were not so troubled). Typically, as a white state-education professional noted:

> My father, an overseer but well-liked by blacks, thought God had made the races separate. He'd be turning over in his grave if he knew these changes had occurred. As a young girl, however, I knew something was wrong about blacks being forbidden entry by the front door. Many students undergoing that experience, in academy or public school, became twenty years later the core of the new generation. They now seek to live with blacks in a fashion far removed from the old attitudes.

Many whites also remember how raw the white emotions were over the civil rights movement, and for many that emotional outpouring was distasteful. A young writer described his reactions to one of the events that changed the perceptions of many. During a civil rights protest in Batesville in the mid-1960s, an old black couple's car broke down amid white crowds, and nearby whites tongue-lashed them.

> These were whites using them to object to change. *The bottom line of racism is when you vent your feelings on everyone because of skin color.* So race is the scapegoat—so immature an attitude, even though human. But this behavior is at its lowest level—macho, compensatory—because you get high in running down others. We whites could get mad at "outside agitators," but when you saw some local whites' reactions against blacks, you knew those had to be changed. These events crystallized lots of whites.

As a next stage in cognitive development, some whites reported changes in their perception, and the details are revealing:

Over the last twenty years I see the emergence of a new generation largely untainted by old prejudices. [Local educator]

I see this in education today. The new generation, without the
earlier prejudices, wants to engage on a professional peer basis. From
my position in supervising local schools, I find both races are interacting with respect for one another much more, now that the opportunity exists to do so due to law. The mix of state mandates and
interracial professionalism is a major element in Mississippi's educational reform, and federal law started it. [State educator]

I noted changes in attitudes about desegregation, when whites,
discussing the same group over two periods of time, moved from describing "those nigger teachers" to "my personal friends." [Writer]

State politics have changed greatly. Historically, all local politics
had bad leadership; there was no local source of news about public
affairs except from these politicians. Our people look on politics as a
social, entertaining event, a prolonged celebration every four years.
Politicians are bigger than life, good at entertaining and at justifying their failures in dealing with power in the state. So citizens were
victims of ignorance, and thus "the closed society" label. But blacks
getting the vote is the key to all changes. With that vote, where once
it was easy to identify local white power structures, that is no longer
possible due to black votes. [Governor's assistant]

One result [of legal change] is one that the city council never had
years ago. Laws from the state and Washington cause us to *look at
the minority's interest as it is one of the rules you now play by.* In
redistricting the council, we almost put Willie King out of his council job. But that was changed due to Washington and getting more
complete data from the university on census tracts. Lots of give and
take in all this. So we fixed the numbers right racially, after the feds
asked more and more questions. [City councilman]

These accounts point to changes in white attitudes about how blacks
strive for professional norms and how whites must fit "the rules you live
by" in public life. A changing appreciation of black interests, often institutionalized as a result of law, involves a growing awareness about the
problems of blacks. Recall that under the traditional culture, there was
little concern about such problems; blacks were never seen as having their

own agenda, and if they did, nothing was done about it. But today, some whites reach out to meet their needs.

For example, two white teachers of black history and minority studies differed in their mode of instruction; only one shows, by implication, a concern for black students. This teacher observes, "I don't say to my class what I'd not say outside of it; I tell it straight. I'm very frank about what happened." By dealing directly with the old prejudices and discrimination, this instructional approach projects a concern for what had happened historically to blacks. However, the second teacher observes, "I stick to the books and give little to current events. I'm worried about white parents' objections due to one case I had."[11] This teacher reflects a common concern about community disapproval in such "political" courses that is found not only in Panola but elsewhere in the nation. That attitude leads to the classic blandness found in such courses as many teachers try to avoid trouble; but that blandness also protects educators from harrassment.[12]

A common theme among white Panolians in this generation was that they had learned much about the complexity of blacks' lives and about whites' outlooks. We noted this earlier, in a white lawyer's account of a black farmhand's attitude to the desegregation of schools. Three accounts from north and south Panola illuminate the process.

A white school board member in north Panola found that a confrontation with one black leader had provided important lessons about other blacks. In this case, a white confronted a black leader and his group for using "hateful" language. He had called black opponents "Uncle Toms" and whites "racist" when both races, the board member noted, were actually trying to deal with complex school problems. This black leader, he complained, had ignored rules by which the board operated, thereby creating confusion there and in the black community. Slowly, pressures rose in the black community against this black leader; equally unhappy white views were reflected in the local Sardis newspaper. And slowly, the white board member found that there was little black support for this man except from his small group. This discrediting by many blacks of another black was seen by the white member as a "learning experience" for him about significant differences among blacks. He "kept communication lines open to people who can think," regardless of their color.

In a second case, a white alderman in Batesville came to realize that his perceptions about some blacks were false. "I found I had once thought of blacks as lesser persons, but now, after observing Willie King and Leonard Morris, I found something new about them." While many may see such black leaders as role models for other blacks, they also serve whites by opening their minds to black potential.

One white official acquired a deep awareness of this change in racial perceptions. He came to see beyond the black leaders to the blacks in the community, realizing that their problems were real and required changing one's mind in dealing with them. His observations explore this new relationship between races, one that was unknown a quarter century ago.

In my experience in this job I had a growing awareness of what poverty means and what might be done for blacks. Clearly, we need more public housing costing $60,000 or less. I wonder on my own if I could buy lots for such buildings and make them biracial. No, not in the Delta, because no one wants to lead on this. One white builder in Batesville was earlier blackballed for several years for building a home for a black man.

[The more I look at race today] I see racial tensions everywhere of a kind we did not have to deal with decades ago. I am working with a new and permanent county group dealing with poor areas, ad hoc and biracial. I now think we need a new and permanent local government agency in this county to deal with race relations. There is a need for a mix of races to decide such matters.

You know, these black leaders are pivotal to either race, but they also face different needs from each race. [In my government work,] whites usually discuss economic matters, especially on land questions; but blacks are concerned with filling out forms in order to get some subsidy. Before, however, blacks had no one in office who could do this for them. Different cultures cause these different behaviors, and they cause the failure of social programs designed to help them. One black leader, I found, was slow in his numbers and never asked questions unless he actually understood the matter. So now I generally keep repeating materials until he clicks on and asks questions, showing he understands.

I'm thinking of leaving [my] church to create a multiracial church. [They] spend $15,000 for a black church in the black neighborhood, but they don't let blacks into [our church] gym; the first is defined as "mission outreach" but not the latter. I asked my minister why he didn't hire blacks and was told he wanted only the best qualified person. But I pointed out that his jobs required no qualifications; all he does is train any new person for the job. I asked him, "Why wait for change when you could start it here?" I got no answer.

In this complex awareness of a new agenda and new ways of coping with it, many whites also show that they are far removed from the old culture. In this quotation we see a white viewpoint that is far from the recalcitrant one of a quarter century ago. Such changes indicate a pragmatic, in some cases bordering on transformed, outlook.

Reflecting on the Awareness of a New Reality

This chapter has sought to use different data, drawn from observations of change reported in newspapers and in interviews with Panolians, in order to define the new racial reality in this county and elsewhere. The data presented here while few, are quite typical, and they show clearly what has taken place decades after the new law. There is a larger theoretical explanation of this social change with which the next chapter deals, but we can infer the nature of this experience from the words of those involved.

First, all are aware that *they live amid change in racial relations*. Western history in the modern era has made change a commonplace in life; it is much like Tennyson's "the old order changeth, yielding place to new." The conditions facing both races in the South in the last quarter century were truly those in which "the old order changeth." The details of that process were illustrated quite fully and in detail in newspaper content, language changes, and personal experience. However, living with change in any era is painful because our old self composed of thought and action is compelled to alter; we must examine the old reality in light of a new one thrust upon us. As the social critic Eric Hoffer once noted, "Broken habits are as painful and difficult as broken bones." That seems as true for institutions as for individuals. Change alters the old by creating new situations that operate in tension with the past, an interaction that itself creates even more change.

A second common experience is that when federal law began providing blacks with more votes, schooling, and jobs, *nonlegal changes also occurred*. Not least was a change in perceptions among whites so great that a new attitude about blacks was required. Clearly, violence departed quickly in this county, leading to other kinds of racial contact. Also, language in public discourse altered, though a fainter racial dislike continues among many whites. Editors, despite cultural differences, opened their pages to news from the black community. So it was that changes emerged in Panola's society that were not spurred directly by law.

A third common experience is that *a special nonlegal change occurred when linkages were formed between blacks and whites to bring black needs to official circles*. These linkages went beyond electing officials appointing citizen committees—often biracial—that emerged in many communities. Some were designed to deal with nonracial matters, for example, cleaning streets or cemeteries in Sardis or setting up an all-county team to explore economic development. Blacks emerged to challenge official actions affecting their neighborhood, such as police shootings, redistricting plans, or neighborhood facilities. This change brought out individual leaders who mobilized latent discontent against specific, visible problems; not all of these efforts were successful, as in the case of the discredited black activist in the Sardis school controversy.

Other black linkages emerged when state and federal regulations sat in as invisible partners on every local decision. Whites came to learn of the need to think about possible consequences for black leaders and their constituents before they took any action. As a white noted earlier, "Look at the minority's interest, as it is one of the rules you now play by." These new linkages between blacks and white officials were often episodic, and they did not always meet black needs, but their presence marked a new racial reality.

That reality was that public officials who were allocating resources had to think beyond whites and become more responsive and responsible to blacks who for so long had been ignored. That goal had been the hope of civil rights workers who had entered the South almost thirty years before, and who had lived, and, sometimes died, with that hope. That goal also permeated the arguments for the legal changes in the 1960s and the consequent development of federal and state bureaucracies to implement the legislation.

As the newspapers, people's language, and personal comments have shown, these legal changes were accompanied in time by changes in perceptions among some, maybe many, whites. Much of that transpired in the generation after passage of the new laws. The new generation has not been grounded in the bitter racial enmity of the old traditional culture but has grown up in a new culture struggling to redefine race relations. One hallmark of the New South that emerges from this study is an openness to the other race. To use an image suggested by one of the epigraphs that introduce this book, the subjective impression one gets is that of the blind compelled to see the new reality.

Of course, it is not a full change, for the old stereotype has been transformed into a new white stereotype about blacks, involving law and discrimination. National polls show much agreement between the races on many social issues,[13] like abortion, drug dealing, patriotism, belief in God, and morality. But the races differ sharply on whether blacks are better off, on the need for more laws to reduce discrimination, or the preferential treatment for blacks and minorities through affirmative action. The white stereotype of the mid-1990s drove a strong political reaction in elections and referenda across the nation to block many public programs for reasons of "fairness." Insightful use of questions designed to measure racial attitudes unobtrusively showed in 1991 that southerners were more likely to be angry about some form of nondiscrimination (e.g., neighborhood integration). All Americans, however, are hostile about affirmative action, but at the same time want to help blacks.[14] This recent change may be rooted in more basic changes in the national political system. Current studies show that race has dramatically altered issue evolution in the two major political parties, and may even have hastened the decline of class as a factor in American politics.[15]

It is important to note that, in both the Old and New South, the races continue to be separate. That lack of racial contact hinders the development of a total new reality of racial relations. As the public arena was compelled toward desegregation, the private arena of church, friends, and clubs remains segregated, as the next chapter explains. That understanding of differences between the civil rights era and the present opens the way to developing a theory to explain the nature of law and social change, with applications to Panola and the South.

10 | The Theoretical Context of Race and Law

The events I have described, and the reflections offered by both races, serve to introduce an explanation of how law works to change people's lives. We have seen that law, when implemented, changes reality, which then changes behavior and, in time, attitudes. But we have also seen that the individual's response to law changes both immediately and over time. How is it possible to incorporate these individual changes in a larger explanation of a general theory of law and social change that is based on the Panola experiences?

The Alteration of Attitudes

While white attitudes toward blacks have altered during the law's implementation, the nature of such attitudes is subject to many qualifications. A brief review of the research shows a dramatic shift nationwide, just as we have seen in Panola County, but the problem of understanding those attitudes still remains.

Whatever item is used on polls to judge tolerance, prejudice, or discrimination, there is considerable ambiguity in America's racial attitudes. However, the polling evidence over some decades yields some significant conclusions. Americans' attitudes are ambivalent at best,[1] often unstructured,[2] difficult to tie directly to any ideology,[3] and not held firmly across time (the news media's position can shift over decades).[4] But all analysts agree that in recent times bigotry and discrimination have sharply declined but hardly disappeared.[5] Indeed, as one of the best analysts concludes, racial attitudes over thirty years have undergone a "radical transformation when prejudice and discrimination have gone from the accepted fact of American life, with substantial legal support, to an activity that is prohibited by law and fundamentally offensive to most Americans."[6]

For example, the old explanation of the racial gap, that blacks were "innately inferior," no longer dominates white views; over the years the percentages supporting this view have decreased greatly among whites. But many today, even those who lack traditional prejudices, think that blacks lack motivation.[7] Prejudice is stronger in metropolitan areas, when the black proportion of population increases, and support of racial integration sharply declines among whites.[8]

The changes in attitude are not specific to particular age cohorts, so that the young are not necessarily more liberal and elders more conservative; surprisingly, there is much variation within any given age group. A thorough review of that evidence concludes, "People do not have an inevitable tendency to become more conservative as they grow older."[9] This "life cycle" model of change in racial attitudes finds little support in current research, nor is there support for the "generational" model where people retain their original views as they age.

Rather, the clearest evidence is that both younger and older citizens become more tolerant as society changes around them. As society has become more tolerant in recent decades, all age groups also move in that direction. Thus, all three age groups in the nation today, compared with the same age groups twenty years earlier, show an increase in political tolerance and racial attitudes. The gap between the South and other regions has considerably narrowed. But southern differences do exist, linked to the more tolerant views of the younger generation, that is, to generational replacement.[10]

This book has demonstrated that such changes in cognitions, attributable to the force of law, have evolved over a quarter century in one section of the most segregated and prejudiced state in the Union. To understand these changes we traced several kinds of change in the small society of Panola County as new realities began to emerge in its politics, schools, and economy. We need finally to trace consequences for local institutions, which carry dominant values into the future, and for local individuals, who must operate among these changes. As an introduction to this analysis, we can review two events that occurred in Mississippi in 1994, which focus our attention on the racial reality of the New South.

Church Burnings in Mississippi—1994 Response

It is important to establish the baseline by which we can compare change. Before and immediately after the passage of the civil rights acts of the mid-1960s, the South was a cauldron of white intimidation and violence against black citizens in both private and public sectors of life. In that history to claim civil rights, the battle was carried out primarily by "local people." The key were those persons in black communities who quite literally put their lives on the line to create new rights in Mississippi and the South in the face of massive white recalcitrance.[11]

The Violence of the South in the 1960s

The reasons for violence by these recalcitrants were clear to most whites in the South, even if they did not cite it; they were threatened by "Communists" and "liberals." These outsiders were overthrowing their traditional culture by challenging their politics, lowering white men's status — and seeking their women.[12] For many southerners, it was the Yankee invasion all over again. In response, many whites used intimidation and violence, for they saw themselves in combat, and many more whites condoned these actions by their own acquiescence to the violent ones. From 1960 on, there were stories in each southern state of murders, shootings, bombings, beatings, arrests, imprisonments on minor or nonexistent charges, and a continuing psychological warfare against the "outsiders."

In Panola County alone from April 1964 to March 1965, at least forty acts of violence appeared in the files of the Civil Rights Division of the U.S. Department of Justice, most occurring in mid-1964 during the "Freedom Summer."[13] These acts included legal harassment by public officials and threats by law officers; but private white citizens accounted for most of the harassment and assaults. Among the incidents was the destruction by fire of a black church in Batesville. Such acts of arson, usually at night, were one of the violent reactions of the Old South to black protests and new federal laws. For a while in the 1960s, church burnings seemed to be the favorite outdoor sport of the Ku Klux Klan or allied whites. The arsonists saw this action as not only safe (acting at night against a scattered and defenseless people). But it was also a blow against black leaders who had often encouraged "freedom riders" in the South, those young northerners who descended on the South to assist voter registration.

At the center of the violence in Mississippi was the town of McComb, in the southwest of the state. In two months of 1964 there had been twelve racial bombings in and near McComb, plus the usual nightly attacks on black homes, all under Ku Klux Klan efforts. Under urging of the local editor, Oliver Emmerich of the *McComb Enterprise-Journal*, such violence began to change.[14] Nine whites of some prominence were sentenced to suspended sentences of probation unless the arson and bombings stopped. They did.

Burning Churches in Mississippi in 1993

That old past was suddenly revived in the spring of 1993. Shouting racial epithets, three young men burned two black churches in two counties in southwest Mississippi. What happened then reflects a basic alteration from the procedures of the Old South, a major change from an earlier day.[15] In short order, the arsonists were captured, tried, and convicted on state and federal charges of violating civil rights; they received the maximum sentence of three years in jail and a large restitution fine. More significant was what occurred next; over three hundred whites and blacks from McComb and Magnolia rebuilt those black churches. What was even more significant was that these events helped unite further both races; as one white noted, "It bonded people together who had lived here all their lives without really getting to know each other."

This event was one of many signals of major change in the New South; clearly none of this was possible a quarter century ago. As the *New York Times* reported, "It was a reminder that . . . the enduring imagery of the Mississippi's violent past does not go far toward describing life there today." On the other hand, this area was not a racial utopia; many whites were unhappy about what happened to the arsonists. But there was the other white reaction that is seen in the prosecution of arsonists and the rebuilding of churches. One white noted that "the rebuilding is the greatest thing to happen [here] in a long time. But I think that most people feel a lot of wrong has been done over the years, and this was the one thing we could do to make it right." As an older black who remembered the earlier church bombings, observed, "This is different altogether, as different than daylight and dark. There's room for improvement, but it's 99 percent better than it used to be."

After the first church was rededicated in the spring of 1994, a group of former civil rights activists from the "long, hot summers" of the 1960s met in this county to commemorate those deeds. With great surprise, they were amazed at the changes around them in racial behavior. As one white activist noted, in her time the only local white woman who befriended her was compelled to leave town. Knowing the old reality and seeing this new reality, she felt that "I was incapable of saying anything. I just couldn't connect these two realities." One black pastor said during the rededication of the new church, "We think that this is something that will go on and on."[16] In late summer 1994, the new churches, built primarily by white contractors, held integrated services.

But it is still not paradise for either race. In two years, from 1994 to 1996, over thirty black churches were burned throughout the South. There had been barely one incident during each year from 1987 to 1994. Police believed that the Ku Klux Klan or "skinheads" (a new American version of fascism) were involved. Some white churches helped in rebuilding these black churches, President Clinton deplored it publically, and a Republican congressional committee investigated the situation in mid-1996.[17]

While there was no evidence of a conspiracy (as black leaders feared), and although white churches were also burned in this period, the motivation of the whites who burned black churches was clearly reflective of the behavior of recalcitrants of the past.

The Murder of Blacks—1994 Response

Panolians were involved in another sign of change, the court case of the murder of a black civil rights activist thirty years earlier. In the winter of 1994, a Panola County jury of twelve plus two alternates was selected; they were men and women, white and black. They sat in judgment of a white man who had expounded the traditional hate philosophy of the Ku Klux Klan for many decades. The jury found him guilty, and a white judge sentenced him to a life sentence. The case suggests another major turning point in Panola's adjustment to a new racial reality.

The Murder of Medgar Evers, 1963

In June 1963, as the civil rights protest picked up in Mississippi, Medgar Evers, a field representative of the NAACP, was murdered in Jackson. The event became national news because, to the national media, it made clear to many outside the South what white resistance meant to civil rights for blacks. Evers was murdered by a single shot in the back in his front yard at night, leaving his wife and three small children to find him dead in a pool of blood. This was not the first murder of a black in this era, of course, but Evers was the highest official in that largest of Mississippi cities. Other murders of lesser blacks received very little attention until the wave of protest picked up steam.

From the beginning the police had believed that the assassin, firing from a honeysuckle bush that hot night, was Byron De La Beckwith, a white supremacist. The rifle that had been left behind was of the kind that Beckwith had once owned, and police found his single fingerprint on the rifle's telescope. In 1964, two trials were held, but two white, male juries brought in hung decisions. Informal accounts[18] indicate that these juries were sharply divided, with an even vote on the first and a small majority to convict on the second trial. It is important to remember that amid all the violence and passion of many whites in that feverish period, there were still some whites who did oppose racism. Afterward, amid all the racial furor that followed, Evers was regularly seen as a martyr, one of the costs of attempting to change the Old South.

Beckwith then retired to Tennessee; the case remained open, though it was generally believed closed. However, it was reopened in 1993 when a young state prosecutor in Jackson found that the jury of the second trial may have been screened by a "state sovereignty commission" that was designed to block racial change. It is another sign of change that this commission of important state figures, long wrapped in secrecy, was uncovered by a Jackson newspaper, which challenged the commission's authority. Maybe more significant, the prosecutor found six new witnesses, some of whom would testify that Beckwith had bragged over the years about having killed Evers. And finally, the prosecutor believed that a new generation of both races could today review the case without the old racial passions.

Beckwith was prosecuted again in late 1993, and a state judge decided to try him in Jackson, the state capital, the county of Evers's death. However, in order to ensure fairness, the judge wanted to pick jurors removed from this scene and decided to select them from Panola County. For four hundred dollars each, the members of this jury heard testimony for fifteen days in a Jackson courthouse decorated with a frieze that showed slaves picking cotton.

The Beckwith Trial: The Jurors' Personal Reactions

When Panolians thought about the case before the jury selection, many feared they would be called. They believed this was an old case from another age over a matter that they regarded as deeply distasteful. For several reasons, the news did not sit well in the county for both races. They feared what violent men might do, they thought it unlikely there would be a conviction for a murder now thirty years old where memories would be uncertain, and they saw Beckwith as a tired man in his seventies. Regardless of their fears, the judge in Batesville picked eight blacks (five women and three men), and four whites. This jury was clearly unlike that of the earlier trials in gender, race, and culture.

It is important to understand the context of their effort, because much of it was not only frighteningly new but deeply emotional. As a prelude, these Panolians[19] were escorted by bus for the two-hour trip to Jackson by police cars with lights ablaze. Every day they attended court surrounded by a police escort forming a wall against the feeding frenzy of the national media; one member recalls the media people shouting that they would pay money to anyone for talking after the trial. The presence of the police was clearly necessary, but many in the jury feared that someone could shoot them. Other changes in their routines were also upsetting. They were separated from family and friends, a major dislocation in the comforting sense of place that one knows in small-town America. Sequestered in a motel, they had no newspapers or television to pass the time, could not talk about the trial, and toward the end could not move from room to room. Each constraint was by itself an unknown and unsettling condition in their lives. But combined with an atmosphere of history and violence in a trial setting they had not known, it is not surprising that all underwent emotional upheaval by the end.

The elements of the trial were also new, partly because many had never heard of the murder or the assassin; a few members were infants or not yet born when the murder occurred. Their newness to the case upheld the county judge's decision to find less biased juries in this county. As Leonard Morris had said before the trial, "If anyone can have a fair trial in Mississippi, it would be in Panola County." Further, the physical evidence of photographs of the murdered body shocked everyone. The contrasting evidence from both sides, as one noted, held them spellbound and sometimes confused. One juror was sometimes ill but decided to "tough it out." Sleep was irregular, food was sometimes below their standard of home meals, and, basically they were isolated from one another except for meals. In the last days, their deliberation as a jury was emotionally exhausting.

It is not surprising that at the end of the trial, some were crying, partly for the two families, but also over the deep emotions that were tapped in the jury's deliberation. For many members, daily services were provided by a minister on the jury, and frequent prayers helped sustain them against this intrusion in the private gardens of their personal lives. Afterward, one juror returned home only to spend three days apart from the family, thinking, feeling, and crying about these events. The jury had agreed not to talk about their deliberations to anyone; in the months afterward, they saw one another very little, avoided all comment, and turned down requests for interviews.

The Beckwith Trial: The Case and Decision

What the Panola jury confronted was a case in which they found the prosecution argument was overwhelming; there were many witnesses and much physical evidence (Beckwith's presence on the scene of the shooting and his ownership of the rifle).[20] This the jury found convincing in the prosecution evidence. Other witnesses testified that Beckwith had bragged in the years since the early trials that he had killed Evers. Some witness testimony consisted of depositions from persons in earlier trials who were now dead. Behind the prosecution evidence were the views of a man who had repeatedly used racist words, a backdrop for explaining his use of violence. On the other side, the defense had only a few witnesses who said that at the time of the murder he was with them some distance away. Beckwith did not testify, surprising the jury; newspapers reported that this omission was crucial to the final decision. After all, the jury had seen him every day and had expected his statement in defense.

The foreman in the jury's deliberations was a black minister, Elvage

Fondren. There is little evidence of personal or racial interactions before the final vote was announced. One juror recalled to the author that there had been three divided votes on the first day, each with a majority to convict. It was clear by that evening that there were some sharp divisions here, and a hung jury seemed likely. But on the morning of the next day, two votes led to a consensus, but just how that consensus was reached is unclear, despite the author's effort to contact every juror.

Reactions to the conviction and life sentence[21] were decidedly different from Beckwith's earlier trials. Then, he had the support of the Citizen's Council, a middle-class and professional group opposing any civil rights for blacks. At an early trial while awaiting the result, he had sat with the state's governor in a "good old boy" scene. Afterward, when he had returned to his residence in Greenwood, there were public signs saying "Welcome Home." In 1994, however, the governor gave a brief statement that justice had been done. The state newspapers were filled with congratulations, noting that a long delayed injustice was now corrected. As an Ole Miss historian concluded, "We are free of a very ugly incident in which a man not only committed a heinous crime, but bragged about it with an arrogance that had to shame any decent person. We've now resolved that." While some white views critical of the decision were published, it was the general view by both races that justice had been achieved. Shortly after the decision, a group of both races held a service of thanksgiving at Evers's statue in Jackson.

Reaction in the black community was everywhere enthusiastic. Mrs. Evers, who with her children had attended the whole trial, quickly and emotionally declared that justice had been done to the memory of her husband. At an emotional leave-taking before the jury's departure, Reverend Elvage Fondren, the black foreman from Batesville, said, "When the decision was made . . . we were sad, but glad." Spent emotionally, they wanted to leave the case in the past and get on with their lives. As the Reverend Fondren said of Evers, "What he stood for means more now that it did during his lifetime. Now, the testament is coming into place."

Observations on Violence in the New South

Veteran observers of the Old South had shown that race was its central cultural value, and that the use of violence was the control mechanism.[22] But reactions to church burnings and Beckwith's trial show clearly that the control mechanism was weakened severely, if not gone; what was left for the recalcitrants were random acts of church burning. Note the prompt response today of state and federal officials in McComb and Hinds counties, and the frantic effort in 1996 at all levels of government to find the arsonists. But what is far more significant is that biracial juries in Mississippi voted to convict the violence of whites. In such events, a new generation, maybe intentionally, was correcting the older treatment of blacks, bit by bit, sometimes reluctantly, but persistently.[23]

Other changes contributed to the New South's changed racial attitudes. The Klan had been weakened by the late 1960s, and the clandestine linkages that had facilitated violence were gone. Yet another change lay in the modern media's stance against all violence, as seen in Panola's weeklies and the dailies in Jackson and Memphis. The media today provide news of the change in race relations, which reaches all but the most remote southerner, and that news helps shape the new racial reality.

Such changes in the new culture cause black perceptions to be far more optimistic than one might expect. This optimism is widely prevalent among black leaders and citizens. As Julian Bond, a veteran black leader of the civil rights movement, put it clearly: "You know, Mississippi is a place where some of the most horrendous events of the civil rights period happened, some of the things that ought to make us ashamed to be Americans. . . . But compared to what it was thirty years ago, or fifty years ago, it's literally night and day."[24]

We have shown how two counties responded recently in dealing with one of the most visible signs of racial domination in the traditional culture. There are important theoretical reasons why these changes have occurred in the individuals and institutions, a consideration to which we now turn.

The Theory of Law and Change

When the force of law intrudes on life, when it challenges as improper accepted behavior and attitudes, then a complex process of adaptation to law takes place. We see this process happening when federal civil rights law first intruded on the traditional culture of Panola County and the South, and widespread white resistance continued for some time. This reaction was a contest between the old ideas on the one hand, and the new ones that the law calls forth. But what the law seeks in new behavior, and indeed in attitudes, may not be quickly found. In Shakespeare's *Henry IV*, Part 1, when Glendower claimed that he could call "spirits from the vasty deep," Hotspur responded, "But will they come when you do call for them?" This section is about those elements of the call of law and the spirit of compliance.

As no law is automatically self-executing, its administration requires advocates with the will and purpose to generate the new reality that the law seeks. When new values seek to replace old ones, there is considerable variation in how individuals respond. If the tasks of compliance are to succeed, then strong implementation is required to alter the old reality that citizens had known for so long. That new reality can generate new perceptions among citizens who may modify their behavior, and new behavior in time can contribute to creating new attitudes about the law's goals. Translating the goals of law into a new reality in this sequence can break down at any stage when it is weakened or strongly opposed. Success can also be blocked by poorly defined legislative goals, tepid implementation by bureaucrats or judges, legislative goals difficult to carry out even when implemented, and outraged citizens work to reject a new reality.[25]

What needs further specification in this theory of law and change is what transpires when both individuals and institutions meet the goals of new law. We develop this theory in terms of the experiences of Panola County over the quarter century discussed throughout this book.

Individual Responses to Legal Goals

Theory suggests that when citizens face law that contradicts their actions or beliefs, there are four possible responses to it. People may adopt responses we will term *recalcitrant, exceptionalist, pragmatic,* and *transformed.* For any class of major legal change, the population affected by implementation may be distributed among these four responses. Specifically, such diverse responses arose among southern whites facing new law on civil rights, for there was no monolithic response—note the number of whites voting to convict Beckwith thirty years ago. Over time, then, the structure of these responses will influence the effectiveness of implementation; that is, the number of people within each response category will shift as the law continues to affect their perceptions and behaviors. Let us review these responses in light of what happened in this county.

The Recalcitrants

At the first stage, when the law makes its entrance, there will be much outrage from the "recalcitrants," who will stick to their old behavior and attitudes, for these have always defined their own reality. Moreover, they will challenge the new law using standard arguments—that it is contrary to tradition, to the Constitution, or even to a higher law. As we review the swirl of events over time in this county and the South, the most noticeable difference in the set of responses over time has been the reduction in the number of recalcitrants. I found their presence pervasive in my first book on the 1960s but a quarter century later they have all but disappeared.

The earlier recalcitrants, laboring in the late 1950s under a weak federal law, had prevented black voter registration, enrollment of blacks in public schools, and the hiring of black employees in industrial plants. Indeed, for the recalcitrants, race was the proper criterion for making decisions, whether for acquitting Beckwith or opposing entry of blacks to votes, jobs, and schools. But as we have shown, this resistance broke down, due to a new and more effective law, to litigation, and to a new generation where old values dimmed over the use of violence. The two Mississippi trials in 1993–1994 epitomized the fading of recalcitrance; note that it would have taken only one white in these trials to block the convictions, but none did.

Much of this white recalcitrance, then and now, suggests a parallel to what individuals feel when first confronting death, that is, denial and anger. Early on, white Panolians and southerners denied what law sought and were angered by its enforcement. The high pitch of emotions among recalcitrants permeated every action in the early resistance. In one sense, it was indeed a kind of death for those rooted in the traditional culture. Old behavior and values about race (as later, in the case of women, elders, and gays) were to be overturned and replaced by new laws imposed from outside the culture and contrary to accepted wisdom.

In dealing with this conflict in ideas and in justifying noncompliance, whites used scapegoating and rationalization, familiar explanations rooted in cognitive dissonance. The goals of such laws, they believed, were "unconstitutional" ideas emanating from the North or from "Communists," often regarded as the same. The motto of the recalcitrants was found in the implacable words of Governor George Wallace confronting federal officials in the 1960s, "Segregation now! Segregation tomorrow! Segregation forever!" It is useful to recall that in 1982, when running again for office, Wallace apologized for his past behavior.[26] But for the recalcitrants, anger and denial irradiated every part of their response. Remnants of that response are still evident in the failure of whites in north Panola to vote for tax referenda for all-black schools that are in dire need of funds, and in the church-burning surge in the South in the mid-1990s. Both are covert ways of concealing this lingering racism.

The Exceptionalists

A second response to the goals of new law is found in the exceptionalists, those who accept some part of the law's new goals while resisting the rest. They provide some justifications for partial compliance, but they also use some of the excuses used by recalcitrants to avoid full compliance. A common example exists in white campaigners for public office. As the poet Cowley said, so argue the exceptionalists: "The world's a scene of changes, and to be / Constant, in Nature were inconstancy."

Thus, when sufficient numbers of blacks became registered, white candidates critical of these laws early on sought black support.[27] Like most politicians, they went where the voters are, so if converting blacks into voters became a legal goal, candidates promptly started knocking on doors in black neighborhoods. If business owners are required to hire blacks, or they think it is the right thing to do for profit, they hire them. The illustration implies the larger point about exceptions. If they enhance personal gain they are pursued, even though other parts of law are evaded or ignored. Note also, though, that this is a partial response only if there is strong implementation that brings higher costs for noncompliance; but the rest of the exceptionalist's reality reflects the older culture.

The Pragmatists

The third response to new law is pragmatism, that is, eventually accepting all the goals of law and modifying behavior, but not attitudes. This change occurs, as with exceptionalism, when the costs of noncompliance exceeds the benefits of retaining the old practices.

Thus, when the U.S. Department of Justice intervened to sue local registrars in this and other southern counties, and then obtained restraining orders, their tough implementation restrained discrimination and opened registration to blacks. For the registrars, especially when many voters are now black, the costs of staying with the old practice becomes exorbitant. However, that transition is not prompt, as recalcitrants can find other ways to hold back social change. Note the protracted effort to pass state laws to "dilute" the black vote, using at-large districts, redrawn district lines, and changing elective to appointive offices. All these laws were designed to dilute black vote but were later overturned in litigation.[28]

It takes time to shift people into the pragmatist response, and here generational replacement may work to create it. By the 1980s, no white leader in Panola County was in power who had once been a recalcitrant. The newer generation of whites seems to have come to their positions by a recalculation of the costs imposed by staying with the old values. White interviewees today condemn the earlier generation's violence and its "blatant racism," an often heard term about the past. Talking at the most personal level, many whites volunteered a rejection of much in that past and even expressed shame about it. That is why we hear terms today among whites like "progressivism" or the "New South," which I have adopted in this book to mark the new and pragmatic attitudes that reject the racial part of the Old South.

There are several indicators of a new kind of recalculation in white estimates. One is suggested by the change seen in the white use of "blacks" rather than "niggers," mentioned in chapter 9. When asked about this change, whites in the new reality said there were penalties for using the old label. Not least of these was the challenge of blacks about using those terms in public. For example, in mid-1994, a black man in Batesville in a newspaper letter criticized the use of the term "nigger":

> Today I experienced a painful feeling and shame for my race. While in justice court with a friend, with blacks and whites sitting in the lobby, a business owner and some other white males came out of court and into the lobby. [They] got into an argument, about what I don't know. The business owner made the statement to the man that he would send two big old black niggers to beat him up. I have been in this business owner's store several times in the past. But now, if he were the last store in Panola County, I would drive to Memphis rather than go in his store. This is 1994 and if he thinks that blacks are niggers, he doesn't need my money and I sure don't need his business. All races should feel the same way about a business owner using words like that.[29]

As this letter shows, many blacks could stand up to challenge old terms even in public. Consequently many whites had learned such terms had to be dropped in public. As the letter writer says, "This is 1994."

Another recalculation of costs was the clear effort by white leaders, especially in Batesville, to incorporate a few blacks into political and economic circles of decision making—albeit *without permitting them any dominance.* As one black leader noted, the "oneness principle" of whites permitting just one black as leader in one type of office still prevails today. Blacks in power were relatively few, and all accepted "progressive" ideas about economic development. But some circles still remain closed to blacks, even in Batesville; as already noted, it was only in 1994 that the first black was admitted to the Rotary Club. Finally, note that such recalculations of the pragmatists arise due to a force that intervened from outside the community—federal and state laws. As blacks agreed fully and whites mostly, without that law there would have been no change or recalculation in the face of the traditional culture.

The Transformed

The fourth response of whites to the goals of new law is like the final stage of recognizing death—acceptance. Some whites become transformed, that is, they adopt fully the new behavior and attitudes called for by the law's goals. The hallmark of this group is a rejection of the traditional view of thinking; they find instead not merely acceptance of the new law but endorsement of its objectives. Lengthy interviews with many people of both races make clear that some whites do indeed fit into this category. Black leaders point to some persons like this, and some whites express their own psychological change to the author. The numbers are not that great, though, but still far larger than when the author first rode the dusty back roads of the county over a quarter century ago. It is an aspect of change that needs more study, for we saw something of this transformation in the two contemporary episodes recounted earlier in the chapter.

Without this response it is difficult to explain the leadership of some whites, such as former Superintendent David Cole in leading the desegregation of south Panola's schools. Like many others, he recognized as a child that white discrimination was basically unfair, an idea that was reinforced later when he was a young adult reforming schools in this district. He worked then with a supportive board of mostly whites from the Hill culture to meet court orders, federal statutes, and administrative regulations. The idea driving all these officials was the need to provide good schooling to all children. The judgment of local blacks who know him support this judgment, and the author's review confirms it in numerous school experiences and in student attitudes (chapters 6, 9). It is clear, on the other hand, that in north Panola the failure to establish a similar transformational leadership contributed to the grave problems its schools have suffered since desegregation began.

The Distribution of Responses

Several theoretical points underlie these four white responses. First, at any time, whites respond in all four ways, but over time the numbers in each category can shift. Further, the distribution of responses among whites will shift in reaction to weak or strong implementation by courts or bureaucracy. These in turn create pressures to change reality that will produce further changes in perceptions. For example, the recalcitrants dominated the early years of civil rights but weakened later (although a few still lurk in the night in the present generation—witness recent black church burnings). Today, most whites are pragmatists, but the younger they are the more likely they are to have transformed, as shown in chapter 8. Whether young or old, they had earlier rejected the violence of the old values and had recalculated the cost of continuing them in the face of a new reality, as their images of blacks became more varied.

Polls also show that much of the change is attributable to younger whites. Table 10.1 shows strong support as early as 1981 for integration in schools and neighborhoods in Mississippi. Of course, the state's support is less than in the rest of the South and in the nation as a whole. But support is surprisingly strong—seven out of ten whites accepted these changes in a state where 90 percent of all students are in public schools. Other polls show that while the races in this state may differ on economic or social policies, on the issue of civil rights, however, the similarity of support is

Table 10.1   White Support of Integration: Mississippi, South, and Nation, 1981

Locale	School Integration	Neighborhood Integration
State	69%	58%
South	74	56
Nation	86	65

Sources: Data on the nation and the South are from National Opinion Research Center; state data are from Social Science Research Center, Mississippi State University. They are reported in Stephen Shaffer, "Public Opinion and Interest Groups," in *Mississippi Government and Politics,* Dale Krane and Stephen Shaffer, eds. (Lincoln: University of Nebraska Press, 1992), 64.

indicative of a changed reality. By 1981, 67 percent of whites supported the Voting Rights Act. However, while supportive of school integration, only 21 percent of the whites supported busing, the only method that courts have found that is feasible to accomplish the aim of that law.[30]

Such polls also show that much of this overall change is attributable to younger whites who are even more supportive of such issues. The findings here confirm the studies of Panola students (see chapter 7) who showed tolerant racial views. In a 1981 poll, Mississippians under age thirty had supported school integration compared to those over age sixty by 80 to 49 percent; the support for open housing was 65 compared with 34 percent. The younger group exceeded the older on a range of other issues (e.g., women's rights, the Equal Rights Amendment, abortion, gun control, labor unions, and welfare and health care spending).

As the analyst of these data concluded, "As time passes and elderly Mississippians are replaced by their off-spring, the state should continue to become more tolerant and to reflect more closely the political orientations that have existed nationally."[31] In our terms, the old hates and fears of the past are weakened by a new generation that includes the transformed—few at first and more over time—living in a new reality with new attitudes about civil rights. Here, full acceptance, even enthusiasm, for a law's goals will be the norm that was once anathema to the recalcitrants of the traditional culture.

What was true for Mississippi was equally true for the rest of the South. White congressional incumbents from the Ninety-first to the Hundredth Congresses had become far more liberal on civil rights issues.[32] Polls show native white southerners having more nonracist views between the early 1970s and early 1990s on such matters as interracial marriage (43 vs. 62%), neighborhood housing desegregation (43 vs. 71%), open housing laws (23 vs. 46%), and voting for a black as president (64 vs. 80%).[33] Moreover, the gap between southern and nonsouthern narrowed sharply on such issues.

These figures on the attitudinal shift in race and other civil rights issues may seem exceptional, given the past culture and its racial violence, but similar charges have occurred elsewhere in American society. As one scholar has noted, law has been instrumental

> in reshaping in less than a generation this nation's views about racism; in altering in even a shorter time police attitudes toward criminal behavior; in ennobling the city dweller as the backbone of American democracy; in imparting an understanding of poverty; in recasting our ideas about leisure; in maintaining certain attitudes of good sportsmanship apparently essential to a competitive market economy, in stemming religious prejudice; in establishing height-ened standards in public service. . . . Judiciously used, law can and does manipulate our deep-rooted attitudes, our personality.[34]

Institutional Responses to Legal Goals

If enforced law shapes individuals, does it work upon institutions such as those in politics, education, and the economy? Each institution controls a special aspect of life for individuals, providing the means for fulfilling their life goals.[35] As we noted in Panola County, in responding to law these institutions changed in some—often major—respects. But in some insti-tutions that lie outside the reach of civil rights law—such as churches—a counterexample exists, which demonstrates the culture's reluctance to change completely.

Relevance of Law to Different Institutions

The success of law is seen when its goals become *institutionalized*, that is, when they are incorporated within the norms and activities of the institu-tion and are put into practice. These legal goals then become institution-alized as correct, justified, served, and endorsed. Institutionalization can occur, for example, when a political system over time provides policies that undergird its own values and provide services and protections to indi-viduals.[36] Indeed, the study of comparative education among nations finds that a nation's laws reflects dominant values that are reflected in many school practices like curriculum, finance, and governance.[37] Even private schools come to match the institutional requirements of public school-ing. Legal controls have indirect influence as, for example, the standards of private schools are changed to fit those of the public schools. For ex-ample, accreditation of a school creates considerable parallelism between the private and public schools of Mississippi and the South.[38]

The law's effects on economic institutions are designed to influence the search for profit. Set in the private sphere, this institution's balance of costs and benefits, which is designed to yield personal profit, can be altered by law in the form of regulatory policy.[39] Indeed, over time the very definitions of "cost" and "benefit" can be altered by law. Recall the legal shift from the acceptance of slaves as "property" to the rejection of slavery, or the imposition of restrictions on industrial and environmental practices. Such impositions coming from government cause businesses to expend much effort to block its regulatory hand, an opposition that historically has run from slavery, child labor, trade unionism, and unfair trade practices, to environmental controls. It is then no surprise to find that a recent ranking of the most powerful interest groups in Mississippi shows that business had four of the top six groups with power.[40]

As another kind of institution, churches have a special relationship to law. They normally work within the political system, often reinforcing and supplementing it, and much church support exists for the body of law. That support has consequence, for religion helps reinforce a faithful person's behavior and attitudes. However, our Constitution precludes a reciprocal relationship between religion and government, as government cannot regulate this institution. This contrasts with law's power over political and educational institutions, a distinction useful for later analysis.

It is important that we do not see each institution as being simply uniform, for there is much division within and among them. These groupings are not monolithic monsters dominating the nation, despite the parade of imaginary horribles raised by ideologues of the Right and the Left. There are institutional conflicts, which may confuse the public when they see an institution's leaders sometimes opposing government. Sometimes the conflict may be sparked by one section of government blocking implementation of another section's rulings. Thus, for example, in order to block a new federal law, political opponents at the state or local level may limit its budget or block implementation; this occurred throughout the federal enforcement of civil rights, especially under Ronald Reagan.[41] In the institution of education, state and local school leaders during early segregation opposed court orders or even abandoned the public schools. Similarly, religious leaders use the First Amendment against any effort at regulating that institution.

In short, where law can reach into lives through strong implementation, individuals and their institutions adapt to the new norms of behavior and attitudes. Despite individual differences in response to law's goals, it is the force of implementation that gradually brings an agreement, either grudging or acceptance, to those goals. Yet in other institutions not affected by law, such as religion, the traditional patterns of attitudes and behavior can be maintained by their leaders.

Institutional Changes in Panola

The whirl of events in this book should not make us lose sight of the deep underlying institutions of social life that underwent change in this county after the civil rights laws of 1964 and 1965. A brief review of the decades since then will focus on these structures as they became altered by the laws or resisted them. The structures form a pattern of institutional response to implementation and its incorporation into individuals' behavior and attitudes.

Decades of Change

The political system of Panola County was the first institution exposed to new law. However, in the first decade after the Voting Rights Act of 1965 there was limited change for blacks, even though more blacks had registered and voted.

Yet the political institution was itself undergoing some change. Local whites could not block registration of blacks because federal intervention was brought on by court orders and citizen pressure. And pragmatic politicians now sought the benefits of black votes, so slowly some public services did respond to some black needs. Meanwhile, in this first decade black candidates for public office did appear but were ignored in elections. In the institution of education, wealthy white recalcitrants had deserted north Panola schools for new private institutions; south of the river, school desegregation began seriously despite preliminary disturbance. The economic institution also began to alter in the first decade; some pragmatic plant managers, more active than others, began slowly to hire some blacks for entry-level jobs. However, in an institution where the law did not have any effect, that is, in the white churches, the response was primarily recalcitrant, though a few ministers did individually caution against the use of violence in this era of social unrest.

In the second decade from the mid-1970s to the mid-1980s, the county's institutions made major changes, except again for religion. The old and traditional political regime in Batesville was overthrown by a younger generation of white pragmatists. A few black elected officials slowly emerged throughout the county. Local public services for blacks had begun to improve; this improvement was still slow, partly because county or local officials were still dominated by recalcitrants or exceptionalists. Typical of this resistance was the reluctance of police forces to hire blacks in any number except the few working in black areas.

Clear differences continued between the two sections of the county. Again, black candidates were ignored in county elections, but some were just emerging in local government. The north Panola schools did not hire a black superintendent, where over 90 percent of the students were black; its student achievement record declined sharply. On the other hand, south Panola schools had undertaken an array of desegregation activities, as the pragmatists and a few transformationals came to dominate. Industry was opening up even more for black jobs (though still at entry level) as more plants emerged, managed by the Batesville new biracial, pragmatic progressives. Again, however, where law did not apply, as in white churches, little change took place; none took on black members.

In the next decade, from the mid-1980s, changes from the decade before were developing fully, despite some institutional reluctance to change. Blacks appeared in all elective bodies of local government, though fewer than their percentage in the population; in hamlets with many blacks they captured most seats. Public services for blacks were slowly improving, but again, there were proportionately fewer in the police force or in home amenities services (e.g., sewers, water). The south Panola schools were fully desegregated, except for alumni reunions, which were private functions. But little of this change in schools existed north of the river where the system remained totally segregated; no blacks headed school district administration. Plant managers in both sections of the county were completely pragmatic. They were wide open to hiring blacks, and most did so in large numbers; for the first time in this decade a few blacks became supervisors. In white churches, where law could not reach, there was still no desegregation.

In 1996 this growth in racial relations in local institutions continued even more fully, for all but religion and to an extent the schools. A black had been elected to the state legislature with a large plurality of white support. Two of five county supervisors were black, and a third might appear before the year 2000. Blacks were on local councils in all communities or were mayors in the hamlets across the county where black constituencies dominated. These black officials were closely linked to improving public services, which were increasingly distributed as the criterion of *need* replaced that of race. This was a criterion of public service that was spurred by ever growing state mandates, as Mississippi moved toward modernism. More blacks had appeared as municipal and county police (a police lieutenant was appointed in Batesville). Services for home amenities for this group also improved, but public housing and storm drains were still needed.

Elsewhere in the county the split in public education remained. The private school had a small student population but still no blacks. There was, finally, a black superintendent in the north Panola schools, working hard with the school staff to improve its lowest ranking in the state. But the news in 1995 of his failure to control finances left that district in control of a state agency. In Batesville, Superintendent Cole had moved on to become president of a community college in Tupelo, and his successor, Tommy Wren, was staying the course that Cole and others had helped set. (Incidentally, the first desegregated class reunion occurred in 1994.) Large numbers of blacks were working in local plants, and a small number was emerging in middle-level positions. At a higher level, black professionals were appearing in the private economy, as well as in local and state administrative offices. Once again, though, the religious situation remained unaffected by these changes.

Institutional Change and Stasis

We have shown in summary form that in politics, education, and industry, national law could and did reach into the internal operations of institutions themselves. First, national voting registrars replaced local ones, and later, when the state instituted a second stage of discrimination in the form of vote dilution, litigation overturned the practice. Statutes and administrative orders restructured public schools so they became desegregated. State laws shaped their curricula and assigned them textbooks that dealt with blacks in society. Affirmative action, litigation, or business leaders' attitudes had altered the hiring practices of both industry and local government, and there were opportunities for more blacks in the professions. In all these institutions, there was some variation in results, but at the local level it was clear that major changes had taken place. It is in these details that we have learned the meaning of "the old order changeth."

Confirmation of these legal and social changes appears in the reports of local observers. Black and white leaders agree that without legal intrusion there would have been little change in the traditional culture. A few whites thought some change would have occurred anyhow, but it would have taken longer; significantly, no black leader expressed this thought. From the perspective of observed change in these institutions, all those polled agreed on the pivotal if not exclusive role of law in this social change.

Of course, it was not federal law alone that produced all these changes, but the law served to crystallize other, reinforcing factors of change. With law, black leaders could encourage followers to improve their quality of life, and the black community would be free from the pervasive fear of violence from whites. With law, local white leaders adapted to new agendas for their community, not only for whites but also for blacks who had been long ignored. With law, new standards of public service were instilled that emphasized professional goals, including personnel performance. With law, new features of social life could develop to bring together both races in common goals about jobs—again, unknown in the past.

Law did not work alone for all the changes we have seen in Panola. However, it was the sovereign key that opened other possibilities of creating a new reality from which new behaviors and cognitions emerged. Notwithstanding the changes, all observers agreed that much is still needed to improve racial relations; even more prevalent was a clear awareness of the need to reduce the great poverty found in both races.

The counterexample of law's effects on institutions and individuals appears in the religious institution. No law affected religion, and certainly few argue that it should, given our constitutional protections. Consequently, the reactions of the churches to racial change were immune to law, thereby helping them continue a traditional culture as a wall against modern encroachment. We should note, however, that some ministers in the early days of this law did make efforts to reduce violence by voicing their cautions, and some did encourage recalcitrants to obey the law. It may be significant that many Batesville leaders of progressivism were members of the First Baptist Church; no interviewees claimed, however, that the church led in these changes. This silence is rather like that of the dog that Sherlock Holmes did not hear barking in the night.

It is clear that the church leaders' responses to social change were individual, but they overlay an institution whose tradition provided few incentives to adapt. Whether Baptist (largest membership), Methodist, or other, behind the reluctance of their leaders was the underlying value about race that many whites shared and which only private institutions can today maintain. Despite biracial minister councils or "mission" efforts in black areas by white ministers, most white-only churches have done little to encourage biracial recruitment within their churches. The only option for change in these institutions does not lie in the law. Rather, it lies in a continual racial education outside the church, which will finally lead a new generation of church members to ask—in their terms—given the openness of God's love, why this traditional closed door?

Circles of Racial Acceptance and Rejection

The interaction of individuals and institutions in this great social change has produced a complex world of racial interaction. In the traditional culture, the interaction was quite simple; there, no blacks exercised any authority in any institution affecting whites. But today, there exist three worlds: one in which blacks do have authority, another in which they do not, and yet a third where the question of authority is still being resolved. This mix of interactions requires us to employ the concept of *circles of racial interactions* to understand what occurred, and to relate them to these social changes.

The Concept of Circles

In our daily lives we interact with a wide range of persons who are more or less close to us and who have more or less influence on our lives. We move with easy familiarity across that range of contact, which runs from close to remote connections, from, say, spouse to president. Some of our interactions are with those working in an institution, whether casually or intimately, say, the mail person or the priest. These different patterns of interaction we may designate as different kinds of "circles," that is, as ranges of personal contact that have greater or lesser interest for the individual. Implicit in this concept of circles is a personal calculation of the costs of entering or rejecting them, a process that produces three types of circles: *intimate, compulsory,* and *symbolic.*[42]

One circle defines itself in terms of matters so close to defining one's own life or personality that we may term it *intimate.* Here are our closest friendships, our mating, dating, and marrying arrangements, and the pull of religion. This circle is the private garden of life, which we build or maintain against threats from the public garden, which hovers uncertainly outside our intimate wall. In this circle, members share a familiar and comforting similarity of personal values and feelings. A second set of circles is defined by our contact with larger groups outside the private garden where we must indeed mix with those who are not our intimates, who may, indeed, be different from us. These connections form the *compulsory* circle that includes school, workplace, and neighborhood. There is some option here for a person to move out of one's circle, but then it is only a move to another parallel one. Because there is a need for these circles, one must work with others who may not be like us. In this circle, as with others, all its members share a collective context that is set by the circle's social norms. These norms are imposed on us by others to whom we accommodate in order to share the benefits of the circle—for example, learning, income, and community.

What lies behind the definition of the third circle is the fact that all persons share at a symbolic level common values and public opportunities that are granted them. Every person in this *symbolic* circle shares in a society that is undergirded by a government. Consequently, everyone operates within symbolic circles, which encompass broad arenas of life. This normal sharing provides most citizens with common qualities of a national culture. We see these, for example, in matters of government like voting access, consumer and job opportunities, and protection of person and property under law. A similar set of symbolic circles arise in popular culture, for example, supporting one's home team or admiring entertainment cult figures. Baseball has become the *lingua franca* of Americans, and many admire Elvis Presley even beyond his death. The point is *not* that all of us are in one symbolic culture (e.g., admiring the lad from Tupelo, Mississippi), but rather that some interactions do not involve personal contact, and there are outlets for symbolic contact.

There are certain problematic aspects of these multiple circles that surround the individual's life, for example, the problems of overlapping boundaries among these three circles. That is, do schools lie in both the last two circles or just one? Does residence lie in the first two circles? The answers here may indicate how individuals recognize differences among the circles in order to judge how to distribute their personal resources through participation in each one. We can see what these estimates are by looking at how people expend their time and other resources in joining and sharing or in avoiding and separation. The circles represent where one expends most effort—that is, expending mostly in the intimate, while participating, almost without awareness, in the other two circles. For most people, choosing to marry is really not the same value as going down to vote; going to a church service is, for some, more important than upholding freedom of the press.

Circles and Civil Rights

Another question arises that is central to this book. How does law alter opportunities to those who claim discrimination within these circles? Civil rights law may be defined as seeking opportunities for the rights of one group by restricting those of another. Granting blacks the right to vote dilutes white voters' power over public resources. But in some circles there is no legal right to be asserted. Thus, in the most intimate circles of marriage, friendship, or religion, there is more freedom from law to pursue these definitions of self. Exceptions have arisen for behaviors in the intimate circle if they can be claimed, for example, to injure others, as in the case of miscegenation. Apart from these exceptions, personal freedom is based on social norms that encourage citizens to do as they wish without legal constraint.

In the compulsory circle, law has intervened, as in the case of discrimination in schools and jobs, where civil rights have been denied. Much has been accomplished in people's lives by such laws in this circle, as we have seen. But there still remain problems, since law alone does not provide sufficient resources to increase options for those seeking them. That is a critical finding of this study; witness the wide extent of poverty in this region, as noted earlier.

Finally, in the symbolic circle, of concepts common to all people, law has intervened to protect civil rights and liberties, such as voting and due process of law. The key to this circle has been the political will and energy of some leaders to make law effective. Such leaders are needed to define these rights and to pursue them through all public avenues; if effective, leaders attract others who respond to those values, which is the essence of the "transformational leader."[43]

In the symbolic circle there are opportunities to alter reality by the use of persuasion and politics, as we have seen in Panola's voting, schooling, and jobs. These values seem hazy for they are not ever fully defined. But it is this quality that is the key to the "symbolic." Such ideas motivate leaders who identify with these values and whose new definitions society over time will accept. But acceptance of the new definition is not full, or its meaning may change. Yet these definitions of values form the ideational basis of a society whose broad goals are always in the process of becoming. In his inaugural address President Lyndon Johnson, whose support and signing of the 1964 Civil Rights Act unleashed the forces of change seen in this book, referred to America as a nation that was always becoming. Laws become powerful instruments to turn this emergent idea of a nation into reality.

The Circles of Panola County

This general concept of circles helps explain what we found in Panola County. Here, law's influence was directed primarily at the symbolic circle in politics and at the compulsory circle in schooling and jobs. Federal efforts had used a battery of statutes, regulation, and litigation against discrimination in voting, hiring, and schooling. But law was not designed to touch the intimate circle, where little change actually took place.

It was the presence of this new external force that enabled many black voters to vote in the local political systems of this county and the South. Note, though, the early and great anger of white recalcitrants over this breaking of the circle that had traditionally always excluded blacks. With the new law, they confronted a new biracial reality of politics. The response of most whites was to reshape politics at the local level—and switch to the Republican party nationally. The traditional view enjoyed a local victory, though, with whites still dominating elective and appointive office in the county. Ironically, that "victory" occurred at a time when state mandates, professional standards, and corporations increasingly constrained their local control.

Similarly, in Panola County desegregated schooling was at first strongly opposed by the most recalcitrant and the most wealthy; the latter could opt out by fleeing to private schools. In the rural South where black proportions are high, public schools are now segregated for blacks because of white flight. Nevertheless, there still remains much desegregation of public schools, as noted earlier. Despite its recent slowing, it is still a historic change for this region, which has seen more change than other regions.[44] Finally, the third circle, the intimate, still remains closed. White churches in the county remain white, interracial dating and marriage are almost unknown, and social activity is primarily segregated, with the exception of events sponsored by local government.

Within each circle, the effects of civil rights law clearly varied. In the circle where law was most active and fully implemented, the conditions for blacks did change, constituting a new reality for them and for whites as well. Thus, black registration compelled candidates and other officials to listen to black concerns and slowly to remedy them. Some blacks secured elective office, but only when the constituency was at least 60 percent black.

In the compulsory circle, more schooling created a new sense of opportunities that moved black Panolians to graduate from high school and to attend junior colleges and state universities. More blacks became professionals. These advances caused new perceptions of reality that were previously unknown to either race. Also, where jobs were opened to blacks, white managers could see that some blacks were quite capable, and a few were promoted. Black professionals appeared in new positions in the public and private sectors, which were reported in local newspapers for both races to read about. For example, the *Southern Reporter* carried a 1994 interview with the black police chief of Como, once the center of Delta plantocrats. In short, law-impelled changes for blacks in the larger circles had brought in a new reality, which was observed by whites, who slowly came to modify their traditional behavior in important respects.

Moreover, white attitudes toward blacks were also modified, so that whites heavily supported these new rights of blacks, as table 10.1 shows. This shift of attitudes was also a sign of a new generation of whites which was more open to this reality. The shift changed the nature of white response from recalcitrant to pragmatist, with some transformational responses. Finally, in the most intimate circle, little had changed in a white person's sense of the place of blacks. For whites who seek to find the reality of the Old South, the white churches and private clubs still provide it.

The Sense of Place and Social Change

Thus it was that the Old South was altered to create this mix of conditions that makes up the New South. Circles outside the intimate have been changed to fit new requirements of law. That shift involves

— a changed two-party system,
— an industrial explosion,
— a new immigrant population from the North,
— federal laws redefining civil rights for blacks,
— state law mandating local government to provide better, fuller, and more racially aware public services.

Each of these new elements goes against a major part of the traditionalism of the past. Individuals and institutions have altered, all within one generation. Power has shifted to blacks where they have a solid black constituency. Their representatives come to power with a new orientation, not simply of group protection but of new ideas—shared by some whites— about the economy, about jobs, and about addressing the pervasive problems of those at the bottom of life's scale.

Much of this change is centered in the state of Mississippi, although other southern states have improved faster. When scholars recently asked colleagues in Mississippi to identify key changes as of 1992, they reported new conflict between "modernism" and "traditionalism."[45] Old conditions persist; for example, an outdated constitution, an inequitable and inefficient tax system, an outmoded county government, and a poor population amid protected wealth. But everywhere they looked, in the state's institutions and practices, in citizens' opinions, and in public policies, they found even more change in the rest of Mississippi than we have found in Panola County.

The importance of these changes is due to different forces, one of which we have explored, that is, the force of federal law, which is the key to all the others. But more important, the changes are reported in a state that was once formerly reviled by outsiders. Before, when southerners might complain about race issues in their own state, they could make themselves feel better by saying, "But there's always Mississippi." In that state today, however, there is much to learn about how Americans adapt to social change. What some might regard as the region most bound by the past has undergone in a bare quarter century more change than most regions have known. Willie Morris, one of the state's foremost writers, wrote in 1981 about small towns undergoing change:

> I believe that what happens in a small town in Mississippi with less of a population than three or four apartment complexes on the West side of Manhattan Island will be of enduring importance to America. Its best instincts only carried the day, and still may fall before anything really gets started (for we are mature enough in our failures by now to know how thin is the skein of our civilization). How many other little towns would have done nearly so well?[46]

In closing a book about Panola County's first confrontation with federal law, I wrote that "the county's leadership has realized that social change is a reality which must be faced and accommodated."[47] Since then, change has met with surprising success, considering the past. It was not the old leadership that brought change about, but a new generation, and it took people of both races to get this far. Adaptation to change was not overnight, of course, and was not final; it was gradual yet persistent. Nevertheless, some aspects of this community are the same as they ever were; there is still, for example, much poverty.

My earlier book closed with a metaphor of olive trees, which take twenty years to produce fruit but yet may live one thousand years. I said then that "[t]he olive seed has been planted and its first roots are moving down into the black soil along the Tallahatchie." Thirty years later, both blacks and whites can agree with the old phrase "We ain't what we was." Do not look into the South and misjudge it—as Shakespeare said, "Presume not that I am the thing I was." That symbolic olive tree is bearing its first blossoms, where once there had been nothing but a scraggy tangle. Like all such blooms, they suggest the possibility of another reality, which is yet to come.

Appendix A | Student Sense-of-Self Questionnaire

Student Sense-of-Self Study
Panola County Research Project

Instructions

The questions that follow will help us to understand what students here and in other states think about themselves and the world around them. There are no right or wrong answers to these questions, so just put down what you think or do. Do not put your name on this sheet, because we want this to be very private. REMEMBER: no one will know how you answer.

For each question, choose the answer that most fits what you think. After selecting your answer, check an (X) in the space to the right or circle an answer. Leave blank any question on which you have no opinion or which you don't understand.

Take your time and put down your general feeling.

Introduction about you

(Circle answer or fill in.)

a. Sex: Male   Female
b. Race: Black   White   Other
c. Present grade in school: 6   9   12
d. Overall report card grade: A A/B B B/C C C/D D Less
e. School district: North Panola South Panola North Delta
f. What does your parent do for a living?
g. Do you plan to go to college?:   Yes   No   Don't Know
h. What do you plan to do for a living?

1. In the last two years:

	Often	Sometimes	Never
a. When you talked with your friends, did you ever talk about public problems, that is, what's happening in the country or in your community? (mark an x)	——	——	——
b. Did you ever talk about public problems with any of the following people? (mark an x)			
1) Your family	——	——	——
2) People where you work or play	——	——	——
3) Community leaders, such as a club or church	——	——	——

2. Have you voluntarily participated in the following groups during the last two years? ("Voluntarily" means you were not hired by the group. "Active Participant" means you attended meetings or events. "Member Only" means you are on a list so that you are kept informed of meetings and events.) **Mark answer with an (X).**

	Active Participant	Member Only	Not At All
a. Youth organization	——	——	——
b. Church or church-related activity (not including worship activities)	——	——	——
c. Political clubs or organizations	——	——	——
d. Organized volunteer work, such as in a hospital	——	——	——
e. School club or organization	——	——	——
f. Literary, art, discussion, music, or study group	——	——	——

3. These questions are on how you feel about people. Mark answer with an (X).

	Agree Strongly	Agree	Disagree	Disagree Strongly
a. A working mother of pre-school children can be just as good a mother as the woman who doesn't work.	——	——	——	——
b. It is usually better for everyone involved if the man is the achiever outside the home and the woman takes care of the home and family.	——	——	——	——
c. Men and women should be paid the same money if they do the same work.	——	——	——	——
d. A woman should have exactly the same educational opportunities as a man.	——	——	——	——
e. Women should be considered as seriously as men for jobs as business executives or politicians.	——	——	——	——
f. Whites and blacks should be paid the same money if they do the same work.	——	——	——	——
g. A black person should have exactly the same educational opportunities as a white person.	——	——	——	——
h. Blacks should be considered as seriously as whites for jobs like business executives or politicians.	——	——	——	——

4. Now we have some questions about living with another race. Mark with an (X) in all but one case.

	Mostly Black	Mostly White	About Even
a. How would you describe your friends at school?	——	——	——

b. When you play with friends out of
   school, are they

c. Is the closest friend of your age
   (circle)

	Black	White	Other
	Often	Sometimes	Never

d. How much contact do you have
   with persons of another race in:
   1) sport
   2) church
   3) community groups (like scouting, 4H, others)
   4) social events (like parties,
   dances, shows, others)

e. In your opinion, is there a problem
   with race relations in your:
   1) school
   2) neighborhood
   3) community
   4) nation

5. Now some questions on how you feel about life. Mark with an (X).

	Agree Strongly	Agree	Disagree	Disagree Strongly
a. I take a positive attitude toward myself.	—	—	—	—
b. Good luck is more important than hard work for success.	—	—	—	—
c. I feel I am a person of worth, on an equal plane with others.	—	—	—	—
d. I am able to do things as well as most other people.	—	—	—	—
e. Every time I try to get ahead, something or somebody stops me.	—	—	—	—
f. Planning only makes a person unhappy, since plans hardly ever work out anyway.	—	—	—	—

g. People who accept their condition in life are happier than
those who try to change things. —— —— —— ——

h. On the whole, I am satisfied
with myself. —— —— —— ——

i. What happens to me is my own
doing. —— —— —— ——

j. At times I think I am no good at
all. —— —— —— ——

k. When I make plans, I am almost
certain I can make them work. —— —— —— ——

l. I feel I do not have much to be
proud of. —— —— —— ——

m. This school gives me very
positive feelings. —— —— —— ——

n. I am relaxed and confident
while at school. —— —— —— ——

o. I have pride in this school. —— —— —— ——

p. I feel that school is important. —— —— —— ——

q. School will help me very much
when I am grown up. —— —— —— ——

6. As you think about the time when you will come of age to vote in elections, mark with an (X) each of the following statements about your feelings.

	Agree Strongly	Agree	Disagree	Disagree Strongly
a. It isn't so important to vote when you know your party doesn't have a chance to win.	——	——	——	——
b. A good many local elections aren't important enough to bother with.	——	——	——	——
c. So many other people vote in the national elections that it doesn't matter much to me whether I will vote or not.	——	——	——	——

d. If a person doesn't care how an election comes out, he or she shouldn't vote in it. —— —— —— ——

e. Everyone has a duty to be active in politics. —— —— —— ——

f. One takes care of one's duty as a citizen if one votes regularly. —— —— —— ——

g. Voting is the only way people like me can have any say about how the government runs things. —— —— —— ——

h. People like me don't have any say about what the government does. —— —— —— ——

i. Same as h, but applied to the time when you come of voting age. —— —— —— ——

j. Sometimes politics and government seem so complicated that a person like me can't really understand what's going on. —— —— —— ——

7. Thinking about some public issues, how do you feel about the following? Mark with an (X), but leave blank if you have no opinion.

For each issue, think first:

"The government in Washington ought to . . ."

	Agree Strongly	Agree	Disagree	Disagree Strongly
a. see that everybody who wants to work can find a job.	——	——	——	——
b. not concern ourselves with problems in other parts of the world.	——	——	——	——
c. help people get doctors and hospital care at low cost.	——	——	——	——
d. see that blacks get fair treatment in hiring and housing.	——	——	——	——

e. see to it that big business corporations don't have much say
   about how the government is
   run.   —   —   —   —

f. act just as tough as Russia and
   Communist China do.   —   —   —   —

g. keep soldiers overseas where
   they can help countries that are
   against Communism.   —   —   —   —

h. see to it that labor unions don't
   have much to say about how the
   government is run.   —   —   —   —

i. stay out of the question of
   whether white and black chil-
   dren go to the same school.   —   —   —   —

j. let our state set its own rules on
   who can vote in elections.   —   —   —   —

Appendix B | Regression Tables of Student Responses

Table B.1 ANOVA Tests of Total and Desegregated Sample of Students

	Public Discussion	Volunteer work	Racial Contact	Political Efficacy	Public Policy Preferences	Racial Composite Score
			Total Sample			
Race	.650	.263	.000 *	.000 *	.000 *	.000 *
School type	.000 *	.015 *	.000 *	.000 *	.029 *	.484
Age	.243	.180	.000 *	.007 *	.003 *	.000 *
School grades	.000 *	.000 *	.132	.000 *	.014 *	.005 *
College plans	.000 *	.000 *	.070	.000 *	.020 *	.115
			Desegregated Sample (South Panola)			
Race, total	.000 *	.002 *	.000 *	.000 *	.015 *	.993
Race, 6th grade	.105	.124	.000 *	.009 *	.159	.000 *
Race, 9th grade	.653	.745	.000 *	.000 *	.000 *	.000 *
Race, 12th grade	.727	.214	.000 *	.000 *	.010 *	.000 *

* = significant by t-test, two-tailed, pooled variance estimate.

Table B.2 Regression of Student Characteristics on Scales

Variable	b	S.E.	B	Sig.	b	S.E.	B	Sig.
	Discussion of Public Problems				*Volunteer Work*			
Parent								
occupation	.012	.011	.041	.241	.026	.011	.083	.017 *
Female	.032	.029	.036	.272	.077	.030	.083	.011 *
Age	.033	.006	.181	.000 *	−.004	.006	−.023	.474
Desegregated	−.002	.055	−.002	.967	.095	.057	.096	.093
College plans	.120	.035	.117	.000 *	.175	.036	.167	.000 *
School grades	.031	.009	.112	.001 *	.028	.010	.100	.003 *
Black	.049	.037	.054	.179	.039	.037	.042	.300
Segregated black	−.019	.068	−.017	.784	.137	.070	.125	.049 *
(Constant)	.507	.098			.373	.099		

    Multiple R .270   Multiple R .273
    R sq. .072   R sq. .075
    Signif. F .000   Signif. F .000

Variable	b	S.E.	B	Sig.	b	S.E.	B	Sig.
	Gender-Race Liberalism				*Racial Contact*			
Parent								
occupation	.022	.014	.051	.121	−.009	.008	−.038	.267
Female	.331	.039	.262	.000 *	.049	.023	−.069	.035 *
Age	.061	.008	.235	.000 *	−.013	.004	−.091	.005 *
Desegregated	−.018	.074	−.014	.802	.181	.044	.238	.000 *
College plans	.103	.046	.072	.026 *	.067	.027	.083	.015 *
School grades	.041	.012	.106	.001 *	.004	.007	.018	.603
Black	.122	.048	.097	.012 *	.118	.029	.166	.000 *
Segregated black	−.103	.090	−.069	.250	.051	.053	.060	.345
(Constant)	.023	.128			.763	.076		

    Multiple R .408   Multiple R .269
    R sq. .167   R sq. .072
    Signif. F .000   Signif. F .000

Variable	b	S.E.	B	Sig.	b	S.E.	B	Sig.
	Self-Esteem				*Political Efficacy*			
Parent								
occupation	.007	.011	.021	.533	.000	.012	.000	.991
Female	.002	.030	.002	.940	.159	.035	.135	.000 *
Age	.030	.006	.155	.000 *	.069	.007	.287	.000 *
Desegregated	−.240	.056	−.233	.000 *	−.093	.066	−.074	.159
College plans	.138	.035	.127	.000 *	.210	.042	.157	.000 *
School grades	.077	.009	.263	.000 *	.061	.011	.170	.000 *
Black	.004	.037	.004	.908	−.152	.044	−.129	.000 *
Segregated black	−.180	.069	−.159	.009 *	−.096	.081	−.069	.237
(Constant)	.183	.098			−.439	.116		

    Multiple R .401   Multiple R .473
    R sq. .161   R sq. .223
    Signif. F .000   Signif. F .000

Table B.2   *Continued*

Variable	b	S.E.	B	Sig.	b	S.E.	B	Sig.
	Public Policy Preferences							
Parent occupation	.005	.010	.017	.636				
Female	.086	.027	.104	.002*				
Age	.026	.006	.156	.000*				
Desegregated	.032	.519	.036	.537				
College plans	.014	.033	.015	.658				
School grades	.013	.009	.050	.148				
Black	.041	.034	.049	.234				
Segregated black	.015	.064	.016	.810				
(Constant)	−.060	.091						

Multiple R .206
R sq. .042
Signif. F .000

Table B.3   Summary of Significant Regression Results on Student Scales

	BEHAVIOR			ATTITUDE			
	Public Discus- sion	Volun- teer work	Racial Contact	Race/ Gender	Political Efficacy	Self- Esteem	Public Policy Prefer- ences
Personal Variable							
Black		+		+	−		
Parent Occupation		+					
Female		+	−	+	+		+
Age	+	+	−	+	+	+	+
Institution (Compared to segregated whites)							
All Desegregated			+				−
Segregated Black		+					−
Interest in Schooling							
College Plans	+	+	+	+	+	+	
School grades	+	+		+	+	+	

Note: Significance at least .05 (most are .00 or better); beta signs as indicated.

Table B.4 Regression of Race-School Types on Student Scales

Variable	b	S.E.	B	Sig.	b	S.E.	B	Sig.
	Discussion of Public Problems				*Volunteer Work*			
Deseg. black	.070	.055	.069	.201	.135	.056	.130	.016*
Female	.034	.029	.038	.240	.077	.030	−.021	.010*
Age	.034	.006	.180	.000*	−.003	.006	−.020	.514
College plans	.129	.035	.125	.000*	.173	.035	.164	.000*
Parent								
occupation	.014	.010	.044	.196	.021	.011	.067	.049*
School grades	.030	.009	.107	.002*	.031	.010	.108	.001*
Seg. black	.056	.056	.051	.323	.191	.058	.171	.000*
Deseg. white	.020	.051	.022	.694	.112	.052	.118	.032*
(Constant)	.480	.092			.365	.094		

Multiple R .271
R sq. .074
Signif. F .000

Multiple R .277
R sq. .076
Signif. F .000

Variable	b	S.E.	B	Sig.	b	S.E.	B	Sig.
	Gender-Race Liberalism				*Racial Contact*			
Deseg. black	.115	.972	.081	.113	−.014	.033	−.022	.668
Female	.333	.039	.261	.000*	−.035	.018	−.062	.050*
Age	.061	.008	.236	.000*	−.011	.000	−.094	.002*
College plans	.110	.046	.077	.017*	.056	.021	.087	.007*
Parent								
occupation	.025	.014	.059	.070	−.005	.006	−.024	.461
School grades	.041	.012	.106	.001*	−.000	.006	−.000	.999
Seg. black	.009	.074	.006	.908	−.170	.034	.−.250	.000*
Deseg. white	−.035	.067	−.027	.605	.095	.031	.164	.002*
(Constant)	−.003	.122			.882	.055		

Multiple R .412
R sq. .179
Signif. F .000

Multiple R .372
R sq. .138
Signif. F .000

Variable	b	S.E.	B	Sig.	b	S.E.	B	Sig.
	Self-Esteem				*Political Efficacy*			
Deseg. black	−.201	.055	−.190	.000*	−.217	.065	−.166	.001*
Female	.000	.029	−.000	.980	.157	.035	.133	.000*
Age	.031	.006	.159	.000*	.070	.007	.285	.000*
College plans	.147	.035	.136	.000*	.212	.041	.159	.000*
Parent								
occupation	.009	.010	.028	.397	.002	.012	.006	.860
School grades	.077	.009	.267	.000*	.061	.011	.171	.000*
Seg. black	−.152	.056	−.133	.007*	−.227	.067	−.161	.001*
Deseg. white	−.222	.051	−.228	.000*	−.076	.060	−.063	.212
(Constant)	.131	.092			−.468	.109		

Multiple R .405
R sq. .164
Signif. F .000

Multiple R .467
R sq. .218
Signif. F .000

Table B.4 *Continued*

Variable	b	S.E.	B	*Sig.	b	S.E.	B	Sig.
	Public Policy Preferences							
Deseg. black	.066	.051	.071	.196				
Female	.089	.027	.106	.001 *				
Age	.026	.006	.154	.000 *				
College plans	.015	.032	.016	.648				
Parent occupation	.005	.010	.017	.622				
School grades	.011	.009	.044	.198				
Seg. black	.043	.052	.044	.407				
Deseg. white	.019	.047	.023	.684				
(Constant)	−.042	.086						

Multiple R .204
R sq. .041
Signif. F .000

* Significance is at least .05 or better.

Table B.5 Summary of Significant Regression Results: Institutional, Personal, and Schooling Variables

	BEHAVIOR			ATTITUDE			
	Public Discussion	Volunteer work	Racial Contact	Race/ Gender	Political Efficacy	Self-Esteem	Public Policy Preferences
Institution (Compared to segregated whites)							
Seg. blacks		+	—	—	—		
Deseg. blacks		+	—			—	
Deseg. whites		+	+			—	
Personal variable							
Parent occupation		+					
Female		—	—	+	+		+
Age	+	— *	—	+	+	+	+
Interest in schooling							
College plans	+	+		+	+	+	+
School grades	+	+		+	+	+	

Notes: Beta significance at least .05; their signs are as indicated.

* Significance is .514.

Table B.6 Difference of Means Tests: School Population Types and Student Scales

Student Scale	School Population Type					
	DesW DesB	DesW SegW	DesB SegW	DesB SegB	SegW SegB	DesW SegB
Public discussion	.800	.332	.269	.620	.150	.442
Volunteer work	.951	.382	.421	.223	.074	.214
Racial contact	.000 ***	.000 ***	.272	.000 ***	.000 ***	.000 ***
Race composite score	.369	.002 ***	.010 **	.000 ***	.118	.000 ***
Political efficacy	.000 ***	.008 **	.000 ***	.736	.000 ***	.000 ***
Self-esteem	.479	.000 ***	.000 ***	.584	.000 ***	.936
Race-gender	.017 **	.061?	.783	.017 **	.051?	.805
Public Federal policy preferences						
New Deal liberal	.000 ***	.024 *	.171	.026 *	.868	.005 **
Populist	.672	.637	.830	.134	.462	.040 *
States rights	.143	.803	.558	.925	.594	.172
Cold war warrior	.000 ***	.005 **	.464	.354	.870	.000 ***

Notes: In each row, the group named first in the column head has a significantly different score than the group named second.

DesW = desegregated whites; DesB = desegregated blacks; SegW = segregated whites; SegB = segregated blacks.

Significant differences are indicated by separate estimate if significance of F <.05; otherwise by pooled estimate: significance levels are *.05; **.010; ***.000; ? slightly over .05 level.

Table B.7 Larger Mean in Significant School Type Comparisons

Student Scale	PAIRS OF SCHOOL TYPES					
	DesW DesB	DesW SegW	DesB SegW	DesB SegB	SegW SegB	DesW SegB
Public discussion	—	—	—	—	—	—
Volunteer work	—	—	—	—	—	—
Racial contact	DesW**	DesW***	—	DesB***	DesW***	—
Racial composite score	—	DesW***	DesB**	—	DesB***	DesW***
Political efficacy	DesW***	SegW***	SegW***	—	SegW***	DesW***
Self-esteem	—	SegW***	SegW***	—	SegW***	—
Race-gender	DesB**	SegW?	—	DesB**	SegW*	—
Public policy preferences						
New Deal liberal	DesB***	SegW*	—	DesB*	—	SegB***
Populist	—	—	—	—	—	SegB*
States rights	—	—	—	—	—	—
Cold war warrior	DesB***	SegW***	—	—	—	SegB***

Notes: In each row, the group named first in the column head has a significantly different score than the group named second.

DesW = desegregated whites; DesB = desegregated blacks; SegW = segregated whites; SegB = segregated blacks.

In t-tests, cells without designation lacked any significance; otherwise, significance levels are *.05; **.010; ***.000; ? near .05.

Notes

1 Setting the Community Scene

1 The term "black" is used here, and "Negro" in our earlier book on Panola County, on the same principle—let people call themselves what they wish. In both eras these were what most African Americans termed themselves.

2 A full chronicle for Mississippi is given in Neil McMillen, *Dark Journey* (Urbana: University of Illinois Press, 1990).

3 A full analysis of the first years of federal law is set out for Panola County in Frederick Wirt, *The Politics of Southern Equality* (Chicago: Aldine, 1970).

4 Jerome Kirk and Marc Miller, *Reliability and Validity in Qualitative Research* (Beverly Hills, Calif.: Sage, 1986), 30.

5 Kirk and Miller, *Reliability and Validity*, 30.

6 See James Silver, *Mississippi—The Closed Society* (New York: Harcourt Brace & World, 1966).

7 E.g., John Dollard, *Caste and Class in a Southern Town* (New Haven, Conn.: Yale University Press, 1937).

8 V. O. Key, *Southern Politics in State and Nation* (New York: Knopf, 1949).

9 Figures cited below are drawn from the earlier study of Panola, in Wirt, *Politics of Southern Equality*, chapter 2.

10 The fullest account of the consequences of that move north is found in Nicholas Leman, *The Promised Land* (New York: Vintage, 1991), 7.

11 McMillen, *Dark Journey*, 126.

12 This orientation is based on David Easton, *A Framework for Political Analysis* (Englewood Cliffs, N.J.: Prentice-Hall, 1965); quote at 12.

13 Albert Kirwan, *Revolt of the Rednecks* (New York: Knopf, 1949).

14 Key, *Southern Politics*, 239.

15 William Percy, *Lanterns on the Levee* (New York: Knopf, 1941), cited in Key, *Southern Politics*, 240.

16 F. Glenn Abney, *Mississippi Election Statistics, 1900-1967* (University: Bureau of Governmental Research, University of Mississippi, 1964), State Administration Series No. 25; Richard Chesteen, "The 1948 States Rights Movement in Mississippi," master's thesis, University of Mississippi, 1964.

17 Figures cited in Walter Lord, *The Past That Would Not Die* (New York: Harper & Row, 1965), 25; identification of the single registrant was given me by the U.S. Department of Justice whom I interviewed—an extremely old man in a bare shack. A system of legal segregation, called the Jim Crow laws, emerged

after the Civil War; Charles Wilson and William Ferris, eds., *Encyclopedia of Southern Culture* (Chapel Hill, N.C.: University of North Carolina Press, 1989), 214. The "politics of the [people] disenfranchised" by these laws in Mississippi is found in McMillen, *Dark Journey*, chapter 2. The regional account is the classic C. Van Woodward, *The Strange Career of Jim Crow* (New York: Oxford University Press, 1955).

18 The most sensitive account is Dollard, *Caste and Class in a Southern Town.*

19 We rely here on David Minar and Scott Greer, eds., *The Concept of Community* (Chicago: Aldine, 1969), ix–xii; the volume reflects the multidimensional nature of the subject.

20 David Minar and Scott Greer, "The Concept of Community," in *The Concept of Community*, Minar and Greer, eds., ix.

21 Wirt, *Politics of Southern Equality*, 48–49.

2 Regional Changes in the South, 1970–1990

1   John Egerton, *The Americanization of Dixie* (New York: Harpers, 1974).

2   Daniel Elazar, *American Federalism*, 2d ed. (New York: Crowell, 1972), 90–120.

3   T. Harry Williams, *Huey Long* (New York: Knopf, 1969), 187.

4   An extended development is found in Earl Black and Merle Black, *Politics and Society in the South* (Cambridge, Mass.: Harvard University Press, 1987), chapter 2.

5   Timothy O'Rourke, "The Demographic and Economic Setting of Southern Politics," in James Lea, ed., *Contemporary Southern Politics* (Baton Rouge: Louisiana State University Press, 1988), 20. For fuller review, see David Perry and Alfred Watkins, eds., *The Rise of the Sunbelt Cities: Urban Affairs Annual Review*, vol. 14 (Beverly Hills, Calif.: Sage, 1977), and Bernard Weinstein and Robert Firestine, *Regional Growth and Decline in the United States* (New York: Praeger, 1978).

6   The local needs and national response are developed in Kirkpatrick Sale, *Power Shift* (New York: Random House, 1975); and Perry and Watkins, eds., *Rise of the Sunbelt Cities.*

7   O'Rourke, "Demographic and Economic Setting," 24–25.

8   Development of these three factors are expanded in Black and Black, *Politics and Society in the South*, chapter 2.

9   The following information is drawn from Stuart Rosenfield, "Employment Patterns in the Nonmetropolitan South," in *Emerging Issues in the Rural Economy of the South*, Proceedings of conference on Emerging Issues in the Rural Economy of the South, sponsored by Southern Growth Policies Board et al., Birmingham, Ala., January 13–14, 1986 (Mississippi State: Southern Rural Development Center, 1986).

10 Dann Milne, "Migration and Income Opportunities for Blacks in the South," *Southern Economic Journal* 46, no. 3 (1980): 913–17; see sources cited here about this effect. On housing, see Douglas Massey and Nancy Denton, "Trends in the Residential Segregation of Blacks, Hispanics, and Asians: 1970–1980," *American Sociological Review* 52 (1987): 802–25.

11 Wallace Huffman, "Black–White Human Capital Differences: Impact on Agricultural Productivity in the United States South," *American Economic Review* 71, no. 1 (1981): 94–107.

12 W. W. Falk, "Rural Youth and the Labor Force," in Don Dillman and Daryl Hobbs, eds., *Rural Society in the United States* (Boulder, Colo.: Westview, 1982), 94–102.

13 Lewis Smith, Vernon Briggs, Jr., Brian Rungeling, and James Smith, Jr., "Wage and Occupational Differences between Black and White Men: Labor Market Discrimination in the Rural South," *Southern Economic Journal* 45, no. 1 (1978): 250 57. See also Charles Hirschman and Kim Blankenship, "The North-South Earnings Gap: Changes during the 1960s and 1970s," *American Journal of Sociology* 87 (1981): 388–403.

14 James Smith and Finis Welch, "Race in Poverty: A Forty-Year Record," *American Economic Review* 77 (1987): 152–58.

15 Albert Karnig and Paula McClain, "The New South and Black Economic and Political Development: Changes from 1970 to 1980," *Western Political Quarterly* 38 (1985): 539–50.

16 Will Campbell, "Staying Home or Leaving," in Peggy Prenshaw and Jesse McKee, eds., *Sense of Place: Mississippi* (Jackson: University Press of Mississippi, 1979), 19, 21–22.

17 V. O. Key, Jr., *Southern Politics in State and Nation* (New York: Knopf, 1949), 4.

18 Editor and contributors spell out the transformation in this traditionalist society in Lea, ed., *Contemporary Southern Politics.* For specific changes in Mississippi, see Dale Krane and Stephen Schaffer, eds., *Mississippi Government and Politics* (Lincoln: University of Nebraska Press, 1992).

19 The fullest review of these effects on all aspects of the political system of the South are in Black and Black, *Politics and Society in the South.* The debate is seen in Edward Carmines and James Stinson, *Issue Evolution* (Princeton: Princeton University Press, 1989) and Alan Abramowitz, "Issue Evolution Reconsidered: Racial Attitudes and Partisanship in the U.S. Electorate," *American Journal of Political Science* 38 (1994): 1–24.

20 John Green and James Guth, "The Transformation of Southern Political Elites," in Lea, ed., *Contemporary Southern Politics,* chapter 3.

21 Ally Mack, Mary Coleman, and Leslie McLemore, "Current Trends in Black Politics: Prospects and Problems," in Lea, ed., *Contemporary Southern Politics,* 113–15.

22 *Black Elected Officials: A National Roster 1990* (Washington, D.C.: Joint Center for Political and Economic Studies, 1990).

23 *Black Elected Officials,* 12.

24 1996 data from Michael Barone and Grant Ujifusa, eds., *Almanac of American Politics 1996* (Washington, D.C.: National Journal, 1995), vi–xii. Variations can be found in John Van Wingen and David Valentine, "Partisan Politics: A One-and-a-Half, No-Party System," in Lea, ed., *Contemporary Southern Politics,* 136–42.

25 Paul Beck and Paul Lopatto, "The End of Southern Distinctiveness," in Laurence Moreland, Tod Baker, and Robert Steed, eds., *Contemporary Southern Political Attitudes and Behavior* (New York: Praeger, 1982), 171. For a state-by-state analysis, see Alexander Lamis, *The Two-Party South,* 2d ed. (New York: Oxford University Press, 1990) and Jack Bass and Walter DeVries, *The Transformation of Southern Politics* (New York: Basic Books, 1976).

26 On such measures as budgets, personnel numbers, and program changes, Re-

publican presidents opposed most civil rights advances for blacks; the evidence is seen in Steven Shull, *A Kinder, Gentler Racism?* (Armont, N.Y.: Sharpe, 1993), and *The President and Civil Rights Policy* (New York: Greenwood, 1989).

27 W. Wayne Shannon, "Revolt in Washington: The South in Congress," in William Havard, ed., *The Changing Politics of the South* (Baton Rouge: Louisiana State University Press, 1987), 662.

28 Bass and DeVries, *Transformation of Southern Politics,* 377–79.

29 Charles Bullock III, "The South in Congress: Power and Policy," in Lea, ed., *Contemporary Southern Politics,* 187.

30 Bullock, "The South in Congress," 187–93, and Black and Black, *Politics and Society.*

31 Merle Black and Earl Black, "The South in the Senate: Changing Patterns of Representation on Committees," in Robert Steed, Laurence Moreland, and Tod Baker, eds., *The Disappearing South?* (Tuscaloosa: University of Alabama Press, 1990), 19.

32 Edward Carmines and Harold Stanley, "Ideological Realignment in the Contemporary South: Where Have All the Conservatives Gone?" in Steed et al., eds., *The Disappearing South?,* chapter 2.

33 Individual chapters in Dale Krane and Stephen Schaffer, *Mississippi Government and Politics* (Lincoln: University of Nebraska Press, 1992), provide the details for the following judgments.

34 Larry Sabato, "New South Governors and the Governorship," in Lea, ed., *Contemporary Southern Politics,* 194. His insights are used below.

35 Following drawn from E. Lee Bernick, Patricia Freeman, and David Olson, "Southern State Legislatures: Recruitment and Reform," in Lea, ed., *Contemporary Southern Politics,* 214–41.

36 Quote and events following drawn from Edward Wheat, "The Bureaucratization of the South: From Traditional Fragmentation to Administrative Incoherence," in Lea, ed., *Contemporary Southern Politics,* 263–81.

37 The course of this history in education, health care, and housing policies is fully detailed in Paul Peterson, Barry Rabe, and Kenneth Wong, *When Federalism Works* (Washington, D.C.: Brookings Institute, 1986).

38 Following drawn from Ronald Marquardt, "Judicial Politics in the South: Robed Elites and Recruitment," in Lea, ed., *Contemporary Southern Politics,* 242–62.

39 *Black Elected Officials,* 9–22.

40 Frank Parker, *Black Votes Count* (Chapel Hill: University of North Carolina Press, 1990).

41 Documentary evidence is set out for the worst of the states, Mississippi, in Neil McMillen, *Dark Journey* (Urbana: University of Illinois Press, 1990), chapter 3; for the other southern states, see Harry Ashmore, *The Negro and the Schools* (Chapel Hill: University of North Carolina Press, 1954).

42 The events leading up to this complex case are clearly set out in Richard Kluger, *Simple Justice* (New York: Knopf, 1976). Reactions against it are shown in Numan Bartley, *The Rise of Massive Resistance* (Baton Rouge: Louisiana State University Press, 1969).

43 See the compilation by states in Reed Sarratt, *The Ordeal of Segregation* (New York: Harper & Row, 1966), 363.

44 Greene v. County School Board of Kent County, 391 U.S. 430 (1968); Alexander v. Holmes, 396 U.S. 19 (1969); and Swann v. Charlotte-Mecklenburg Board of Education, 402 U.S. 1 (1971).

45 See reports of the U.S. Commission on Civil Rights during the 1970s, e.g., *Reviewing a Decade of School Desegregation, 1966-1977, Fulfilling the Letter and Spirit of the Law,* and *Twenty Years after Brown* (Washington: U.S. Government Printing Office, 1977, 1976, 1977).

46 In Freeman v. Pitts, 503 U.S. 467 at 89-120 (1992), a majority of the Court would not abandon all desegregation orders, but "[t]he district court may determine that it will not order further remedies in the area of student assignments where racial imbalance is not traceable, in a proximate way, to constitutional violations."

47 Data below are drawn from Gary Orfield, *Public School Desegregation in the United States, 1968-1980,* and Orfield with Franklin George and Rosemary George, *School Segregation in the 1980s* (Washington: Joint Center for Political Studies, 1983, 1987).

48 Orfield, George, and George, *School Segregation in the 1980s,* 1-2.

49 Orfield, George, and George, *School Segregation in the 1980s,* 14-17.

50 For a review of this research, see Stephen Wainscott, "Consequences of School Desegregation," in Steed et al., eds., *The Disappearing South?,* chapter 5.

51 Following drawn from Wainscott, "Consequences of School Desegregation."

52 Kenneth Meier, Joseph Stewart, and Robert England, *Race, Class, and Education* (Madison: University of Wisconsin Press, 1989).

53 Lascelles Anderson, "School Desegregation: A Social Science Statement," amicus curiae petition, in Freeman v. Pitts, 503 U.S. 467 (1992).

54 Earl Hawkey, "Southern Conservatism 1956-1976," in Moreland et al., eds., *Contemporary Southern Political Attitudes and Behavior,* 48-72; the same author, "Public Opinion in the South Today," in Lea, ed., *Contemporary Southern Politics,* 34-57, and Edward Carmines and Harold Stanley, "Ideological Realignment in the Contemporary South," in R. Steed et al., *The Disappearing South?* (Tuscaloosa: University of Alabama Press), chapter 2.

55 Hawkey, "Public Opinion in the South Today," 57.

3 Panola's Pre-1970 Response to Civil Rights

1 United States v. Duke, 332 F.2d 759 (C.A. Miss., 1963) (5th Cir., 1964).

2 Rich accounts of the Mississippi violence are found in John Dittmer, *Local People* (Urbana: University of Illinois Press, 1994); and Charles Payne, *I've Got the Light of Freedom* (Berkeley: University of California Press, 1995).

3 This process is described in detail in John Kingdon, *Agendas, Alternatives, and Public Policies* (Boston: Little, Brown, 1984).

4 Evidence on Panola County is detailed in Frederick Wirt, *Politics of Southern Equality* (Chicago: Aldine, 1970), chapters 6-7.

5 Data and sources are from Wirt, *Politics of Southern Equality,* chapter 10.

6 On origins of the Civil Rights Act of 1965, see Gary Orfield, *The Reconstruction of Southern Education* (New York: Wiley-Interscience, 1969), chapter 3.

7 Details are provided in Wirt, *The Politics of Southern Equality,* 199-207.

8 Green v. School Board of New Kent, 391 U.S. 430 (1968).

9 The material in this section is abstracted from data in Wirt, *Politics of Southern Equality*, chapter 12.

10 The material in this section is abstracted from Wirt, *Politics of Southern Equality*, chapter 13.

Part II Introduction

1 The design is drawn from John Brewer and Albert Hunter, *Multimethod Research* (Newbury Park, Calif.: Sage, 1989).

2 Drawn from Harriet Nathan, *Critical Choices in Interviews* (Berkeley: Institute of Governmental Studies, University of California, 1986).

4 Local Politics and Black Empowerment

1 For the region, see V. O. Key, Jr., *Southern Politics in State and Nation* (New York: Knopf, 1949); for Mississippi, see Neil McMillen, *Dark Journey* (Champaign: University of Illinois Press, 1989).

2 Frederick Wirt, *Politics of Southern Equality* (Chicago: Aldine, 1970), part 2.

3 A review of the harshest penalties is found in William Randall, *Ku Klux Klan* (Philadelphia: Chilton Books, 1965).

4 For Mississippi, see Wirt, *Politics of Southern Equality*, chapters 4–5; John Dittmer, *Local People* (Urbana: University of Illinois Press, 1994); and Charles Payne, *I've Got the Light of Freedom* (Berkeley: University of California Press, 1995). For the South, see Earl Black and Merle Black, *Politics and Society in the South* (Cambridge, Mass.: Harvard University Press, 1987), chapters 4–5.

5 In this first reference to these interviews, I draw the reader's attention to the parameters of their use. All the interviews were with then key actors in political and economic matters ($N = 95$), 63 of whom were white (blacks then had little contact with politicians, and if they did, the circumstances were usually unfortunate), and most had direct knowledge of the events and actors. For these interviews, as with all others, three requirements were maintained. I provide no names with quotations because I respect the interviewees' efforts to explain matters that my promise of anonymity helped promote. Second, a triangulation methodology (using the same questions for different persons) ensured internal validity when interviews agreed what had happened. On this methodology, see David Fetterman, *Ethnology Step by Step* (Newbury Park, Calif.: Sage, 1989), 89–92. The third requirement was that the same questions were put to persons active in the three areas of study: politics, schools, and jobs.

6 On widespread rural practices and the friends-and-neighbors approach, see Key, *Southern Politics in State and Nation*.

7 His efforts to seek federal grants for farm and local business interests by working with federal legislative allies had foundered due to his sloppiness in missing application deadlines.

8 It was symptomatic that when Ferguson was defeated, his mayor's desk was filled with parking tickets that had not been processed, apparently those of his friends.

9 Old-time business leaders do note that Mayor Ferguson inadvertently helped future industrial development. He succeeded in getting TVA electricity into

Batesville from lines in Alabama as cheap power for use by his supporters, despite the attraction of having Mississippi Power and Light to stay with the town. While Sardis did stay within MPL, Batesville did not. Later, TVA's cheap electricity would be an inducement to attract industries to Batesville.

10 The investigation operated like a movie script. On the day of a statewide check of the books of such boards, investigators met before dawn in selected central sites within the state, were given their county assignments, and headed to the county courthouses to be the first order of business for the supervisors that day.

11 Gerald Gabris, "The Dynamics of Mississippi Local Government," in Dale Krane and Stephen Shaffer, eds., *Mississippi Government and Politics* (Lincoln: University of Nebraska Press, 1992), chapter 11.

12 Wirt, *Politics of Southern Equality*, 160.

13 The following review was based on a content analysis by two graduate students at the University of Mississippi, School of Journalism, and the University of Illinois, College of Communications. They used a detailed form for summarizing the news according to topic (politics, education, economy, government, race, and other). These were sampled by the author for reliability. The author cross-filed the results under those topics and later summarized them in the text that follows here and elsewhere in the book.

14 Peter Bachrach, and Morton Baratz, "Two Faces of Power," *American Political Science Review* 56 (1962): 632–42.

15 Wirt, *Politics of Southern Equality*, chapter 7.

16 Clifford Finch began the gubernatorial practice of openly proclaiming against racial discrimination, but in the 1960s he had fought black registration as a state attorney in Batesville; see Wirt, *Politics of Southern Equality*, 190, 205. His change of heart was one that numerous other whites also made in working with the black community when they got the vote. A symbolic figure of that change (a building is named for him in Batesville), his career in state politics was ultimately frustrated.

17 Data from *Black Elected Officials: A National Roster 1990* (Washington, D.C.: Joint Center for Political and Economic Studies Press, 1991). On the actions of John Doar and the Justice Department's strategy, see Wirt, *The Politics of Equality*, chapter 4.

18 Frank Parker, *Black Votes Count* (Chapel Hill: University of North Carolina Press, 1990), xv.

19 This judgment is reflected in the reform's history, e.g., Samuel Hays, "The Politics of Reform in Municipal Government in the Progressive Era," *Pacific Northwest Quarterly* 55 (1974): 157–69. These findings are supported in Willis Hawley, *Nonpartisan Elections and the Case for Party Politics* (Berkeley: University of California Press, 1973). But while persons elected by the at-large and ward systems are different, recent research finds that the policy differences may be marginal; see Susan Welch and Timothy Bledsoe, *Urban Reform and Its Consequences* (Chicago: University of Chicago Press, 1988).

20 The distinctions among these representative roles are drawn from a national sample of councillors in Welch and Bledsoe, *Urban Reform and Its Consequences*, chapter 6.

21 Many of this younger set of leaders came from the nearby hamlet of Pope, a

largely white community of small farmers. While an area of "rednecks," it also produced progressive leaders.

22 Paul Peterson, *City Limits* (Chicago: University of Chicago Press, 1981), chapter 8.

23 The broader professional influence is seen in Frederick Mosher, *Democracy and the Public Service* (New York: Oxford University Press, 1982). For Mississippi, see Gerald Gabris, "The Dynamics of Mississippi Local Government," in Dale Krane and Stephen Shaffer, eds., *Mississippi Government and Politics* (Lincoln: University of Nebraska Press, 1992).

24 These influences are traced in Frederick Wirt, "The Dependent City? External Influences upon Local Control," *Journal of Politics* 47 (1985): 85–112.

25 This classic distinction is explored in James Macgregor Burns, *Leadership* (New York: Harper & Row, 1978).

26 Details are found in Wirt, *Politics of Southern Equality*, chapter 6, 159–61, 165–66. A full review of black leadership in Mississippi is found in Payne, *I've Got the Light of Freedom*.

27 Leonard Morris even entered a "juke joint" and stopped a dice game to call for their help in the campaign. They agreed, but gamblers still bet on whether he could win.

28 Honors began to accumulate, including the presidency of the state's school board association and an alumnus award from Ole Miss (University of Mississippi).

29 Data are found in the mid-November 1992 issues of the two local papers, including some small errors.

30 Designation as "black" and "white" was estimated by local knowledgeables, and are here confirmed by noting the largest versus the smallest votes for candidate Morris.

31 The median votes of these black precincts were Morris 72.9 percent, Clinton 72.1 percent, and Espy 83.6 percent.

32 Frank Parker, *Black Votes Count*, 10. The litigation involved: Allen v. State Board of Elections, 393 U.S. 544 (1969); Conner v. Williams, 404 U.S. 549 (1972); Stewart v. Waller, 404 F. Supp. 206 (N.D. Miss. 1975).

33 *Proposed Redistricting, Panola County, Mississippi: Hearings before Officials of Office of Civil Rights, U.S. Department of Justice*, held in Sardis (May 21, 1985) and Batesville (October 30, 1984, and May 21, 1985).

34 Abigail Thernstrom, *Whose Votes Count?* (Cambridge, Mass.: Harvard University Press, 1987). The response is strongly criticized in Parker, *Black Votes Count*, 11–12, 143.

5 South Panola and Desegregation

1 At least four English patterns are traced in David Fischer, *Albion's Seed* (New York: Oxford University Press, 1989).

2 Willie Morris, *North toward Home* (New York: Houghton Mifflin, 1967), part 1, and *Terrains of the Heart* (Oxford, Miss.: Yoknapatawpha Press, 1981).

3 Explored in Will Campbell, "Staying Home or Leaving," and Peirce Lewis, "Defining A Sense of Place," in Peggy Prenshaw and Jesse McKee, eds., *Sense of Place: Mississippi* (Jackson: University Press of Mississippi, 1979). The small-

town aspects are analyzed in Robert Craycroft and Michael Fazio, eds., *Change and Tradition in the American Small Town* (Jackson: University Press of Mississippi, 1983).

4   A theme most fully developed for football in a small Texas town; see H. G. Bissinger, *Friday Night Lights* (Reading, Mass.: Addison-Wesley, 1990).

5   David Tyack, *One Best System* (Cambridge, Mass.: Harvard University Press, 1974).

6   Alan Peshkin, *Growing up American* and *God's Choice* (Chicago: University of Chicago Press, 1978, 1986).

7   Neil McMillen, *Dark Journey* (Urbana: University of Illinois Press, 1989), chapter 3, which provides the following data and analysis of Du Bois.

8   For example, U.S. Commission on Civil Rights, *Public Education* (Washington, D.C.: Government Printing Office, 1964), including a chapter on Mississippi. For reviews of evidence, see Reed Sarratt, *The Ordeal of Desegregation* (New York: Harper & Row, 1966), and Gary Orfield, *The Reconstruction of Southern Education* (New York: Wiley-Interscience, 1969).

9   The evidence is seen in Gary Orfield, *The Growth of Segregation in American Schools* (Cambridge, Mass.: Harvard University Press, 1993).

10 From a recent report in the *Charlotte Observer*, May 15, 1994, pp. 1 ff. For a longer analysis, see Frye Gaillard, *The Dream Long Deferred* (Chapel Hill: University of North Carolina Press, 1985).

11 Albert Hirschman, *Exit, Voice, and Loyalty* (Cambridge, Mass.: Harvard University Press, 1970).

12 The first years of desegregation are set out in detail in Frederick Wirt, *Politics of Southern Equality* (Chicago: Aldine, 1970), part 3.

13 In Washington, this plan was overseen by Leon Pannetta, later a powerful member of the House of Representatives, and after that, Office of Manpower and Budget director and chief of staff in the Clinton administration.

14 *The Panolian*, September 10–October 1, 1970. Editorials expressed disappointment at this action, noted it was not brought by the OCR, and warned against alleged harassment against black plaintiffs.

15 Pope, a hamlet noted for its "rednecks," also produced the young business leaders and city councilors who would form the new "progressive" attitude of the new political regime.

16 The first two black principals, Robert Hyde and Matthews Landers, were from inside the district; the third, Robert Chapman, was appointed from outside but was originally from Batesville.

17 The sequence of events, in order, are in issues of August 6, January 22, September 9 and 17, December 3, and January 8. Comparing *The Panolian*'s coverage with the *Southern Reporter*'s, we find the ratio for supportive editorials was 9–3, for details of desegregation 18–7, for federal finances for schools 4–2, and for private school news 16–5.

18 Frederick Wirt and Michael Kirst, *Schools in Conflict*, 3d ed. (Berkeley, Calif.: McCutchan, 1992); Catherine Marshall, Douglas Mitchell, and Frederick Wirt, *Culture and Education Policy in the American States* (New York: Falmer, 1989).

19 Larry Sabato, "New South Governors and the Governorship," in James Lea, ed., *Contemporary Southern Politics* (Baton Rouge: Louisiana State University

Press, 1988). The conditions in the rest of the American states is shown in Frederick Wirt, "State Education Politics and Policy," in Virginia Gray, Herbert Jacob, and Kenneth Vines, eds., *Politics in the American States*, 4th ed. (Boston: Little, Brown, 1983).

20 Those forces are explored in Frederick Wirt, "The Dependent City? External Influences upon Local Control," *Journal of Politics* 47 (1985): 83–112.

21 The textbooks, respectively, are Margaret Branson and Fred Coombs, *Civics for Today* (Boston: Houghton Mifflin, 1980); and William Hatcher and Joseph Parker, eds., *Civics and Law for Mississippi*, 2d ed. (Brandon, Miss.: Magnolia Publishing, 1987).

22 Robert Hardgrove, *American Government: The Republic in Action* (Orlando, Fl.: Harcourt Brace Jovanovich, 1986); William McClenaghan, *Magruder's American Government* (Newton, Mass.: Allyn and Bacon, 1987); Lewis Todd and Merle Curti, *Triumph of the American Nation*, vol. 2 (Orlando, Fl.: Harcourt Brace Jovanovich, 1986).

23 A full record of all these documents was provided for the author's analysis by Dr. Dolores Barnett, curriculum supervisor, South Panola School District.

24 One white teacher asks blacks to select and research a famous black person, so that for one day the student would act and dress like that hero (sports and entertainment figures regularly prevail).

25 My earlier book, *Politics of Southern Politics*, on Panola's early civil rights involvement, was never purchased in any school district of the county, despite several notices to these authorities in the early 1970s.

26 This theme is explored in Frederick Wirt, "The Uses of Blandness: State, Local, and Professional Roles in Citizenship Education," and a review of the textbooks in Daniel Katz, "Federalism in Secondary School American History and Government Textbooks," both in Stephen Schecter, ed., *Teaching about American Federal Democracy* (Philadelphia: Temple University, Center for the Study of Federalism, 1984).

27 This framework is set in the systems analysis of David Easton, *A Framework for Political Analysis* (Englewood Cliffs, N.J.: Prentice-Hall, 1965).

28 Data provided by Superintendent Cole's deputy, Bobby Carlisle, South Panola School District.

29 Cole introduced the author to a brilliant graduating senior whom he had encouraged to become qualified and to return later as a future superintendent in this district. He was black. When Cole left for the presidency of a Tupelo junior college in 1992, his successor, Tommy Wren, had years of administrative experience within this district. He was white.

30 Variations in representation types in local councils nationwide are reviewed in Susan Welch and Timoth Bledsoe, *Urban Reform and Its Consequences* (Chicago: University of Chicago Press, 1988), chapter 6.

31 By 1970 alone, the county's schools had received about $900,000 from Title I funds, split about evenly between the north and south Panola schools, and another $475,000 to south Panola for remedial education, plus $65,000 from Emergency School Assistance for curriculum revision, multiethnic materials, teacher training, etc. *The Panolian*, April 30 and November 5, 1970.

32 However, the board's recent redistricting plans had to meet the OCR challenge. Activity was reviewed in a printout of all counties, provided by OCR, in which

the author checked both public school systems. Exceptions arise in the 1990s redistricting of south Panola's system; it was reviewed, disapproved, and then approved after changes by the Voting Rights Section of the Department of Justice, according to OCR representative, David Hunter.

33 Results calculated from annual data provided by Superintendent Cole's deputy, Bobby Carlisle, South Panola School District.

34 While teachers lament that the grades of blacks are disappointing and often point to lack of parent support, another reason may lie in other pressures on these same students. As anthropologist Signithia Fordham's recent work is showing, in northern schools, black students cannot reconcile being academically successful with maintaining status in their group. Their fear is loss of racial identity, often leading to peers discouraging school achievement. See review in *Education Week*, June 9, 1993, pp. 6–7.

35 *The Panolian*, June 20, 1990.

36 Earlier grades were omitted due to research that shows the students in these grades lack views about events external to family and school life. See Richard Dawson and Kenneth Prewitt, *Political Socialization* (Boston: Little, Brown, 1969).

37 Superintendents in the three school systems not only approved this research, but made all their facilities available. With assistance from administrators and teachers, tests were administered in separate assemblies under the author's mentoring. All students in grades 9 and 12, all grades 6 in north Delta and north Panola, and a large sample of grade 6 in south Panola were covered. Translating these data into computer analysis was funded by grants from the Spencer Foundation and the University of Illinois Research Board. Analytical help was provided by Dawn Anthony, Social Science Quantitative Laboratory, and Alan Young, Department of Sociology, University of Illinois.

38 Reliability tests provided scores around .70 for all items but the set of public policies; the exception testifies to the proposition, familiar in political science, that social and foreign policies do not combine into a single ideology. The range of answers in these Likert-type scales were in often–never or agree strongly–disagree strongly scales. Each number shown is the mean score of the responses within that scale and was used for later analysis.

39 Dawson and Prewitt, *Political Socialization.*

40 Robert Hess and Judith Torney, *The Development of Political Attitudes in Children* (Chicago: Aldine, 1967).

41 These tests occurred while the Soviet Union was dissolving and with the Berlin Wall already down.

42 In August 1990, during preschool conferences in the three school systems, almost all teachers (294) responded to the slightly revised instrument; in south Panola, there were 111 white and 34 black teachers.

43 This use of "lines" is fully explicated for politics in Earl Black and Merle Black, *Politics and Society in the South* (Cambridge, Mass.: Harvard University Press, 1987).

44 James McGregor Burns, *Leadership* (New York: Harper & Row, 1978).

45 Samuel Krug, "Instructional Leadership: A Constructivist Approach," *Educational Administration Quarterly* 18 (1993): 432–45; Martin Maehr and L. Fryans, Jr., "School Culture, Motivation and Achievement," in Carole Ames and Martin

Maehr, eds., *Advances in Motivation and Achievement* (Greenwich, Conn.: JAI Press, 1989), vol. 6.

46   Frederick Wirt, "Administrators' Perceptions of Policy Influence: Conflict Management Styles and Roles," *Educational Administration Quarterly*, 25 (1989): 5–35.

6   Two Responses to Desegregation in North Panola

1   The theory, with modifications, is drawn from Alfred Hirschman, *Exit, Voice, and Loyalty* (Cambridge, Mass.: Harvard University Press, 1970).

2   By 1965, 76 percent of all county students were black in north Panola and 56 percent in south Panola. One key measure of school quality is the pupil-teacher ratio; for whites it was 1–23 and for blacks it was 1–34 (analysis from data provided in *The Panolian*, April 29, 1965). An earlier state study had found in the county an even wider range of racial disparities: Bureau of Educational Research, School of Education, *The Report of a Survey of the Public Schools of Panola County* (University: University of Mississippi, December 1955) (mimeo). Its results are reported in Frederick Wirt, *Politics of Southern Equality* (Chicago: Aldine, 1970), 197.

3   An early account of the first year appears in the *Memphis Commercial Appeal*, July 26, 1965. Interviews of these pioneers and later officials are used in what follows.

4   Since the Civil War, when they were solicited as substitutes for black farm hands, the Chinese had thrived throughout the Bible Belt but always on the side, mostly as local merchants and always as Protestants. The culture survives in Wally Pang and his restaurant in Batesville's main business street.

5   One veteran kept two volumes of a scrapbook of these documents, which is abstracted below.

6   Editorials in *The Panolian*, January 8, January 22, July 23, August 6, 1970; on August 27, Hunt Howell's editorial advised parents not to withdraw from local public schools, even if they are "unhappy." The newspapers' restraint on inflaming the public was noted in the 1960s in Wirt, *The Politics of Southern Equality*, 144.

7   Following drawn from Mississippi Private School Education Association (MPSEA) documents on teacher certification and accreditation, including interview material with officials in 1990.

8   *The Panolian*, April 23, 30, 1970.

9   One local source noted that MPSEA gave the North Delta Academy an "A" rating in 1990. That rating is less than the "AA" rating and is designed for small schools that cannot meet state or MPSEA standards. Only two private schools did have state accreditation in 1991, reduced from about forty, because of new state reforms that private schools could not meet—plus the heavy paperwork required.

10   At that date, there were 2,299 students enrolled in north Panola, 2 percent of whom were white, while 32 percent of the 135 teachers were white. Information provided by the office of Superintendent James Harris, April 17, 1991.

11   One sign is the sharp decline of whites leaving for other schools in the earliest years; compare data in *The Panolian*, April 29, 1965; March 12, 1970.

12   White expectations were that anything black-controlled was bound to be poorly

organized, if not dirty. As a black principal recalled, when whites entered his school in the early years, they were surprised at how clean and organized the school was.

13 An account of the process by which this happens is developed in Frederick Wirt and Michael Kirst, *The Political Dynamics of American Education* (Berkeley, Calif.: McCutchan, 1997), chapters 1, 7; Wirt and Leslie Christovich, "Administrators' Perceptions of Policy Influence: Conflict Management Styles and Roles," *Education Administration Quarterly* 25 (1989): 5–35.

14 Account drawn from both newspapers, October 12–November 6, 1980. The stories differed in some respects: south Panola's *The Panolian* noted whites had fled, while the Delta *Southern Reporter* noted that the Voters League and NAACP voted not to support the boycott; it editorialized against loss of state money for absences and ignored the ending of the boycott when the board acted to meet some claims.

15 Following accounts drawn from survey of the *Southern Reporter* in these years.

16 *Southern Reporter*, July 11, 1991.

17 These concepts are set out in Samuel Krug, "Instructional Leadership: A Constructivist Approach," *Educational Administration Quarterly* 18 (1993): 432–45; Martin Maehr and L. Fryans, Jr., "School Culture, Motivation, and Achievement," in Carole Ames and Martin Maehr, eds., *Advances in Motivation and Achievement* (Greenwich, Conn.: JAI Press, 1989), vol. 6.

18 Reviewed in Robert Crowson, "The Local School District Superintendent: A Puzzling Administrative Role," *Education Administration Quarterly* 23, no. 3 (1987): 49–69. Another aspect of this office is reviewed in Wirt and Christovich, "Administrators' Perceptions of Policy Influences: Conflict Management Styles and Roles."

19 The test used was the Stanford Achievement Test Series, 8th ed., whose results were provided by Superintendent Harris; data are drawn from the Mean National NCE columns. Later figures are drawn from the state's district summary reports on functional literacy for April 1990.

20 Those judgments are probably inflated, though, to judge from the 1994 SAT tests for juniors and seniors planning to attend college. Among the 152 Mississippi districts north Panola ranked 150 in the test scores of its students; its ACT test mean of 15.1 compared unfavorably with those of south Panola at 20.0 and Senatobia at 20.9, and the state's highest score at 23.5. *Southern Reporter*, September 29, 1994.

21 A review of the current crisis in this leadership is shown in Wirt and Kirst, *The Political Dynamics of American Education*, chapter 7. The halcyon days of earlier leadership are detailed in David Tyack, *One Best System* (Cambridge, Mass.: Harvard University Press, 1974).

22 *Southern Reporter*, May 7, October 8, June 18, 1992.

23 Crowson, "The Local School District Superintendent."

24 In 1991, the system introduced an alternative learning center for students who were under discipline that was designed after consulting with other districts.

25 Both newspapers covered this event in great detail in these years.

26 At the end of 1991, 38 percent of its teachers were white, the principals were all black (though the vocational-technical school director was white), and in the central office 40 percent were white.

27 Much detail emerged in issues of the *Southern Reporter* (February 23, March 2, March 9, 1989), and in all interviews of board members.

28 A review of these roles in education is explored in Dale Mann, *Policy Decision Making in Education* (New York: Teachers College Press, 1975).

7 The Results for Students in Different Systems

1 These cultural influences are demonstrated in Alan Peshkin, *The Relationship between Culture and Curriculum*, and Leslie Fyans, Jr., and Martin Maehr, *School "Culture," Motivation, and Achievement* (both from Urbana: National Center for School Leadership, University of Illinois, 1990).

2 For a review of this literature, see W. Russell Neuman, *The Paradox of Mass Politics* (Cambridge, Mass.: Harvard University Press, 1986).

3 Randall Ripley, *Policy Analysis in Political Science* (Chicago: Nelson-Hall, 1985), 69. For supporting evidence, see Benjamin Page, *Who Gets What from Government* (Berkeley: University of California Press, 1983).

4 The coherence of these scales in each list is measured by alpha scores, which are respectively, .539, .562, .528.

5 This term refers to items based on widely used research analysis.

6 The coherence of alpha scales was, respectively, .717, .702, .624, and .076. The last scale on policy attitudes was then broken down into subscales based on factor analysis, shown later in table 7.2.

7 The alpha score was .510.

8 Compare William Wilson, *The Declining Significance of Race* (Chicago: University of Chicago Press, 1980), with Dale Marshall, "The Continuing Significance of Race: The Transformation of American Politics," *American Political Science Review* 84 (1990): 611–16, and Edward Carmines and James Stimson, *Issue Evolution* (Princeton, N.J.: Princeton University Press, 1989).

9 Norman Nie, Sidney Verba, and John Petrocik, *The Changing Voter* (Cambridge, Mass.: Harvard University Press, 1979); and especially the role of education in Raymond Wolfinger and Steven Rosenstone, *Who Votes?* (New Haven, Conn.: Yale University Press, 1980).

10 The numbers and scaling of these answers were:
    127 Professional-managerial
    195 Business (retail trade, business services, self-employed)
     47 Agriculture
    373 Personal services and operatives
    243 "Work" unspecified
     82 Unemployed
    174 No answer; not included in this scaling.

11 Robert Weissberg, *Political Learning, Political Choice, and Democratic Citizenship* (Englewood Cliffs, N.J.: Prentice-Hall, 1974); M. Kent Jennings and Richard Niemi, *The Political Character of Adolescence* (Princeton, N.J.: Princeton University Press, 1974); and Roberta Sigel and Marilyn Hoskin, *The Political Involvement of Adolescents* (New Brunswick, N.J.: Rutgers University Press, 1981).

12 Education is clearly a quality that determines voting; see Wolfinger and Rosenstone, *Who Votes?*

13 Students may inflate their grades, and probably many do, but in that case a

curve of grades still exists, although higher. That result is acceptable in this analysis.

14 See sources in note 11.

15 Research reviewed in Neal Krause, "The Racial Context of Black Self-Esteem," *Social Psychology Quarterly* 46 (1983): 98–107.

16 One other possibility exists in the data on younger students. The high school students had nine to twelve years of desegregation experience, while sixth graders have had less. Something in the younger person's experience encourages more racial contact, but in the older ones encourages less. Whether it is the peer or maturation influence cannot be determined without another review before these sixth-graders graduate.

17 A technical explanation of this finding may be that there is too little variation in the occupations to create a useful variation. But the numbers shown in note 10 find considerable variation. Note 10 does not show the number on welfare, but clearly this is not an agricultural society. It may be that the large number in the category of unspecified "work" may fuzzy the distinction in the analysis. But that designation should be markedly lower in the analysis, because anyone with a parent who was a professional or business owner would know about his or her occupation, while someone whose parent assembled a thermos jug in a nearby plant might not.

18 Richard Dawson, Kenneth Prewitt, and Karen Dawson, *Political Socialization*, 2d ed. (Boston: Little, Brown, 1977).

19 The government policy head shown in table 7.1 was broken down into subsets for table 7.2, which describes the policy content. Thus, "New Deal liberal" refers to a policy of government providing aid for those who need it economically. "Populist" refers to the power of big business and big labor in government. "States rights" refers to Washington staying out of schooling on racial matters and permitting the state setting of voting requirements. Finally, "Cold war warrior" refers to those seeking American involvement in international affairs. The table is expressed so that any significance is found in the direction of the label. Items appear in appendix A.

20 A state-by-state review is found in Arthur Link, "The Progressive Movement in the South, 1870–1914" in Patrick Gerster and Nicholas Cords, eds., *Myth and Southern History*, vol. 2, 2d ed. (Urbana: University of Illinois Press, 1989).

21 Support for these actions was stronger among senior school students, but not middle and elementary students; indeed, teachers' scores on these two measures were higher significantly (.000 level for each set of teachers).

8   The Local Economy and Political Regimes

1 Gunnar Myrdal, *The Political Element in the Development of Economic Theory* (Cambridge: Harvard University Press, 1954). Myrdal notes that "it is vain to attempt to isolate a purely economic problem from its political setting" (p. 185).

2 Susan Hansen, "The Politics of State Taxing and Spending," and Bruce Williams, "Regulation and Economic Development," in Virginia Gray, Herbert Jacob, and Robert Albritton, eds., *Politics in the American States*, 5th ed. (Glenview, Ill.: Scott, Foresman/Little Brown Higher Education, 1990), 333–77, 479–526.

3 Paul Peterson, *City Limits* (Chicago: University of Chicago Press, 1981).

4 Peterson, *City Limits*, chapter 2. A historical review and the consequence of these linkages are set out in Paul Kantor, with Stephen David, *The Dependent City* (Glenview, Ill.: Scott Foresman/Little Brown, 1988).

5 Such development patterns are reviewed in Timothy O'Rourke, "The Demographic and Economic Setting of Southern Politics," in James Lea, ed., *Contemporary Southern Politics* (Baton Rouge: Louisiana State University Press, 1988), 9–33.

6 Poverty affects not only income but also attitudes. Surveys in this state have found that rural poor blacks are more fatalistic, suspicious, alienated, and less trusting than rural poor whites. See Woong Cho, *Socio-Economic and Psychological Attributes of Rural Poverty in Mississippi*, Research Bulletin 17, (Lorman, Miss.: Alcorn State University, 1982).

7 The thesis and its supporting data are developed in Frederick Wirt, "The Dependent City? External Influences on Local Control," *Journal of Politics* 47 (1985): 83–112.

8 Bryan Jones and Lynn Bachelor, *The Sustaining Hand*, 2d ed. (Lawrence: University Press of Kansas, 1993).

9 Bryan Jones, "Social Power and Urban Regimes," *Urban News* 7, no. 3 (1993): 3.

10 Jones, "Social Power and Urban Regimes."

11 The following is drawn from Dale Krane and Stephen Shaffer, eds., *Mississippi Government and Politics* (Lincoln: University of Nebraska Press, 1992); see especially their chapters, "The Origins and Evolution of a Traditionalistic Society" and "Tradition versus Modernity in Mississippi Politics," 24–42, 270–88.

12 Christopher Jonson, "Poor Relief in Antebellum Mississippi," *Journal of Mississippi History* 49 (1987): 2–3.

13 Donald Nieman, "The Freedmen's Bureau and the Mississippi Black Code," *Journal of Mississippi History* 49 (1978): 91–118.

14 David Sansing, "Congressional Reconstruction," in Richard McLemore, ed., *A History of Mississippi*, vol. 1 (Hattiesburg: University and College Press of Mississippi, 1973), 578–89.

15 V. O. Key, Jr., *Southern Politics in State and Nation* (New York: Vintage, 1949).

16 A literary review of Faulkner's writings is found in Richard King, *A Southern Renaissance* (New York: Oxford University Press, 1980), chapters 4–6.

17 The classic study of this group is Albert Kirwan, *Revolt of the Rednecks* (Lexington: University of Kentucky Press, 1964).

18 Charles Hamilton, *Progressive Mississippi* (Aberdeen, Miss.: Gregg-Hamilton, 1978), 184–85.

19 Donald Mosley, "The Labor Union Movement," in McLemore, ed., *History of Mississippi*, vol. 2, 254–73.

20 The seminal community studies of Mississippi culture appeared in 1937. On Indianola, see John Dollard, *Caste and Class in a Southern Town* (New Haven, Conn.: Yale University Press, 1937); on Natchez, see Allison Davis, Burleigh Gardner, and Mary Gardner, *Deep South* (Chicago: University of Chicago, 1963).

21 A concept first drawn in Dollard, *Caste and Class in a Southern Town*.

22 Information drawn from *Panola County and City Population* and *Mississippi Statistical Summary of Population 1800–1980*, both from Mississippi Power & Light Co., Economic Research Department, February 1983.

23 The old account is that at the end of any year, black sharecroppers would say they were doing all right if it just weren't for the cost of "de ducks," that is, the deductions owners kept for housing or store goods. Note that no one oversaw the planters' accounts, and so they were not held accountable to blacks.

24 Many aspects of this control found in Panola County were first delineated in Key, *Southern Politics*. The "old families" in Panola County included Pointers, Shorts, Hayses, Taylors, Swangos, and Wests.

25 The fine details of this educational accountability in early days are found in Neil McMillen, *Dark Journey* (Urbana: University of Illinois Press, 1989), chapter 3.

26 The religious linkage is discussed in Liston Pope, *Millhands and Preachers* (New Haven, Conn.: Yale University Press, 1942).

27 Evidence of these viewpoints are found scattered through Hunt Howell and Macey Randolph, eds., *History of Panola County* (Hurst, Tenn.: Curtis Media, for Panola County Historical and Geneological Society, 1987).

28 The blacks who got land at that time became civil rights supporters in the 1960s movement; see the linkage in Lester Salamon, "Follow-ups, Let-Downs, and Sleepers: The Time Dimension in Policy Evaluation," in *Public Policy in a Federal System* (Beverly Hills, Calif.: Sage, 1976).

29 This pattern is seen in Key, *Southern Politics*.

30 See also Frederick Wirt, *The Politics of Southern Equality* (Chicago: Aldine, 1970), chapters 4–6 for details.

31 However, Ferguson lacked voting support throughout the county. He was defeated for the state senate in the 1960s by a Sardis lawyer, William Corr, who was followed later in that seat by Batesville's Charles Nix, who as a Democrat held the office from 1972–1988. But Ferguson retained the mayoralty in Batesville for many years.

32 This account is based on interviews with merchants, bankers, politicians, media figures, and black leaders in the county. Their statements on events were overwhelmingly congruent on the sequence and strategies set out here.

33 By 1980, state reports showed that the rise of manufacturing was the main reason for increases in per capita income, especially in high-paying industries (*The Panolian*, March 13); nearly 20 percent of all firms were new (*Southern Reporter*, August 7); the largest source of state income was manufacturing, which by 1978 was up over a decade from 18 to 20 percent (*Southern Reporter*, Sept. 25); and farming hit hard times (*The Panolian*, December 25). Those trends continued. By the early 1990s, cotton was still the biggest farm product in this county, but farmers took home less for three years in a row (*The Panolian*, December 18, 1991).

34 Note how the Hill whites had earlier used this term to apply to helping the poor, to discouraging unions and corporations, and to holding down blacks. Clearly, the content of "progressive" changes, for the modern version is quite different—except on unions.

35 There were many members from the Hill culture town of Pope, a few miles south of Batesville. Some became leaders in Batesville banks, schools, and government, but others fit the stereotype of redneck—and were called that by the first group.

36 His son was later to be central to economic developments in Batesville, as

noted later. By one current analysis, Dunlap was ranked eleventh in the state in the wealth of a privately held corporation (tire sales), with about $145 million sales annually.

37 The group rejected one applicant with unions, but by the early 1990s unions were found in two firms, Kroger and United Parcel Service.

38 Reviewed in Stephen Shaffer and Dale Krane, "Tradition versus Modernity in Mississippi Politics," in their *Mississippi Government and Politics.*

39 For a review of these changes in the state, see Gerald Gabris, "The Dynamics of Mississippi Local Government," in Krane and Schaffer, eds., *Mississippi Government and Politics*, chapter 11.

40 Clarence Stone, *Regime Politics* (Lawrence: University Press of Kansas, 1989).

41 Both stories are in *The Panolian*, September 21, 1994.

42 Drawn from interviews with local business leaders and a review of strategies in John Howell, "City-County Teamwork Keeps Batesville Booming," *Mississippi Business Journal*, November 1988, 34–36.

43 Private borrowers would put up collateral so that if the business failed the town did not end up running it. These funds paid for expanding firms, which in turn added new jobs and interest payments returning back (about 7%) to the fund. In short, this policy was treated like an insurance fund, whose additions contributed to further economic development.

44 *The Panolian*, October 5, 1994.

45 Mayor Baker fits well recent research on the many roles of leadership in small town offices. One sample in North Carolina finds their strong roles were as leader of ceremonies and presiding leader; smaller but important roles were those of external ambassador and promoter, community spokesman, team builder, and administrative liaison; but there is only a limited role as goal setter, organizer, and negotiator. See the research of James Svara, "Mayoral Leadership in Council-Manager Cities: Preconditions versus Preconception," *Journal of Politics* 49 (1987): 297–327, and "Leadership in Cities and Counties: Comparing Chairpersons and Mayors of Council-Manager Governments," paper prepared for the American Political Science Association convention, San Francisco, 1990.

46 See the chamber report in *The Panolian*, November 6, 1991.

47 Wren's estimate was hard to confirm. Chapter 7 found that South Panola's achievement scores, compared to the state averages, were in the middle range.

48 John Howell, "City-County Teamwork," and a letter to the Batesville Chamber of Commerce Director from the Delta Council of Mississippi's economic analysis, June 22, 1993.

49 Research on the equity of representation of new black office holders in the South finds that black, compared to white, office holders have a larger agenda of local problems. The black focus is on poverty and unemployment, while also supporting economic development. But that black concern involves redistributive policy, which is better addressed by external, not local, governments. See Carmine Scavo, "Racial Integration of Local Government Leadership in Southern Small Cities: Consequences for Equity Relevance and Political Relevance," *Social Science Quarterly* 71 (1990): 362–72.

50 Concepts developed in Jones and Bachelor, *The Sustaining Hand.*

51 Stephen Elkin, *City and Regime in the American Republic* (Chicago: University of Chicago Press, 1987), 41.

52 James Button, *Blacks and Social Change* (Princeton, N.J.: Princeton University Press, 1989), 187. His chapter 6 covers subsequent statements, and explains the actions of the business leaders.

53 Both races' leaders cooperated fully in early 1994 when the county faced a devastating ice storm. A photograph in the *Southern Reporter* showed the black mayors of Crenshaw and Como, a black supervisor, and the white mayor of Sardis discussing crisis plans.

54 The local newspaper carried much of the criticism of this move; he changed the salary from $6,000 part-time to $15,000 full-time.

55 Events are drawn from *The Panolian* and the *Southern Reporter* without reference to publication dates except for the year listed.

56 The worry was justifiable. Sam Walton created a successful organization rooted in small towns, whose values he cherished, but his results were devastating for local businesses. Its success, based on low prices and service, overwhelmed local businesses, and worse, its profits went out of town. One study of thirty Iowa towns shows the devastation and loss of local leaders. See Alan Ehrenhalt, "Up against the Wal-Mart," *Governing*, September, 1992, 6–7. Even worse news for Batesville, a new factory outlet of forty-eight stores was opened in the mid-1990s. Its customers, drawn from a 150-mile radius including Memphis, would draw 20 percent of its customers locally. *The Panolian*, April 13, 1994.

57 Another sign of the changing times was a fifty-year-old cotton gin that was dismantled and sold to a firm in the nation of Peru.

58 Albert Myles et al., *A Study of Commercial and Industrial Establishments in Panola County, Mississippi: A Management Perspective* (Mississippi State: Mississippi State University, PRO-MISS Team report, October 1933).

59 The following material uses a form of analysis basic to the formal study of policy analysis; a useful introduction is found in Randall Ripley, *Policy Analysis in Political Science* (Chicago: Nelson-Hall, 1985), chapter 3; citations are from this source.

60 The numbers and sources are provided in Wirt, *Politics of Southern Equality*, 242–43.

61 Richard Couto, *Ain't Gonna Let Nobody Turn Me Around* (Philadelphia: Temple University Press, 1991).

62 Ripley, *Policy Analysis*, 69–70. For a review of this evidence, see Benjamin Page, *Who Gets What from Government?* (Berkeley: University of California Press, 1983).

63 The earlier conditions in the county were set out in Wirt, *Politics of Southern Equality*, chapters 12–13.

64 Evidence is noted in Wirt, *Politics of Southern Equality*, 243–44.

65 The theoretical reasons for local limitations are found in the classic Peterson, *City Limits*; the historical details of these limitations are found in Dennis Judd, *The Politics of American Cities*, 3d ed. (Glenview, Ill.: Scott Foresman, 1988).

9 Local Perspectives on Race and the Law

1 Southern Poverty Law Center, *Intelligence Report* (Atlanta: SPLC, 1993). The next quarterly report did feature one incident from Mississippi.

2 Stories about Boy and Girl Scouts were reported separately, as both races had their own troops (e.g., three all-black girl scout troops are reported in *The Panolian*, February 5, 1992, 13B). The first photo of one desegregated troop of Girl Scouts appeared in *The Panolian* in 1989, which also had desegregated photos in its "kids" section and a full-page spread on a forty-year employee of the newspaper who was black (May 26, 1989).

3 But Avant was reported in another meeting to *calm* in public another black supervisor who had claimed racial bias in a separate matter. *The Panolian*, January 8, 1992.

4 Bill Minor, column in *The Panolian*, January 15, 1992.

5 *The Panolian*, March 18, 1992. Town, county, and state law offices cooperated on the task, converting a courtroom into a facility for processing and holding the prisoners.

6 Deil Wright, *Intergovernmental Grants System* (Washington, D.C.: Advisory Commission on Intergovernmental Relations, 1982), 122.

7 Frederick Wirt, *The Politics of Southern Equality* (Chicago: Aldine, 1970).

8 The concept that language shapes our thoughts and has control over the speaker is traceable to Benjamin Whorf, *Language, Thought, and Reality* (Cambridge, Mass.: MIT Press, 1956). The concept that language is the keystone to understanding culture runs through the writings of many cultural anthropologists, starting with Edward Sapir, *Culture, Language, and Personality* (Berkeley: University of California Press, 1956).

9 Details of this process are seen in David Fetterman, *Ethnography Step by Step* (Newbury Park, Calif.: Sage, 1989).

10 Paul Sniderman and Thomas Piazza, *The Scar of Race* (Cambridge, Mass.: Belknap Press of Harvard University Press, 1993).

11 A senior student had questioned in class the wording of the Fifteenth Amendment (on the right to vote) and then brought in a parent also to question it. The teacher claims that neither had ever read the amendment.

12 Surveyed in Frederick Wirt, "The Uses of Blandness: State, Local, and Professional Roles in Citizenship Education," in Stephen Schecter, ed., *Teaching about American Federal Democracy* (Philadelphia: Temple University, Center for the Study of Federalism, National Institute of Education project, 1984).

13 See the variety of polls assembled in "Public Opinion and Demographic Report," *The American Enterprise*, September/October 1991, 81–87.

14 James Kuklinski and Michael Cobb, "Racial Attitudes and the 'New South,'" *Journal of Politics*, May 1997. James Kuklinski, Paul Sniderman, Kathleen Knight, Thomas Piazza, Philip Tetlock, Gordon Lawrence, and Barbara Mellers, "Racial Prejudice and Attitudes toward Affirmative Action," *American Journal of Political Science*, May 1997.

15 A complex analysis of the national political system is developed convincingly in Edward Carmines and James Stimson, *Race and the Transformation of American Politics* (Princeton, N.J.: Princeton University Press, 1989), and Robert Huckfeldt and Carol Kohfeld, *Race and the Decline of Class in American Politics* (Urbana: University of Illinois Press, 1989).

10 The Theoretical Context of Race and Law

1 Jennifer Hoschschild, "Disjunction and Ambivalence in Citizens' Political Outlook," in *Reconsidering the Democratic Public;* George E. Marcus and Russell L. Hanson, eds. (University Park: Pennsylvania State University Press, 1993); and Hoschschild, *What's Fair?* (Cambridge, Mass.: Harvard University Press, 1981).

2 "Racial policy preferences should be viewed as tentative, equivocal judgments that are the result of deep value conflict. . . . [T]emporary judgments . . . are always subject to revision," in Howard Schuman, Charlotte Steeh, and Lawrence Bobo, *Racial Attitudes in America* (Cambridge, Mass.: Harvard University Press, 1985), 17. See also John Zaller, *The Nature and Origins of Mass Opinion* (Cambridge: Cambridge University Press, 1992).

3 While there is some current effort to link critical views of blacks with conservatism, current analysts believe there is a very special kind of conservatism that actually supports some blacks. But discrimination is not encouraged by any particular ideology—indeed, it is most often absent. See Paul Sniderman, Thomas Piazza, Philip Tetlock, and Ann Kendrick, "The New Racism," *American Journal of Political Science* 35 (1991): 423–47, and Paul Sniderman and Thomas Piazza, *The Scar of Race* (Cambridge, Mass.: Belknap Press of Harvard University Press, 1993).

4 Paul Kellstedt, "The Dynamic American Ethos: Value Conflict and Racial Policy Preferences," paper presented to the annual conference of the Midwest Political Science Association, Chicago, 1995.

5 Benjamin Page and Robert Shapiro, *The Rational Public* (Chicago: University of Chicago Press, 1992); William Mayer, *The Changing American Mind* (Ann Arbor: University of Michigan Press, 1992), chapter 6.

6 Mayer, *The Changing American Mind,* 128.

7 James Kluegel, "Trends in Whites' Explanations of the Black-White Gap in Socioeconomic Status, 1977–1989," *American Sociological Review* 55 (1990): 512–55.

8 Mark Fossett and K. Jill Kiecolt, "The Relative Size of Minority Populations and White Racial Attitudes," *Social Science Quarterly* 70 (1989): 820–35.

9 Mayer, *The Changing American Mind,* 188.

10 Michael Corbett, "Bridging the Gap: Trends in Political Tolerance and Racial Attitudes among Southerners," paper presented to the Midwest Political Science Association, Chicago, 1992. For earlier data by the same author, see *Political Tolerance in America* (New York: Longman, 1982).

11 John Dittmer, *Local People* (Champaign: University of Illinois Press, 1994).

12 For statements at that time in local newspapers across the state, see Shirley Tucker, *Mississippi from Within* (New York: Arco, 1965). For white statements in Panola County, see Frederick Wirt, *The Politics of Southern Equality* (Aldine: Chicago University Press, 1970), 128–36.

13 See Panola details and supporting studies in Wirt, *The Politics of Southern Equality,* 128–30.

14 Bill Minor, column in *The Panolian,* July 1994.

15 The following details and quotations on the fires and their aftermath are in the *New York Times,* January 3, 1994, A10.

16 Minor, column in *The Panolian,* July 1994.

17 Reports of *Klanwatch* (Atlanta: Southern Poverty Center, 1996).
18 Reported to author by current Batesville officials who related earlier stories found in newspaper and court circles of that era.
19 What follows is drawn from a private diary of daily events by one member of the jury panel (confirmed by another interview with a second member) and from newspaper accounts. Interviews with officials and the accused are reported in Marganne Vollers, *Ghosts of Mississippi* (Boston: Little, Brown, 1995), whose chapter 26 discusses Batesville.
20 Details are presented in the Jackson *Clarion-Ledger* in late January and early February 1994. Reaction stories appeared there after the verdict on February 4–6, 1994, from which the following quotations appear.
21 Beckwith is serving his term in the Hinds County jail in Jackson. Informal accounts to the author indicate that a decision was made not to send him to the state penitentiary in Parchman due to fear of violence against him.
22 V. O. Key, Jr., *Southern Politics in State and Nation* (New York: Knopf, 1949).
23 The evidence for this proposition is drawn from national polling data that the media—over time—alternate values of individualism and egalitarianism that, in turn, move policy support on such racial matters; see Kellstedt, "The Dynamic American Ethos."
24 "Civil Rights Leader Julian Bond Speaks at Ole Miss," *Southern Register*, Fall 1992, Center for the Study of the South, University of Mississippi, 1992.
25 A detailed review of these factors are explored in Walter Williams et al., *Studying Implementation* (Chatham, N.J.: Chatham House, 1982). A review of national policy is found in Randall Ripley and Grace Franklin, *Policy Implementation and Bureaucracy*, 2d ed. (Chicago: Dorsey, 1986).
26 Earl Black and Merle Black, *Politics and Society in the South* (Cambridge, Mass.: Harvard University Press, 1987), 302.
27 Early evidence in the South is seen in Donald Matthews and James Prothro, *Negroes and the New Southern Politics* (New York: Harcourt, Brace & World, 1966), and in Panola County, Frederick Wirt, *Politics of Southern Equality*, chapter 7.
28 This stage and its defeat are detailed in Frank Parker, *Black Votes Count* (Chapel Hill: University of North Carolina Press, 1990).
29 *The Panolian*, August 17, 1994.
30 Stephen Shaffer, "Public Opinion and Interest Groups," in Dale Krane and Stephen Shaffer, eds., *Mississippi Government and Politics* (Lincoln: University of Nebraska Press, 1992), 67–69.
31 Shaffer, "Public Opinion and Interest Groups," 67–69.
32 Corbett, "Bridging the Gap," 2; see also Black and Black, *Politics and Society in the South.*
33 Corbett, "Bridging the Gap," 14.
34 William Muir, Jr., *Prayer in Public Schools* (Chicago: University of Chicago Press, 1967), 138.
35 The renewed interest in institutions by political scientists stems from the ideas of James March and Johan Olsen, "The New Institutionalism: Organizational Factors in Political Life," *American Political Science Review* 78 (1984): 734–49.
36 This is the heart of the concept of systems analysis framework that links society

to political systems which "authoritatively allocate resources and values"; see David Easton, *A Systems Analysis of Political Life* (New York: Wiley, 1965).

37   This central concept in "the politics of education" scholarship is seen in Frederick Wirt and Michael Kirst, *Schools in Conflict*, 3d ed. (Berkeley, Calif.: McCutchan, 1992), chapter 3. For a particular case, see the symposium in Mobin Shorish and Frederick Wirt, eds., "Ethnicity," in *Comparative Education Review* 37, no. 1 (1993): 1–61.

38   Based on interviews with officers of this state's private school system and a review of its documents.

39   The economic theory for this practice is seen in Lester Thurow, *The Zero-Sum Society* (New York: Basic Books, 1980); the national policy effort of regulation is set out in Randall Ripley and Grace Franklin, *Congress, the Bureaucracy, and Public Policy*, 5th ed. (Pacific Grove, Calif.: Brooks/Cole, 1991), chapter 5.

40   Thomas Handy, "Mississippi: An Expanding Array of Interests," in Jeffrey Berry, ed., *Interest Groups in the Southern States* (Tuscaloosa: University of Alabama Press, 1992), 276. See the state data in L. Harmon Zeigler, "Interests Groups in the States," in Virginia Grey, Herbert Jacob, and Kenneth Vines, eds., *Politics in the American States*, 4th ed. (Boston: Little, Brown, 1983), 100.

41   Reagan appointees in the Civil Rights Division of the U.S. Department of Justice explained that cases involving white discrimination were ignored; see Marissa Golden, *Exit, Voice and Loyalty*, no. 91-18 (Berkeley: Institute of Government Studies, University of California, 1990). A thorough study of this administration shows clear opposition to civil rights by decisions affecting personnel, budget cuts, program changes, etc.; see Steven Shull, *A Kinder, Gentler Racism?* (Armont, N.Y.: Sharpe, 1993), and *The President and Civil Rights Policy* (New York: Greenwood, 1989).

41   A similar distinction, dealing with different levels of discrimination, appears in Herbert Blumer, "The Future of the Color Line," in John McKinney and Edward Thompson, eds., *The South in Continuity and Change* (Durham, N.C.: Duke University Press, 1965), 323–35. The concept of different types of "color lines," both inner and outer, are featured in Black and Black, *Politics and Society in the South*.

43   This concept is expounded fully in James MacGregor Burns, *Leadership* (New York: Harper & Row, 1978).

44   Gary Orfield, *Public School Desegregation in the United States, 1968–1980* (Washington, D.C.: Joint Center for Politics Studies, 1983). But these changes are often disappointing; in Atlanta, the hopes and fears of neither liberals nor conservatives have been realized, see, e.g., Gary Orfield and Carole Ashkinaze, *The Closing Door* (Chicago: University of Chicago Press, 1991).

45   Krane and Shaffer, *Mississippi Government and Politics*.

46   Willie Morris, *Terrains of the Heart and Other Essays on Home* (Oxford, Miss.: Yoknapatawpha Press, 1981, 75).

47   Quotes here and below are from Wirt, *Politics of Southern Equality*, 325.

Index

Frederick M. Wirt is Professor of Political Science at the University of Illinois at Urbana-Champaign and author of *Politics of Southern Equality: Law and Social Change in a Mississippi County*

Library of Congress Cataloging-in-Publication Data
Wirt, Frederick M.
We ain't what we was : civil rights in the new South /
Frederick M. Wirt ; foreword by Gary Orfield.
p.   cm.
ISBN 0-8223-1901-2 (cloth : alk. paper). — ISBN 0-8223-1893-8
(pbk. : alk. paper)
1. Civil rights—Mississippi—Panola County.   2. Panola County
(Miss.)—Social conditions.   3. Panola County (Miss.)—Politics and
government.   I. Title.
JC599.A–Z.U52M6378   1997
323.1′196073076284—DC20   96-32710   CIP